WHAT CHURCH CAN BE

WHAT CHURCH CAN BE

AN OPTIMISTIC VISION

MATTHEW KRUSE

XULON PRESS

Xulon Press
2301 Lucien Way #415
Maitland, FL 32751
407.339.4217
www.xulonpress.com

© 2020 by Matthew Kruse

All rights reserved solely by the author. The author guarantees all contents are original and do not infringe upon the legal rights of any other person or work. No part of this book may be reproduced in any form without the permission of the author, except in the case of brief quotations in critical articles or reviews. The views expressed in this book are not necessarily those of the publisher. For more information, contact Seven Mile Road Church, 84 Green Street, Melrose, Massachusetts 02176.

Unless otherwise indicated, Scripture quotations taken from the English Standard Version (ESV). Copyright © 2001 by Crossway, a publishing ministry of Good News Publishers. Used by permission. All rights reserved.

Scripture quotations marked (NIV) are taken from the Holy Bible, New International Version®, NIV®. Copyright © 1973, 1978, 1984, 2011 by Biblica, Inc.™ Used by permission of Zondervan. All rights reserved worldwide. www.zondervan.com The "NIV" and "New International Version" are trademarks registered in the United States Patent and Trademark Office by Biblica, Inc.™

Printed in the United States of America.

ISBN-13: 978-1-6305-0564-6

"I don't know of another book like this. If you want to know what it's like to do church that's gospel-centered (as opposed to attractional) in a post-Christian context (as opposed to where there's a ready-made customer base) with the aim of planting more missional churches (as opposed to to simply getting big or franchising) from a pastor who's about to enter his third decade doing it (as opposed to a guy who just thinks about it), What Church Can Be is for you. It is engaging, sharp, and rich with hard-won wisdom."

Jared Wilson
Assistant Professor of Pastoral Ministry at Spurgeon College
Author in Residence at Midwestern Baptist Theological Seminary
General Editor of For The Church (and host of the FTC Podcast)
Director of The Pastoral Training Center at Liberty Baptist Church in Kansas City, Missouri

"In the near future, the rest of America will become more secular like the city of Boston or the New England region. My friend Matthew Kruse has written a useful book for doing gospel-centered ministry in such a context as this. Seven Mile Road Church, with its theological vision and missional strategy, has cultivated a network of like-minded churches in the area. I highly commend this book for your consideration. I believe it is a tool that can be used to encourage many future leaders who will be doing ministry in our post-Christian world."

Dr. Stephen T. Um
Senior Pastor of Citylife Presbyterian Church in Boston, Massachusetts
Council Member of The Gospel Coalition
Trainer for Redeemer City to City
Adjunct Professor of New Testament at Gordon-Conwell Theological Seminary
Author of Why Cities Matter, 1 Corinthians (Preaching the Word Commentary), and Micah for You

"Matt Kruse is a 'townie.' That's New-England-speak for a local–a guy who's 'from here.' I've walked the streets of greater Boston with Matt and seen cab drivers, laborers, and random pedestrians greet him by name. This is a man who knows and loves real people in a real place. Matt may be unknown to you–but he shouldn't be. His joyful, provocative, prophetic voice makes me want to be a better pastor and fills me with hope for what church can be. I long for every pastor and church planter to read this book."

Bob Thune
Lead Pastor of Coram Deo Church in Omaha, Nebraska
Founder and co-host of Wednesday Conversation podcast
Author of Gospel Eldership and The Gospel-Centered Life

"This book illustrates the joys and challenges of being church. It has a lovely devotional impact as it warms hearts for the Saviour, urging us toward greater gospel fidelity and commitment to the church family we have the privilege of sharing life with for the sake of Christ and his cause. Given our increasingly marginalized positions as Christians today, Matt's experiences in a post-Christian context are a helpful guide for all those serious about gospel advance through church planting."

Steve Timmis
CEO of Acts29 Church Planting Network
Senior Elder of The Crowded House in Sheffield, England
Co-author of Total Church

"This book is written with the integrity, creativity, and urgency I expect from Matthew Kruse, who has given himself to a fruitful, multiplying New England ministry for nearly two decades. As I read it, I was encouraged and challenged. I'm confident that those who read What Church Can Be will be inspired and equipped. I thank God for Matt and for Seven Mile Road."

Dr. Stephen Witmer
Pastor of Pepperell Christian Fellowship in Pepperell, Massachusetts
Professor of New Testament, Gordon-Conwell Theological Seminary
Co-Director, Small Town Summits
Author of Eternity Changes Everything and Revelation in Crossway's Knowing the Bible Series

"The Seven Mile Road churches have been planted with the goal of fruitfulness, not success. This is because Matt Kruse captured the Biblical blend of being counter-cultural and authentic. In this wonderful volume, he does not mince words, nor "make nice" with the challenges of ministry in a post-Christian setting. Matt has honestly faced the joys and discouragements of church in what the Second Great Awakening would have called, the "burned over" district of America – the places where religion is a dirty word, and church is no longer a culturally safe space. I can surely commend What Church Can Be as a volume that speaks to the heart with a courageous and Gospel-centered honesty."

Dr. Richard Lints
Provost and Andrew Mutch Professor of Theology
Gordon-Conwell Theological Seminary

"Matt has written a book on the church he has lived. This is not a pristine doctrinal treatment of the church, but a broken-in, frayed, grace-filled look at life together in Jesus. By God's grace, I've experienced much of what Matt describes here, but as I read, I found myself wanting more. May every person who reads this book experience more of Christ's favorite thing in the world—his Church!"

Jonathan K. Dodson
Lead pastor of City Life Church in Austin, TX
Founder of Gospel-Centered Discipleship
Author of Here in Spirit, The Unbelievable Gospel, Gospel-Centered Discipleship, and 1-2 Peter and Jude in Crossway's Knowing the Bible Series

"Matt Kruse is a faithful and gifted pastoral leader. I have learned much from him in my previous interactions, and this book has brought further encouragement and insight. His work in Boston is inspiring, and his comprehensive vision of discipleship is instructive. I'm sure this book will be a blessing to everyone who cares about the health, vitality, and impact of his/her local church."

Dr. Tony Merida
Founding pastor of Imago Dei Church in Raleigh, North Carolina
Associate Professor of Preaching at Southeastern Baptist Seminary
Content Director for Acts 29 Network
Author of several books, including The Christ-Centered Expositor, Ordinary, Orphanology, and is general editor and contributor of eight volumes in the Christ-Centered Exposition Commentary Series (B&H)

"Before my family moved to the Northeast to help plant churches, Matt Kruse befriended me through an Acts 29 online pastors forum. I'll never forget him typing at me "It's not that bad! It's just Jersey!" These words were a comfort. Over the years Matt and I have worked together in various capacities to see the gospel planted in Northeastern lands. Matt has maintained a sincere missional focus, a robust biblical theology and a Christ-centered hope as he has plowed the hard grounds of New England. We need to hear what he and the Seven Mile Road communities have learned about planting the gospel in post-Christendom western culture."

Reid S. Monaghan
Founder and President of Power of Change
Assessment Director US South Central Network
Co-host of The Gospel Underground Podcast

"Having just finished reading a draft of Matthew Kruse's captivating new book, What Church Can Be, I am delighted to commend it to you and to recommend its publication. Written in a lively, winsome, disarmingly honest and engaging style, the book describes how God enabled the planting of an interconnected family of Gospel-centered churches in the rocky soil of New England.

One might ask, of course, whether yet another book on church planting is really needed. Indeed, even a cursory search of the Amazon book listings under "church planting" yields literally dozens of volumes devoted to various aspects of the theme. However, what makes this new book uniquely valuable, in my opinion, is that its context is here in New England and its author is not a theoretician so much as a seasoned pastor and church planting veteran with more than a few scars to validate his long years at the task.

What Church Can Be, in short, has the aroma of authenticity. Its insights have been thoroughly field-tested in communities such as Melrose, Malden, Waltham, Kennebunk and Hyannis and its failures have been clearly identified. In the final analysis, however, it is a story that is filled with joy and hope. By God's grace, as its author affirms, it is possible to "build a strong church in a post-Christian context that brings glory to God and life to the people" — the very kind of community that members will "actually love belonging to."

The Seven Mile Road model is not for everyone, of course. Some will find it too theologically restrictive, too passionately relational, too liturgically informal and/or too personally demanding. For those who are hungry to be part of a high-demand, high touch, highly relational and authentically Christian fellowship, however, this might be exactly the book they need to read and study. It is, in my estimation, a story that needs to be told — not, God forbid, to bring glory to the Seven Mile Road movement but because God can use it to inspire, encourage and inform a whole new generation of believers who yearn to serve God more fully and faithfully."

Dr. Garth M. Rosell
Senior Research Professor of Church History
Gordon-Conwell Theological Seminary

"Matt Kruse in one of the best pastoral voices in the northeast that churches all over should hear and have not yet known. I have been blessed to know Matt, work with him in church planting in the northeast, and watch the church he has shepherded, 7 Mile Road, grow and multiply. When someone comes to Terra Nova and tells me there are from 7 Mile Road, I am thankful. They likely know, love, and live church well. Or to say it another way, they have been well pastored."

Ed Marcelle
Lead Pastor of Terra Nova Church in Troy, NY
Northeast Liaison Acts29

"If you're looking for advice on how to plant a church in a post-Christian city with a soul as hard as concrete, this isn't the book for you. But if you want to learn how to love and lead people to experience the grace of the gospel in just such a context, then you couldn't have a better guide than Matt Kruse. What you'll find in these pages are humble but brilliant insights dug out of a decade of planting life-giving churches in Greater Boston and beyond. Each chapter has "you can" written all over it, anchored in both scripture and the gritty and deeply personal story of Matt's life and ministry. He has carefully avoided all the well-worn cliches and unhealthy expectations of church planting. Instead, you'll hear a trusted voice and feel the heartbeat of someone who has been there and still on the front lines, planting churches, strong churches, vibrant and beautiful."

Dr. David Butler
Director of SEND Boston (North American Mission Board Church Planting Collective)
Former Pastor of CenterPoint Church in Concord, New Hampshire

"Matt Kruse has been a friend for over fifteen years. We share the huge honor and humble calling of planting churches in New England. Matt is one of the smartest pastors I know, but even more impressive, he's a holy pastor. Matt's book is desperately needed as a handbook for the normal pastor called to slug it out for decades in hard places. I can't think of many guys I'd recommend to you more highly than Matt Kruse!"

Rev. David Pinckney
Pastor of River of Grace Church in Concord, New Hampshire
Co-Director of the Acts 29 Network's Rural Collaborative

"This is the book I've been waiting for a long time. It is a personal memoir of a real pastor in a real place doing the hard work of gospel ministry. It is also a soundly theological exposition of what the calling to Christian ministry entails. And it is an extremely practical, hands-on book on how to do ministry in a post-Christian context. Matt Kruse is open, honest, and transparent, as well as downright inspirational. I would buy this book by the case to give out to all my colleagues in ministry."

Rev. Paul McPheeters
Pastor of Forestdale Community Church in Malden, Massachusetts

To everyone at Seven Mile Road.

This is your book.

TABLE OF CONTENTS

Why I Wrote xix
How This Book Works. xxiii
The Text xxvii

01 | SPIN CLASS 1
   Church will be death. On recognizing the cost … and paying it anyway.
   I do not account my life of any value nor as precious to myself.
   —Acts 20:24

02 | O_2 9
   Church can be life. | On keeping gospel grace central to everything.
   I commend you to God and to the word of his grace. —Acts 20:32

03 | MELANOMA. 19
   Church can be holy. | On the relentless pursuit of personal holiness.
   How I lived … —Acts 20:18

04 | OPEN BOOKS 33
   Church can be honest. | On moving people from "all set" to "you know."
   You yourselves know … —Acts 20:18, 34

05 | LIGHTS 47
   Church can be humble. | On having no rock stars but Jesus.
   With all humility … —Acts 20:19

06 | TEARS 61
Church can be heartbreaking. | On investing ourselves emotionally in the work.
With tears ... —Acts 20:19

07 | SCARS 77
Church can be resilient. | On not avoiding opposition.
With trials that happened to me through the plots of the Jews ... —Acts 20:19

08 | GUTS 91
Church can be bold. | On having hard conversations.
I did not shrink from declaring ... —Acts 20:20, 27

09 | THUNDER 109
Church can be anchored. | On loving and leading from the words of Scripture.
Teaching you in public and from house to house ... —Acts 20:20
Remember the words of the Lord Jesus." —Acts 20:35

10 | OUTSIDERS 125
Church can be outward. | On moving toward folks who aren't there yet.
Both to Jews and to Greeks ... —Acts 20:21

11 | X-FACTORS 139
Church can be daring. | On taking big risks.
Not knowing what will happen to me ... —Acts 20:22

12 | GLANCES 153
Church can be content. | On embracing our callings and capacities.
My course and the ministry that I received ... —Acts 20:24

13 | LOVE LETTERS 169
   Church can be warm. | On stirring our affections for Jesus's people.
   Care for the church of God, which he obtained with his own blood. —Acts 20:28

14 | WOLVES 181
   Church can be orthodox. | On fighting heresies and those who tout them.
   Fierce wolves will come in. —Acts 20:29

15 | YEARS 193
   Church can be durable. | On marrying frequency and longevity.
   For three years I did not cease night or day ... —Acts 20:31

16 | FRESH WHITE KICKS 209
   Church can be simple. | On refusing materialism.
   I coveted no one's silver or gold or apparel. —Acts 20:33

17 | HANDS 219
   Church can be close. | On living in super tight community.
   These hands ... —Acts 20:34

18 | TEAM 229
   Church can be unified. | On working together for gospel advancement.
   ... to those who were with me. —Acts 20:34

19 | HUSTLE 245
   Church can be hardworking. | On breaking a sweat.
   By working hard ... —Acts 20:35

20 | SPEED BUMPS 257
   Church can be compassionate. | On not running people over.
   We must help the weak. —Acts 20:35

21 | SUPERGLUE 273
    Church can be generous. | On giving (literally) everything away.
    It is more blessed to give than to receive. —Acts 20:35

22 | KITES 295
    Church can be dependent. | On actually praying.
    He knelt down and prayed. —Acts 20:36

Endnotes 311

WHY I WROTE

ALTHOUGH I'VE BENEFITED TREMENDOUSLY from much of what our generation's well-known pastors and church planters have published, a caveat looms over every word of theirs I read: "Yeah, but their context is nothing like mine."

Boston, Massachusetts, is my home, and has been since Larry Legend was working his magic on the parquet floor. It's an absurdly expensive, rabidly liberal, post-Christian city where the gospel is increasingly met with disinterest or disdain. Rapid, Instagramable church growth doesn't happen here. You'll find no churches the size of a Walmart, or Christian radio stations, or Bible verses evangelizing from the bottom of fast-food cups. Nobody tithes or even knows what that means. Inviting my Bostonian neighbors to church is like inviting a Mormon to a strip club. No one here knows the first thing about the Bible, or cares to know. I was sharing a meal once with some folks in our neighborhood and said, "You know how Peter denied Jesus three times?" Everyone stared blankly back at me as if I had asked them to explain calculus.

What little the people here do know about church is not good. Many were raised Roman Catholic, coming of age in a city rocked by one of the ugliest scandals the church has ever known, the words "priest" and "pedophile" now permanently wed in their minds. Some grew up attending the heresy-ridden mainline corpses that pass for churches in our neighborhoods; their last rays of the gospel light were snuffed out decades ago. Others have been bamboozled by prosperity gospel hucksters, or browbeaten by better-than-thou fundamentalists, or beaten down by church politics. The sad result is that to an entire generation of Bostonians, an invite to church sounds as appealing as a root canal without Novocain.

We've spent more than a decade planting the gospel here and have baptized around fifty people. I remember hearing one mega-pastor recount how his church had rented a professional baseball stadium to host its Easter service and thinking, "That's funny, because we've been at this just as long, and I bet you could fit our whole church in the dugout."

I've written this book for those working in contexts like ours. For folks whose city resembles Rome more than Dallas, Ephesus more than Escondido. For the pastor who has to grind—*hard*—for every dollar, every connection, every conversion. For those of us who feel like losers half the time, and lunatics the other half, because our progress is always thirteen steps forward and a baker's dozen back.

For those who are not totally sure that church can still be something life-giving, viable, beautiful.

Here's what I've written to tell you:

You can do this.

By God's grace, you can build a strong church in a post-Christian context.

I know, because I've lived it.

Christianity Today's metrics might tell you that nothing special has happened through the planting of our church, but they'd be lying through their teeth. Although we might not fill a stadium,

I've watched Jesus—through the humble efforts of a relentless, motley crew of men and women—build a gospel-believing, truth-loving, life-sharing, hospitality-showing, culture-crossing, church-planting church that people love being a part of.

Our name is Seven Mile Road Church. As of this writing, our one small church has become eight, and we have one in the womb. None of them is supersized, but Christ's glory has been shown off as people have been loved and led to the grace of the gospel.

If you want to lead or be a part of a church like this but aren't sure it can happen, this book is for you.

HOW THIS BOOK WORKS

THIS BOOK FUNCTIONS AS an exposition, a memoir, and a blueprint, all rolled into one.

First and foremost, it's an extended exposition of Paul's farewell speech (Acts 20:18-35) to his deeply loved brothers serving as elders of the Ephesian church.

No other text has influenced my theological vision for planting and pastoring churches more than this inspired transcript Luke gave us. The first time I memorized these words, I wept as I repented and begged God to mark our ministry with the same fervency, integrity, courage, intimacy, and grace that I saw in Paul's. Almost every strand in the DNA of Seven Mile Road Church can be traced back to these words, so I've built this book accordingly. Every chapter anchors to and meditates on a phrase from Paul's speech. To whatever degree the husks of my stories, reflections, and illustrations house the true meaning of his words, that's the degree to which this book will be helpful.

This also means that nothing I've written is original. I may say it with a Bostonian parlance,[1] but the substance comes directly from the life and ministry of Paul and the missional family who built the Ephesian church with him. The way forward for Christians is always the way backward to the eternal truths revealed in Scripture. Building our churches on the latest fads and trends is suicidal and unnecessary. Scripture is not only inspired, inerrant, and perspicuous; it's also sufficient:

everything we need to lead holy and healthy churches is already written. Whatever we say and do should emerge from the rich soil of God's previously spoken words.

Second, this book is a memoir.

I have 150 favorite Psalms, and Psalm 9 is one of them:

> I will give thanks to the LORD with my whole heart;
>
> I will recount all of your wonderful deeds. (Ps. 9:1)[2]

That's the spirit in which I have written every word in this book.

Not for season tickets to the Celts (courtside) would I trade the joys I've experienced through Seven Mile Road Church, the friendships I've forged, or even the failures I've endured. The Spirit has literally taken the truths of Acts 20 and actualized them in real-time in my soul and in the souls of Bostonians I love. This book is packed with our stories, not to hype us up, but to give Psalm 9-esque glory to God and to infuse in your soul a vision of what's possible for you and your church.

Third, this book is a field guide.

The gospel's advance in post-Christian America hinges on the willingness and ability of the next generation of pastors to build biblically faithful, missionally focused churches among distinct people groups—like the one we planted Seven Mile Road in, north of Boston. (If your city and church's context isn't post-Christian yet, give it a minute.)

The next American pastors need to lead these kinds of churches. Although clear theological vision is essential to this work, at some point the work itself must get done. How about we get busy growing real churches among real sinners in need of real grace? That's what we've been doing for seventeen years, and this book is a field guide for how we've done it. Each chapter not only presses a big theological truth but also articulates some real-life ways to flesh that truth out.

I've written primarily with pastors and future pastors in mind, whether they be church planters, church revitalizers, or those leading established churches. In doing this, I believe I am taking my cues from the text of Acts 20 itself. Paul's speech was not given to a random collection of whoever was by the shore that day. It was given to "the elders of the church." Why these men? They were responsible before God for what happened on the ground. As their holiness, unity, and orthodoxy went, so went the church's. If anyone needs a clear vision of what church can be, it's these men whom the Spirit has made overseers of the work.

Of course, my hope is also that this book could be read beneficially by anyone who is deeply invested in their local church and interested in seeing a biblical blueprint for growing a strong church in their city the way Jesus's apostle Paul did in Ephesus.

THE TEXT

READ THESE WORDS BEFORE you read anything else.

Better yet, memorize them. I'm serious. You'll thank me.

> You yourselves know how I lived among you the whole time from the first day that I set foot in Asia, serving the Lord with all humility and with tears and with trials that happened to me through the plots of the Jews; how I did not shrink from declaring to you anything that was profitable, and teaching you in public and from house to house, testifying both to Jews and to Greeks of repentance toward God and of faith in our Lord Jesus Christ. And now, behold, I am going to Jerusalem, constrained by the Spirit, not knowing what will happen to me there, except that the Holy Spirit testifies to me in every city that imprisonment and afflictions await me. But I do not account my life of any value nor as precious to myself, if only I may finish my course and the ministry that I received from the Lord Jesus, to testify to the gospel of the grace of God. And now, behold, I know that none of you among whom I have gone about proclaiming the kingdom will see my face again. Therefore I testify to you this day that I am innocent of the blood of all, for I did not shrink from declaring to you the whole counsel of God. Pay careful attention to yourselves and to all the flock, in which the Holy Spirit has made

you overseers, to care for the church of God, which he obtained with his own blood. I know that after my departure fierce wolves will come in among you, not sparing the flock; and from among your own selves will arise men speaking twisted things, to draw away the disciples after them. Therefore be alert, remembering that for three years I did not cease night or day to admonish every one with tears. And now I commend you to God and to the word of his grace, which is able to build you up and to give you the inheritance among all those who are sanctified. I coveted no one's silver or gold or apparel. You yourselves know that these hands ministered to my necessities and to those who were with me. In all things I have shown you that by working hard in this way we must help the weak and remember the words of the Lord Jesus, how he himself said, "It is more blessed to give than to receive." (Acts 20:18-35)

01 | SPIN CLASS

Church will be death.
On recognizing the cost ... and paying it anyway.

I do not account my life of any value nor as precious to myself.
—*Acts 20:24*

I WAS AMBLING DOWN MAIN STREET toward the YMCA, hand-in-hand with my wife of twenty-one years. It was our anniversary. Other than Christ, Grace Kruse is the greatest treasure I've ever stumbled upon—the best news ever to walk through the door of my life.

Our conversation that sunny morning was warm. Economical. Knowing. The kind seasoned lovers are graced to have.

> ME: It's our anniversary, Babe. Watcha wanna do?
> HER: You wanna come to spin with me?
> ME: Love to.

Having logged thousands of hours playing pickup in the dead of summer on every blacktop in greater Boston, I figured thirty minutes on a bike in an air-conditioned room would be a breeze.

Ten minutes later, I was strapped into a steely black device that vaguely resembled a bicycle. In front of me were a screen with numbers, strange handlebars, and Velcro pedals. The warning signs were missing or had been peeled off. I didn't know it, but I was a heretic tied to the rack.

"Get up!" "Push it!" "GEARS!!!"

My legs sprung into motion as my eyes found the woman in a tank top yelling at me. The woman—Lisa? Lucifer?—barked ferociously: *Stand. Sit. Sprint. Breathe. Hydrate. First position. Second. Third.* I couldn't keep it straight.

Music blared. Fast. Loud. Country. I hate country.

People began to disrobe around me. Hoodies and tank tops, freshly wrenched from quivering bodies, littered the floor. When I imagined hot, sweaty flesh being a part of my anniversary, I wasn't envisioning a room full of strangers.

01 | Spin Class

Sweat began to pour into my eyes and mouth. Lights zipped from wall to wall, darting like neon squirrels. I wasn't told *the whole room spins* at spin class. Exhaustion and dehydration welcomed nausea to their ranks. My legs grew confused and upset. A chorus of complaint arose from my calves, thighs, and ankles in angry harmony: "Why? What did we do? We will make it right. But please, no more." My lungs joined the protest. My bottom was raw as an oyster.

In my fog I wondered how many men have died on their anniversary.

More yelling: "Breathe, people, BREATHE!" A futile command. The room grew darker. Hotter. Smaller. "Lisa" was saying something to me, but I heard nothing. My wife, seated next to me just minutes ago, seemed miles away, a shade whirling in the distance. I was no longer in spin class. I was in the woods, panicked, alone, chased by wolves and neon squirrels and a woman in a tank top as I pedaled for my life, hoping not to die.

I thought to myself, "I will miss my wife."

Then, suddenly, I was told we were done. I could step off the bike. Clothing was retrieved. Handlebars wiped down. Farewells exchanged. I'd survived. My wife, too.

On our way out, I turned to her and deadpanned, "Next year we go to the movies."

• • •

PLANTING A CHURCH HAS BEEN A lot like that spin class: I had no idea what I was getting into, and it's nearly killed me—multiple times.

What Church Can Be

More than seventeen years ago, the decision to plant the original Seven Mile Road Church happened within a week. I was finishing an MBA at Boston University, and every job I was interviewing for required 70 percent travel for the first few years. We were pregnant with our first son, and I couldn't imagine being away that often in the earliest years of his life. So, I scheduled a conversation with our pastor.

A few minutes in, he asked if I had ever heard of "church planting." I answered no. He then tried to describe what he had recently learned at a conference:

> If I have it right, church planting is basically taking the gospel you've experienced here in our church to the Bostonians you love, and then trying to grow a church out of it. You'd have to build the whole thing from scratch, with only the clear teaching of Scripture and the particularities of your people group to guide you. From what I can tell about you, Matt, you've got an engineer's mind, an entrepreneur's spirit, and a scalper's mouth,[3] so you might be good at it. In fact, they told us to write down all the names of all the people in our church who seem like they might be a church planter, and yours is the only one I wrote.

He had me at "scalper's mouth."

I was ready to say yes right there in his office, but he insisted I give it twenty-four hours and maybe confer with my wife.

I did, and Seven Mile Road was born.

My pastor's sketch of church planting proved true in the essentials. We built a community from scratch, with Scripture in one hand and our context in the other. I used my scalper's mouth a lot. But my pastor left out a few things: loneliness, self-doubt, wolves, false conversions, sleepless nights, and nightmares—lots of nightmares. I constantly dreamt people had finally shown up en masse on a Sunday, only to discover we'd forgotten to put out the chairs, that I'd lost my manuscript, and that I wasn't wearing any pants. By the time I'd dressed and set everything up, everyone had left. Everyone.

In the early years, growing the church was like growing a garden in cement on the windward side of Everest. Our core team was my wife, my parents, one friend, one family from our sending church, three teenagers, and me. I knocked on one hundred doors in the neighborhood and got two women to come to an informational open house, only because we offered free coffee and a sixty-minute respite from their kids. Our church plant hovered around thirty people for years. Self-doubt hounded me: "What happens if I'm not wired for this? Why is it just the same few people here every week? I'm not sure I could lead an angel to profess faith in Christ right now."

Eventually, a thought like the one from spin class hit me: "Is it common for a man to die planting a church?"

If you mean *die* in the sincerest gospel sense, then the answer is *yes*. Trying to grow a gospel-centered church in a post-Christian context will kill you, but in the best possible way. It will wring you dry of every ounce of smugness and self-sufficiency. It will rip out of your hands that sexy prospectus you meticulously designed, toss it in a dumpster, and light the whole thing on fire. It will drop a guillotine through every expectation. It will expose you for the fragile, petty, self-interested sinner you are.

And yet—here is the glory, not only of the gospel itself but also of gospel ministry—*it's where we lose our lives that we finally find them*. Once the seed is dead and buried, the tree can grow. After death, life.

I testify to this fact.

Although planting Seven Mile Road has laid waste to so much of who I thought I was, and has repeatedly driven me to my knees wondering whether we'd survive the next ten minutes, nobody has benefited more from the church's existence than me.

It's not even close.

...

SUMMERTIME IN NEW ENGLAND IS WILD. After three months of snow-shoveling, teeth-chattering, depression-inducing cold (followed by two more months of raw, wet spring) summer barges in like Gandalf at dawn on the fifth day, and we get three months of clambakes, beach days, cherry slush, and the sudden return of Vitamin D.

Oh, and storms.

I'm talking sudden, violent, run-for-your-life thunderstorms. One minute everything is as dry as an Amish wedding. The next, the skies split, and you're soaked.

Imagine standing in a storm like that, holding a bucket, and trying to catch the rain. Ninety seconds in, the bucket is full and running over. An armful of buckets couldn't catch all that rain. A field of buckets would fare no better.

Buckets.

That's the first word that comes to mind when anyone asks me about my experience planting our church. I've always felt my arms were full, unable to catch all the grace the Father was pouring out. It's been uncatchable, incalculable. Yes, the Father took one life from me, but He gave me another, unimaginable one.

01 | SPIN CLASS

...

JESUS'S APOSTLE PAUL UNDERSTOOD THIS TRUTH. Obeying Jesus's call to become the Apostle to the Gentiles meant that everything Paul was and might become would have to die. His identity, his security, and his prosperity were vaporized by his *yes* to Jesus's call on his life. And he was good with it.

Here is how Paul says it: "I do not account my life of any value nor as precious to myself, if only I may finish my course and the ministry that I received from the Lord Jesus, to testify to the gospel of the grace of God" (Acts 20:24).

Nobody can say those words and own them ten minutes into their first ministry task (so maybe pause on getting that arm tattoo). It's not until we've died a few times, dug ourselves out from under a pile of rocks as Paul had to do, and then seen the Spirit somehow bring life out of our destruction, that the beauty—the necessity, really—of Paul's sentiment here can take deep root in our souls. But if you stick with the work long enough, you'll get there. And, like Paul, you won't be complaining, but exulting.

Is it a common occurrence for a man to die in the course of his ministry?

Yes.

And it's totally worth it.[4]

02 | O$_2$

Church can be life.
On keeping gospel grace central to everything.

I commend you to God and to the word of his grace.
—Acts 20:32

THE KANCAMAGUS HIGHWAY STRETCHES thirty-four miles across the scenic northern third of live-free-or-die New Hampshire. Unless you're an avid skier, or a masochist who enjoys sleeping outdoors in ten-degree weather and four feet of snow, you don't go anywhere near the Kancamagus in winter. But on a smoking-hot summer day, it's the place to be. All along the highway are picturesque streams and ponds where you can swim, fish, grill, and shoot off some fireworks (perfectly legal in New Hampshire). If you venture a few hundred yards into the woods, you'll discover a maze of pristine hiking trails, rapids, and waterfalls.

My senior year at St. Dominic Savio Preparatory High School,[5] some friends and I road-tripped north from Boston. We pulled onto the shoulder, and one of our outdoor types hustled us deep into the forest. A thousand yards in we found a waterfall shooting through a rocky overpass and plunging thirty feet into a narrow pool. No signs. No trail markers. No dock or ladders. Just ice-cold nature. My buddy pointed to the rapids and said, "Kid,[6] you gotta do this." I consented. I stripped to my jean shorts,[7] shimmied to the center of the torrent, and pushed off.

Three thoughts hit me in succession over the next ninety seconds:

1. Whoa, this water is rushing faster than I thought.
2. Uh, this drop is much steeper than I thought.
3. Oh no, I'm going to die. In the "live free or die" state.

I plunged under the water, and all the air went out of my lungs. All of it.

You know how when you cannonball off a diving board in most pools, you hit the bottom and then push right up to the surface? I hit no bottom this time. Just a murderous surge of mountain water, hell-bent on drowning me. I had to fight to reach the surface, and then fight to reach the shore, never once taking a breath. I grasped for a ladder but found only wet-slick rock. My head ducked under again.

I then made a decision: I am not dying in New Hampshire.

I struggled to pull myself up. When I did, I flailed on the ground, sucking in the pure oxygen of the White Mountains. Air never tasted so sweet. For ten minutes, all I could do was lie there and breathe.

Replace "oxygen of the White Mountains" with "the grace of the gospel," and replace "breathing" with "believing," and you have the central rhythm of gospel ministry.

The foundational pursuit, the bottom line, of gospel ministry is believing the grace of the gospel. We need grace like we need oxygen. Grace is just as essential in surviving and thriving in ministry as it is in becoming a Christian in the first place.

. . .

I REMEMBER THE FIRST TIME I breathed in the grace of the gospel like it was nine seconds ago.

My father and mother had been plowing the ground of my soul and planting the seeds of the gospel for years. (Dad had converted and been baptized in Vietnam during the war, and Mom had spent her childhood as the daughter of a Puerto Rican Pentecostal pastor.) But it wasn't until April 1985 that my own life showed a harvest.

We were visiting friends in Boston, considering a permanent move from New York. I ended up at a Friday night youth group at a church on the Revere Beach Parkway. This being the eighties, think rock band, flaming swords, songs with hand motions, and wicked saucy pizza. At some point, we all sat in a circle on the stage. One by one we were called on to talk about where we were with Jesus.

No explicit gospel message was given that night. No altar call. No invitation to repent and believe. But Jesus brought my heart to life. Like a baby just out of the womb, sucking in air for dear life, the lungs of my spirit came alive.

I don't remember a word I said, but I remember crying and crying (and crying) in front of a room full of preteens I had just met for the first time. It would seem the Father, in love, aware of my tendency toward pride and self-sufficiency, was humbling me from the start. All I had heard about Jesus that had seemed irrelevant and inconsequential at that point in my life suddenly became true—beautifully and necessarily true. The cross was no longer an odd symbol of some random religion my parents happened to believe. My sins were paid for. Jesus was no longer some goofy, sandal-wearing storyteller. He was God and Savior and Lord. All the playing, pretending, and posturing I had been doing (I was good at it) came crashing down in a heap, and the grace of God in the gospel tore hurricane-like through my soul. I was suffocating under my sin, but Jesus threw open the windows of heaven, and I inhaled.

That is primarily what we are getting at when we build gospel-centered churches. In every conversation, sermon, staff meeting, meal, song, strategy session, and member forum—we are breathing in gospel grace. And not just once. Not just as some "beginning." Believing the gospel of the grace of God is the big idea all the way through our lives with Christ.

See, there is this thing about breathing. Unless you are Jason Bourne or Michael Phelps, you need to breathe every five seconds or so. You don't "get your breathing in" in the morning and hold your breath through the day. Breathing is a continual activity. If breathing is not happening, nothing else is getting done.

In the same way, believing the gospel is not just the front door of the gospel-shaped life or the mudroom for gospel ministry. It is the fuel our lives and ministries run on; the grace of God in the gospel is the air we breathe. And breathe. And breathe. And breathe.

Jesus's apostle Paul knew this. He lived this. And he calls us to do the same.

. . .

TOWARD THE END OF PAUL'S SPEECH in Acts, after he's talked broadly about all the marks of faithful gospel ministry and all the essential building blocks of a healthy church, where does Paul anchor the whole endeavor? After he has charged, threatened, warned, encouraged, and instructed his listeners, what is Paul's bottom line? Where does he land the plane?

The grace of God in the gospel:

> And now I commend you to God and to the word of his grace, which is able to build you up and to give you the inheritance among all those who are sanctified. (Acts 20:32)

Commend means both *commit to something* and *call unto something*. In other words, Paul is telling his listeners that they've heard everything he has to say about doing faithful gospel ministry. And the hinge it all swings on is where the joy, the power, the hope, the fire, the energy, and the strength come from: the grace of God in the gospel.

・ ・ ・

NOBODY EVER TOLD ME THAT. IN fact, I heard the opposite. After breathing grace for the first time, I was quickly discipled into a culture of works. It wasn't so much that I was earning my salvation by being a good person. I knew that wasn't the case. It was more that since salvation had been given to me, I had to toe the line to remain in those "good graces" of God. Jesus had chosen me; now I had to work hard to prove He had made a wise choice. Jesus had died for me; now I had to pay Him back by living a holy life. The baton was in my hands, and I had to run fast and straight or the whole enterprise would collapse.

The pressure sucked the air right out of my lungs, like my plunge into the ice-cold waters of New Hampshire. I couldn't breathe.

It was like that for years, until I came under the preaching of the doctrines of grace.

Coincidentally, this happened during our time at a tiny congregational church where the air smelled like Lysol and old people, but its spiritual air was White-Mountain sweet. For the three years I was there the pastor stood up and preached grace. Grace all the way through. Grace because I was totally depraved and could do nothing to earn or keep my salvation. Grace because the Lord's election of me was not conditioned by anything I could or would do. Grace because the blood of Jesus was shed for my sin—mine—for good. Grace because my salvation was about the Spirit causing an explosion of repentance and faith to overwhelm my soul, not primarily about my making the right decision. Grace because nothing could change the take-it-to-the-bank fact that I belonged to Jesus for good.

In those years, the message came as clear as I knew it to be: "Kruse, you have been saved; you are being saved; and you will

02 | O₂

be saved by grace. So, breathe grace. And don't stop breathing it." From that experience came planting a church, and we've been determined since day one to make sure everyone knows that the primary action is not us working, but us believing: breathing in the grace of God together.

What is a church, really? A bunch of broken people who were nearly drowned in their sin, now lying on their backs, smiling, inhaling the grace of God in the gospel.

What is a pastor, really? A fallen and fragile man who was nearly drowned in his sin, now lying on his back, smiling, inhaling the grace of God in the gospel—and now commissioned to lead others to that same spot on the ground.

• • •

ONE SUMMER THE SIX OF US piled into a one-bedroom hotel room in Long Beach, California, for five nights of family vacation. One of our bucket list items was surfing lessons. I intended to stand on the shore and take pictures like a good dad, but the beach-bum-instructor who ran the joint insisted that I try it, free of charge.

I was forty-three years old. You are not supposed to do things like learn to surf for the first time when you are forty-three. It took me fifteen minutes just to put on the wetsuit. I was in trouble.

On the water, dozens of thoughts raced through my head: "Keep your head up. Don't collide with the other surfers. Watch out for sharks. Catch the wave at the right time. Knees, foot, stand, bend." As I struggled to keep all this straight, a wave snuck up and drove me face first into the Pacific, and I swallowed a meal of salt, sand, and seaweed. I crawled back onto the board and added a new thought to the pile: "Don't get wasted by a wave."

In all this, I had forgotten to breathe. The instructor looked at me, noticed my color shifting from vacation-tan to about-to-pass-out-green, and said, "Hey, buddy, breathe. The air is free."

That is the bottom line of our life together: the grace of God freely given to us in Christ. Yes, we have a ton of work to do, but our foundational rhythm—the lifegiving reality we are tethered to—is for us to be continually floored by the grace of God to us in Christ.

I've found that church can be where that happens, over and over again.

- BLUEPRINTS -

1. Flood your mind and soul with the gospel.

Go after the gospel the way my kids go after Fun Dip: forget that candy stick, rip the package open, and inhale all that sweetness. Start with the Bible. Memorize and meditate on its gospel promises. Familiarize yourself with every biography of grace in there, from Rahab to Elizabeth, Zacchaeus to the woman at the well, the woman of the city to Peter, Paul to Lydia, the Philippian jailer to the Ethiopian eunuch, the Gerasene demoniac to Timothy, Matthew to Moses, Mephibosheth to the thief on the cross. Revel in the gospel of the Psalms and Proverbs and parables and songs and signs and stories. And then go beyond the Bible to every gospel resource you can find. Listen to Dustin Kensrue and Shai Linne and My Soul Among Lions and Austin Stone and Andraé Crouch (his gospel, not his eschatology). Read John Calvin and John Bunyan and Horatius Bonar and Jared Wilson. Podcast Ray Ortlund and Ajay Thomas and John Piper. Get the gospel in you, whatever the means.

2. Thread the gospel throughout your church's liturgy.

Yes, every Christian sermon should be grounded in the grace of the gospel. We are called to preach Christ. But we're also to form liturgies that do the same. It is impossible not to hear the gospel on a Sunday at Seven Mile Road, not only because the sermon shouts it but also because we've crafted a liturgy that whispers it. Every week, we begin by marveling at God calling us together graciously. Then we humbly confess our sin and desperate need of grace. Next we hear from our pastors that our sins are forgiven because of the cross and that we have been declared righteous by God! Hearing God's word is next, and then we are invited to the Table, where we are welcomed to Jesus Christ. And finally, we are sent out into the world, assured of Christ's presence with us. All liturgy long we are breathing in the fresh air of the gospel.[8]

3. Know where your people are tempted to fade from gospel centrality.

We all tend to replace God Himself as our ultimate joy with other, lesser pursuits. So, it's no surprise we build churches that do the same. For some, good works in the community become the point of the church. For others, it's arguing about and buttoning down theology. Or it's generating charismatic experiences, perfecting operational systems, or realizing church growth. Other churches chase engaging in politics, liberal or conservative. Whatever it is your people tend toward most, boldly remind them it's no substitute for God in the gospel.

03 | MELANOMA

Church can be holy.
On the relentless pursuit of personal holiness.

How I lived … —Acts 20:18

FIVE SUMMERS AGO, I BEGAN SHAVING my head. My children and I huddled in our downstairs bathroom, and I was giving my sons their late-summer, homemade, start-of-school haircuts when my youngest daughter piped up, "What about you, Dad? Let's shave the whole thing!" Twenty minutes, one can of shaving cream, and half a dozen bloody cuts later, I saw Kojak staring back at me in the mirror.

Later that night I noticed, for the first time, a big red birthmark right below what had been my hairline. I'd never seen it before. My only thought was "Huh, if I wasn't getting old and going bald, I never would've known that was there." I didn't ask anyone about it, tell anyone about it, or do anything about it. What I didn't know was that it was melanoma, the worst kind of skin cancer you can get. If I didn't take it seriously and deal with it, it would literally kill me.

It was only when my primary care physician referred me to a dermatologist because of my rosacea (yeah, I have skin problems) that I learned the melanoma was melanoma. The lab tested the reddish mole, and a technician called me back immediately. Her tone was straightforward, serious. "Mr. Kruse, you have melanoma." We looked up melanoma on WebMD and fear descended on our home. It wasn't a faithless fear of dying, but a fitting and proper fear. "Whoa. This is not a joke. We can't just ignore this or pretend it's not there. We need this cancer removed." Two months later, I was strapped to a surgical table, and a chatty but skilled surgeon removed the threat.[9]

Every six months now, Dr. Kornbleuth and I survey every spot on my body, even between my toes. We do this because we won't allow any melanoma to take root in this body again. Anything good and enduring that is going to come of my life hinges on an acute awareness and merciless elimination of any sign of that wretched cancer.

03 | Melanoma

If we are to thrive as pastors and church planters, we must approach our sin the same way.

...

THE LIST OF FEARS I CARRY into my life as pastor and church planter is longer than a Billy Joel anthology.

I am afraid …

- that the church will fail.
- that the church will plateau.
- that all of our most devoted people will move. Far away. All at the same time.
- that we will run out of money.
- that we will run out of musicians.
- that people will get sick of listening to me.
- that I will be imprisoned in Walpole State Prison for speaking words of love that our post-Christian world will label as hate.
- that there will be a Judas on our leadership team or in our membership.
- that there will be a kazillion people at church one morning, and I'll forget to bring my manuscript—or put on my pants.

I am scared of all those things and more. But my greatest fear—one that is not petty, faithless, or vain, but holy—is that sin will take root in my life and disconnect my public persona (what I say, how I look) from my private life (who I am). To use Jesus's analogy, I fear that the outside of the cup of my life will beam brightly while the inside is filthy with compromise, lust, deceit, anger, envy, and fear.

This is a pronounced fear for two reasons.

First, I am a wicked bad, super fast sinner.

I know my identity has changed ontologically from sinner to saint because of the grace of the gospel, but Romans 7 remains true in me. I sin the way Usain Bolt runs. The way Ben Shapiro talks. The way Vic Mackey lies. I am perpetually five minutes away from wrecking my life and ministry. Maybe three minutes, actually. I sin downhill.

I was doing a phone interview once with a seminary student charged with interviewing local church planters about the mechanics of launching a church from scratch. Toward the end, she asked, "Have there been any places where you've seen the Lord at work personally in your life?"

My answer began something like this: "Let's see. I am a coward who is terrified to correct sin in our people; an exaggerator who is especially skilled at painting himself in a warm, glowing light; a malcontent who ogles the grass on everyone else's side of the ministry fence; a skeptic who's never actually sure anyone is ever going to come to legitimate, permanent, saving faith at our church; an applause-monger who obsesses over how every sermon goes and is desperate to hear even a sliver of positive feedback."

Second, I am a really good talker.

By God's providence, I have always been good with words. According to my mother (who may or may not be exaggerating), my first word wasn't "duck" or "plane" or "Dada." It was a cleanly stated, grammatically correct sentence. I knelt down on the sidewalk in front of our St. John Avenue home in Staten Island, pointed under our green Plymouth Duster, looked her in the eye, and said, "The ball is underneath the car." In kindergarten, I played Papa Bear (the role with the most lines) in the school play. In sixth grade, I won the city-wide public speaking

03 | MELANOMA

contest. I gave the valedictory address at my high school graduation and the commencement speech at college graduation. I was tapped as the lead presenter on every case study I did during the MBA program at Boston University. At this point in my life, I have taught thousands of classes, preached more than five hundred sermons, and given a dozen talks to packed conference rooms.

I'm blessed with the gift of gab.

This is a grace, but it's also a deceptive muse. It is possible to articulate heavenly doctrine while living like hell; to sound like Adele but live like a devil; to be a room-owning, smooth-talking sinner.

• • •

I HAVE SEEN FIRSTHAND, THE DEVASTATION that comes on Jesus's people and the disgrace it brings to the gospel when pastors allow for this sinful disconnect to fester between their public and personal lives. The church I grew up in is no longer there, because the pastor hid more sin in his closet than E.L. James puts in her books.[10] The Christian undergraduate school I attended deposed its president because he was using school funds to throw sweet-sixteen bashes for his daughters in the Bahamas and ordering school employees to escort red Lexuses from Atlanta to Tulsa for his wife. The city I grew up in is now Hollywood-famous for decades of secret sins committed by rapist priests.

The building Seven Mile Road now worships in was home to a congregation that closed overnight after its young pastor committed adultery with a daughter of the church. This was a sin so devastating to the congregation that after their final service they locked the doors and never returned. When we toured the space with a real estate agent, the congregation appeared to have been raptured. Old coffee sat in the pot, sheet music remained on the music stands, and the pall of the pastor's betrayal still hung thick in the air.

I'm not throwing rocks or slandering the dead. I could easily get to the place where my name is added to that list. And it wouldn't start with having an affair, stealing money, or freaking out on someone in the parking lot.[11] It would begin with my letting seemingly innocuous sin go unaddressed, treating personal holiness as optional as long as my public ministry was intact, buying the lie that the success of my ministry hinges on how I present, not on how I live.

It would begin by letting melanoma live.

• • •

THIS IS WHY THE VERY FIRST words of Paul's speech in Acts 20 have become so precious to me. How does Paul come out of the gate in summarizing his ministry? He says these beautiful, arresting words: "You yourselves know how I lived among you."

Would any American pastor begin a recounting of his ministry with these words?

Unlikely.

Where would we start?

"You know how I taught among you. How I was faithful to the text, crafted thoughtful, relevant sermons, and racked up the podcast subscriptions."

"You know how I strategized among you. How we went multisite and launched missional communities. We even ran that art gallery back in the early 2000s."

"You know how I studied among you. You saw all those universities listed in my bio, right? Those letters at the end of my name? That's the terminal degree."

"You know how I looked among you. Dark-rimmed glasses. Plaid shirts. The Greek word *Koine* tattooed on my arm. Shaved head."

"You know how I succeeded among you. Attendance increases. Successful capital campaigns. Record giving levels. I was even interviewed on that Gospel Coalition podcast for pastors."

Yet Paul starts with none of these. He doesn't first say, "You know about my sermons, my degrees, my doctrine, my books, my accolades." He says, "You know my life. You know how I lived."

Did Paul teach? Yes. Acts 20 is filled with references to Paul's sound doctrine and faithful gospel teaching.

Did Paul strategize? Yes. He was a church-planting monster. A savant. His strategies for missional engagement were brilliant and varied.

Did Paul write theology? Just this little letter to the Romans. He is the most theologically adept author in the New Testament.

And yet, in the opening salvo of his speech, Paul doesn't highlight any of these. He starts with the holiness and integrity of his life. "You know that the ground of my ministry was the unassailable fact that my private life aligned with my public persona." Before anything else that must mark our ministries, he drives first to the necessity of personal holiness.

. . .

THERE IS NO TENSION HERE: Paul lands the plane of his speech with grace despite having taken off with holiness. The same grace that frees us from our sin and the guilt and shame that accompany it propels us into a lifelong war against it.

Thanks to Tim Keller, most evangelicals in America with an internet connection know by now that the grace of the gospel frees us from moralism. Praise God! The gospel life is not a Ninja Warrior course where, if you successfully maneuver all the obstacles fast enough, you win—or, if you fail, train harder and come back next season and try again. Grace demolishes that. It owns up to the fact that none of us can get past the course's first obstacle without breaking both of our legs and drowning in that three-foot pool underneath it. In the gospel, we are just fans in the crowd marveling that Jesus completed the course perfectly for us, slammed on that red buzzer at the end (*Tetelestai!* It is finished!) and then, in grace, shares his success with us.

Yes, and amen.

But a relentless focus on grace and simultaneous rejection of legalism should never swing us toward license. What does Paul say in Romans to his rhetorical interrogator who insinuates such nonsense? "God forbid!" Grace covers sin, yes. But it doesn't free us to continue in it. Grace is rocket fuel, propelling us toward holiness. Once you've breathed in the life-infusing, sin-forgiving, conscience-cleansing, soul-justifying air of grace, you don't waltz back into a life of sin. To do so would be to cheapen grace, to demean the price that was paid to ransom us from sin, to muddy our witness to Christ in the world, and to make a mockery of God. In the grace-filled soul, a desperate love for and holy fear of God embrace each other. This makes unrepented-of hypocrisy untenable in a grace-enveloped life and a gospel-shaped ministry.

We must be able to say, "You know how I lived" with integrity. And we must be vigilant to work toward this end.

. . .

IF THERE HAS EVER BEEN A church that lived this out, it was the one led by the elders Paul addresses in Acts 20.

Paul arrived in their city and preached the gospel, announcing that the living God had acted decisively in history to redeem sinners through the perfect life, atoning death, and vindicating resurrection of Jesus from Nazareth, who was the Christ. A number of them believed this gospel, and a church was born. Then something happened that changed the way the church lived. They moved from not-so-serious about sin and holiness, to dead serious about it.

Some syncretistic Jewish exorcists in town were living in sin, with no true affections for or obedience to Jesus. Seven sons of a priest named Sceva began co-opting Jesus's name in a magical, incantational, self-serving way. They were stringing the right words together with their mouths, but their lives were all wrong. Jesus and His gospel had become a means to personal gain. This sinful pretense grew like a cancer and ended up nearly getting them killed. All seven got beat naked by a single possessed man and chased through the streets of the city.

We laugh when we read that story, but that's not how the Ephesians reacted. Luke writes that "fear fell upon them all, and the name of the Lord Jesus was extolled" (Acts 19:17). A holy fear descended on the city and the church, and they realized the seriousness of their sin in that moment. They saw that the gospel of Jesus and a fraudulent life cannot coexist without serious consequences.

This epiphany triggered a beautiful response in the soul of the church. Men and women began to confess. Luke says that "many of those who were now believers came, confessing and divulging their practices. And a number of those who had practiced magic arts brought their books together and burned them in the sight of all" (Acts 19:17-18). The gist of their confession probably went something like this: "We are not unlike those seven sons of Sceva. We talk about Jesus, and go to church even, but we still have our magic books on the shelf at home. We've believed the gospel, but we still run to our incantations when we need them. And that is not okay. There is dissonance there that needs to die."

I love this. They saw what melanoma was lurking under their hairlines and cut it out. They torched everything in their lives that enabled, welcomed, domesticated, or normalized their old life of sin. They hauled out a big, rusty, metal trash can from behind the church, tossed their sinful ways in it, doused it all with kerosene, and set fire to whatever might drive a wedge between what they confessed and how they lived.

We must do the same. We must live our lives and lead our churches with kerosene in one hand and a ready match in the other, perpetually setting fire to every sign of sin in our souls.

...

THIS IS WHY PAUL'S FIRST COMMAND in his speech complements his first declaration. If "how I lived" is the non-negotiable foundation that all healthy ministry is grounded on, then "pay careful attention" is a non-negotiable rhythm we must give ourselves to.

Here is how he says it: "Pay careful attention to yourselves."

These words strike me in the same way that the lists of pastoral qualifications in Timothy and Titus do. In those texts, I am expecting Paul to emphasize a variety of skills and competencies required to engage in successful pastoral ministry, but he won't do it. Instead, he deals almost exclusively with character. I am expecting Paul to delineate all the practical elements of church life we are supposed to keep a pulse on, but he doesn't do that either. He doesn't first say, "Pay careful attention to your programs, your demographics, your attendance, your website, your budget, your sermons, your retention rates, and your average giving units." He says, "Pay attention to yourselves." Your personal holiness.

That same urgency must become a part of our pastoral lives.

• • •

EVERY JANUARY THE EXECUTIVE PASTORAL TEAM of our little family of churches treks up the coast to Portsmouth, New Hampshire, for an unrushed time of eating wings, watching the Pats play in the AFC Championship game (since they're always in it), praying, and talking on the state of our souls and churches. Downtown Portsmouth bustles all summer and fall, but in January it's emptier than a gun show in Cambridge. We never see temperatures rise above twenty degrees on these trips, and most of our time outside the hotel is spent sprinting to avoid frostbite. We choose Portsmouth in January not only because it's dirt cheap but also to remind ourselves that our call to plant churches in New England is not an easy road. (Not that we've ever forgotten.)

Prior to one trip, I wrote up a three-page document delineating what I saw to be essential convictions and practices if we were going to thrive as brothers leading a family of churches.

Following Paul's example, I started with these words: "Men, we must relentlessly pursue personal holiness without compromise. Lazy, entitled, secret sin in our lives will dampen, damage, or even destroy everything we are trying to do. We cannot give an inch here. Nothing can slow this thing down or spin this thing sideways like sin in our senior leaders."

We are several years and seven church plants into our dream of becoming a family of churches that love and lead New Englanders to the true Jesus, and we've not yet had a major, ministry-tarnishing sin from a pastoral leader. That's not to say it won't happen. But every day that passes, the fruit of our vigilance produces more glory for God, more integrity before our people, and more freedom to put the gas pedal down in our disciple-making mission.

Settle this now in the souls of your leaders and people: whatever it takes, church will be a place where our private lives and our public personas align with our personal holiness.

– BLUEPRINTS –

1. Give the folks on your team and in the church a hunting license for sin in your life.

Being a Bostonian kid, I've never held or fired a gun. (I told a friend from Bloomington, Indiana, this once, and he looked at me the way I'd look at someone who's never seen *Good Will Hunting* or bought a scratch ticket.) But I do know what a hunting license is, and I've given one to all the men I serve with at Seven Mile Road. Any of them, at any time, knows they are free to ask me anything about my life: language, attitude, behavior, marriage, fatherhood, finances, anything. I do not take offense. I do not dodge the question. I need all the help I can get recognizing and rooting out sin in my life.

2. Require that everyone share his or her story of sin and grace on the front end of all gospel communities, ministry teams, leadership development tracks, etc.

At the formation of any new community at Seven Mile Road (leadership team, training track, gospel community), each of us walks the group through the basics of our story of grace and the sharpest areas of sin in our lives. This includes historical sin that Jesus has washed us from and ongoing sin we are currently working hard to mortify. Doing this helps us get a feel for each other's tendencies, weaknesses, and areas of unbelief so that we might help them "pay careful attention" and move in the direction of holiness.

3. Make it a lifelong pursuit to know and love God's law.

It's tragic that the Ten Commandments are being banished from our public squares and consciousness in these United States. The moral law of God—rooted in God's character, written on our hearts, and communicated in the canon of Scripture—is a gift to believers and unbelievers alike. God's law is more useful than a Swiss Army Knife. It drives us to despair of hoping in our own righteousness and to find it in the person and work of Christ. It reveals to us the brilliance of what God is like. It curbs sinful behavior and secures civil order. And it teaches us how God intends for us to live in this world for His glory and our good. We can't be too familiar with or enamored by God's law (see the exuberance of Psalm 119) in our fight against sin. Let's make sure our personal Bible reading and our pulpit ministries are chock-full of exposures to God's law, that we might know what glad obedience looks like. Read and preach Exodus and Leviticus and Deuteronomy and Matthew and James and 1 John.

04 | OPEN BOOKS

Church can be honest.
On moving people from "all set" to "you know."

You yourselves know … —Acts 20:18, 34

WE NEW ENGLANDERS ARE FAMOUS FOR being closed books.

Maybe it's the climate. From Thanksgiving to April Fool's Day, the weather here bounces between blustery and blizzardy, between wow-it's-cold cold and this-is-the-weather-that-killed-the-wooly-mammoths cold. We have the kind of weather that constantly has us trying to get behind closed doors as fast as possible.

Maybe it's the competitive culture that pervades an ambitious city like ours, where the person next to you is likely a threat to your personal advancement.

Maybe it's the near-death experience that driving is around here, requiring us to be constantly on the defensive.

Maybe the British overtaxing us sans representation from across the pond cemented in our psyche a perpetual skepticism of outsiders.

Whatever it is, we do not let anyone in.

When asked to describe the people Seven Mile Road connects with, I use two expressions: *ungospeled* and *all set*. *Ungospeled* speaks to the lack of everyday Christian witness in the lives of most Bostonians. Although church buildings are scattered throughout our main streets and many of our institutions echo a Christian worldview, most people we connect with have zero daily contact with anyone who is remotely evangelical. *All set* is our go-to phrase for deflecting offers for help, unwanted sales pitches, unsolicited invitations to conversation, and anything else that might give any leverage that can later be used against us. *All set* is the red-lettered warning sign we hang on the barbed-wire, chain-link fence that encircles what's really going on in our lives.

The foundational Bostonian disposition: we're all set.

Except we're not.

I count this as one of the most profound things Jesus has done in the life of Seven Mile Road: We have seen a culture grow in which we long to be holy yet are free to admit how and when we're unholy. Our church has become a place where it is okay for people—Bostonians even—not to have it all together. Not to perform admirably all the time. Not to be perfect. Or even close to perfect. To sin, stupidly, repeatedly, even repugnantly at times. But never to settle into that sin or keep anyone from knowing about that sin. Christ by His Spirit has moved us from "all set" to "nope, not set, at all."

Yes, Al Michaels, I do believe in miracles.

Even more profound, Jesus has called me to be the one to lead the way on this. His choice surprises me—not merely because I was raised in New England culture, but because confessing my weakness and sin did not go well for me the first time I tried.

...

LIKE MOST YOUNG MEN SINCE AT least Solomon's time, saying no to my lusts has never come easy. I was introduced to pornography at 15 by four Playboy bunnies doing naked calisthenics behind some wavy lines on channel 88 of a sixteen-inch Magnavox. This led to a confusing and debilitating struggle into my adolescent life. Although I was devoted to Jesus and doing everything I knew to follow him well, the allure of this particular sin, and my inability to simply walk away from it, devastated me.

Worst of all, no one knew. I had mastered the art of appearing "all set." There was—literally—not one person in the world to whom I could say the words "you know" about what was going on with me. Nobody knew.

Halfway through my sophomore year of college, I realized I was growing incapable of meeting a girl, even a sister in Christ, without my mind racing to sexual speculation and objectification. So, I finally decided to let someone in. I was attending a Christian college, so I sat with my dorm's SLDD (Spiritual Life Dorm Director, possibly the worst acronym ever). Being an all-set Bostonian, I employed a coy, third-person confessional stratagem: "So, listen. I've been talking with this guy. He's been wasting a lot of time on video games, and he's plagiarizing on some class assignments, and, uh, um, uh, viewing pornography. He loves Jesus, but he can't break some of these cycles of sin. What do you think I should say to him?"

I will never forget his response.

He paused, looked me in the eye, and said, "Well, let's start here. It's clear that your friend is not really a Christian. If he were, he wouldn't be doing those things."

I was floored.

Everything I had feared to be true about myself was affirmed in three curtly delivered sentences. They were daggers. Eight years of what I thought was a genuine pursuit of obedience to Jesus turned out to be fraudulent. I had failed the Father, the Son, and the Spirit in one fell swoop. I wasn't David or Paul or Peter. I was Saul and Judas and Ananias rolled into one. According to this spiritual authority in my life, I wasn't even a Christian.

I stumbled out of that room as if I'd been coldcocked by Conor McGregor. And I decided, that night, I was never going to confess sin, ever again, to anyone, ever. To do so would be too risky. It would call into question the very identity I had built my life on. No. I was going to double down on my efforts, in private, to stop sinning and start acting like a halfway decent Christian, and maybe advance over time to being a pretty good one.

The subsequent years were a death cycle of attempts at self-righteousness. On the good days, I would hold firm on my commitment not to sin, and I'd feel good about my performance. On the bad days, I would hate myself, feeling I was living alone at the bottom of a well I deserved to be in for the rest of my life.

It wasn't until I was a couple of years into planting Seven Mile Road—yes, ten years after my dorm confession—with the weight of my years of secret sin still hanging like an anvil around my neck, that I risked confessing to someone again.

. . .

KEVIN AND BRIDGET HAD SPENT TWO years serving as missionaries on the Comoros Islands off the eastern coast of central Africa. (Spin the globe a few times, you'll find it.) They pushed pause on their missionary life so Kevin could pursue theological training at Gordon-Conwell Theological Seminary, thirty minutes north of Seven Mile Road. They spent a year tacitly attending our church while getting situated to a new school in a new apartment with a new baby in a new (again) country. It was clear Kev was a "deep-waters" kind of soul. We scheduled some time to talk about their getting more deeply involved in the life of the church. He and I sat on two rickety folding chairs (church plants and comfortable furniture don't mix). I was hoping to cast some vision for what we were going for as a church and how I thought they would be able to both receive and give in meaningful ways.

Instead, I ended up confessing, through tears, aloud, for the second time ever, with no edits and no third-party games, all the sin that marked my life to that point. I don't know how long it took. It could have been hours. I dragged everything out on the table. All the lust. All the deceit. All the selfish ambition. All the people-pleasing. All the fear. All the unbelief. There it was, in all its embarrassing gore.

When I finally stopped, my mind raced back to that college dorm room, the SLDD's condemnation still cutting through my soul. I was waiting for Kev's response of "Wait, you are a pastor? That can't be right."

But that's not what happened. Kev nodded. He shifted slightly in his chair. The silence lingered. His laser-blue eyes never left mine. And then he spoke, but not words of condemnation. Or accusation. Or indictment. Instead, he began to confess his own sin.

There we were. Two grown men involved in ministry, alone in a room, with all our sin sitting in a rickety folding chair next to us.

I have never felt freer in my life. Someone else finally knew I wasn't all set and loved me anyway.

...

THIS IS WHAT THE GOSPEL IS FOR. It's not for building a community that ducks and dodges and hides. It's not for recruiting religious Navy Seals to give all-star performances for Jesus. God's grace in the gospel exists precisely because we don't walk the line. We do sin, fast and furious. And the fallout is bad; our lives, and the lives of those closest to us, get messed up. We need the gospel to experience forgiveness and freedom from all our sin. And, as the grizzled apostle John teaches us, that happens only if we open the books of our lives and come clean in community.

04 | OPEN BOOKS

A.S.A. Harrison's *The Silent Wife*[12] is a dark story about a godless, childless, self-absorbed marriage that implodes. Todd and Jodi are as all set as a couple can be, until they aren't. Right when things are hinging toward really bad (like put-a-hit-out-on-your-husband bad), the narrator says, "In the past she has always been open with her friends, but that was when she was on top of things. Jodi not coping is something they don't need to witness." In other words, this woman is an open book, all about community and authenticity and being real with her girls, until her performance falters. Until the sin in her marriage and her life is exposed. Until Miss Got-It-All-Together becomes Miss-Wicked-Hot-Mess and retreats into the darkness of her sin. I read that and thought, "Wow. I've met lots of Jodis. Jodi needs Jesus. And girlfriends. And a church family in which she is free to be a broken sinner in need of grace."

. . .

WHAT WE'VE SOUGHT TO DO AT Seven Mile Road is build a church culture for the Jodis, where the two words that best define us are no longer "all set" but "you know." An ethos of openness, transparency, vulnerability, honesty, and safety. A community where there is no barbed-wire, chain-link fence around our lives, but instead a willingness to let others in. A church where everyone walks with a limp and nobody tries to hide it.

The words "you know" come directly from Jesus's apostle Paul. He lived this way with his people, as evidenced by his repeated use of that beautiful two-word refrain. His life was an open book. He sat in rooms on rickety folding chairs with the elders and saints in the churches he planted and put his sin on the table. "Blasphemer. Persecutor. Insolent opponent. Chief of sinners. That was me. Wretched Man is still what I am. I'm not all set. I need Jesus, just like you. Now you know."

I love this. And it's my ambition to live with the people Jesus has given me the way Paul did with his.

• • •

THE YEAR WE LAUNCHED SMALLER COMMUNITIES for the first time (we called them "soulcare" communities), we began by training several couples in what we were aiming at. Kevin and Bridget were there along with Grace and me, Rob and Patti, Brent and Jessie, John and Julie, Matt and Laurel, and some others. The training happened in a tiny, first-floor apartment at the Medford Heights apartment complex. The men walked to the common dining area and pulled a table and chairs together. It was time to train on the confession of sin. Without hesitation, I said, "Okay, men, I'll go first. Here are my issues." I took the next ten minutes to confess—honestly, specifically, without edits—the sin in my life, past and present.

For many of these Bostonian brothers, this was the first time they had ever heard a man confess his sin. For all of them, it was the first time they heard a pastor do it. Wait, aren't you supposed to be the guy who's got the Christian thing down pat by now? Aren't you afraid people knowing you still sin will undermine your credibility? Shouldn't you keep these gory details to yourself, or at least talk with someone outside of the actual church?

I finished, and time stopped. Nobody moved. The fluorescent lights buzzed overhead. I swallowed hard.

Then the floodgates opened.

Man after man confessed his sin, great and small, past and present, mundane and extreme. We realized there were no rock stars in the room, no super saints. Just a heaping pile of lust and deceit and bitterness and greed and fear and anger and envy and all the rest, stacked seven feet high on a table.

And we were free of it.

No more pretense. No more facades. Just a brotherhood of broken, sinful, men and the cleansing power of the blood of Jesus Christ.

And this was not a one-shot deal. Ten years later, I am regularly calling and texting the men I serve with at Seven Mile Road and confessing sin or almost sin:

> Hey, it's me. Listen, I'm ten minutes from home, and I know nobody is there, and today has sucked so far, and everything in me is saying to look at porn, and nobody would know, but I'm not going there.

> Yo, just found out that my son stole from his mom again. I'm going to sit with him in a minute and wanted to make sure someone knew about it and holds me accountable to not physically assault him, even though I want to. Bad. Pray for me.

> Kid, headed for a potential new member interview and need to confess something. I do not like this guy I'm sitting with. If this was kickball, I'd pick him last. And I don't want to carry that pettiness into such an important conversation.

By God's grace, this willingness to invite others into the struggle with sin now runs through our entire congregation. I got a call once from a godly young woman in our church whose younger brother was found dead from a drug overdose in the back of a Greyhound bus on its way to Worcester. She had called to get some help with the eulogy, but she ended up confessing sin. "Matt, can I talk with you about something? I don't know what to do with this, but part of me is glad he is dead. He deserved it. I have no compassion for him right now. I know that's wrong." I've had twenty-year-olds call me and confess sexual sin from thirty minutes before. I've had grown men confess affairs hidden for decades. I've listened to angry mothers, lazy husbands, ungrateful daughters, and heroin addicts—all of them admitting what they've done and left undone. And in every case, I have seen the love of God for sinners rush in.

• • •

WHEN MY SON BRANDON WAS SIX, he was messing with my iTunes account and did something he knew he shouldn't do. He changed the name of a song to "blop fart." When I saw it, I sat with him, but he refused to tell me aloud what he did. Because I love my son, and because I know the forgiveness and freedom available (immediately!) in the gospel if we'll freely confess what we've done, I made him sit. I steered him as best I could to confess, but I couldn't do it for him. So, being a Kruse, he sat in his chair a long while, refusing to break.

I waited. And waited. And waited.

Finally, he asked me if he could write down what he had done. What he handed me was one of those things you tuck away and save forever. It read:

> Dear Dad. Here is what I did. I changed the name of the song to blop fart.
> Love, Brandon.

I read it, held him, forgave him, and I was glad God in His grace was shaping his little soul to move from "all set" to "now you know, and I am free."

Church can be a place where people experience that freedom and forgiveness constantly.

– BLUEPRINTS –

1. You first.

Don't believe the lie that runs in church circles that as "the pastor" you can't be real with your people. I had a fellow pastor in Massachusetts tell me once how he couldn't invite his elder board into the struggles he was having because "they couldn't handle it." This is nonsense. Jesus handles our sin, not the elders, or anyone else. And one of Jesus's means of grace to us is other sinners with whom we can walk in the light and receive His forgiveness. This is also a death trap. Keeping up appearances will kill you. The one place you should be safe to struggle and fail and get up and go at it again is among your own congregation. Model this always by being the first one to confess your sin.

2. Press for times of confession to be as concrete as possible.

All of us, New Englanders or not, prefer to avoid confessing that we have sinned. And even when we are willing to admit that much, we favor nebulous to specific. *I lusted and clicked on some terrible videos* becomes "I had a bad day with my eyes." *I disciplined my son in anger* becomes "Boy, he pushed my buttons." *I lied* becomes "I proactively withheld information." *I committed adultery* becomes "I had an affair."

A few years ago, I sat in on a gathering led by a pastor who had committed adultery with a woman on his staff early in his ministry. (He had also been restored in his marriage, which I was super glad about.) Everyone knew that at some point during the day together he would reference his church-splitting sexual sin. When he finally mentioned it, he spoke vaguely about how "we went through the darkest time of our life." I found that equivocation disingenuous. If you didn't already know the story, you wouldn't have known whether he had suffered a tragedy, been the victim of a burglary, gone through a dry spell in his devotional life, or been sinning sexually with a woman he wasn't married to. A commandment was broken here. Lots of them, actually. Let's just call it what it is. Another friend of mine just went through this same thing at his church, and in dealing with it publicly the word *adultery* was never mentioned once. Walking in the light is not confessing that we had a bad day. It's saying that God has revealed to us his beautiful, perfect, holy, moral law, and we've broken it. Full stop.

So, love your people by slowing down and helping them call sin by its name.

I committed adultery.

I lied.

I coveted.

I envied.

I played scared.

I am married, but I pursue and enjoy flirting with women who are not my wife.

I am a woman, but I don't respect my husband, and you should have heard the way I talked to him in front of the kids.

I am lazy, so lazy. I spent twenty-four hours watching college football, which I knew was sinful stewardship of my time. I watched the third and fourth seasons of *Game of Thrones*. In a row.

I love money, love it, so much that I make $100,000 a year but give almost nothing.

Naming our sin like this helps us to see it for what it is. Ugly. Awful. Ridiculous. And it allows us to be forgiven. Christ bled and died to forgive our adulteries and thefts and slanders, not our bad days.

3. Always tie confession to repentance.

We are not confessing sin as some secular therapeutic exercise that helps us feel a little better about ourselves. Nor are we doing it as a badge of honor to show that "we keep it real around here." We are confessing sin so that we might be forgiven of it and free from it and done with it.

A few years ago, there was an art display in Vegas. The curator invited hotel guests to anonymously write down their confessions in a private booth. Then she pinned them up on an artsy display. The confessions were things like "I'm in love with my best friend. … Too bad he's married." "I steal pens from work." "The day I found out I was pregnant with my daughter I stopped using cocaine." "I eat too much cheese." "I'm afraid I'll die alone." The *Huffington Post* published a story on the exhibition and wrote, "Through the project Chang shows how the personal and the public, when intertwined, can increase our happiness and sense of community."[13]

This is faux confession. True gospel confession means not only allowing ourselves and our sins to be known simply but also actually turning from those sins. Always tie confession to repentance and a renewed pursuit of obedience.

05 | LIGHTS

Church can be humble.
On having no rock stars but Jesus.

With all humility … —Acts 20:19

I WAS BORN AT ST. VINCENT'S Hospital in Staten Island, New York. On my first visit to Manhattan that I can remember, I was nine years old, and we were going to see *Joseph and the Amazing Technicolor Dreamcoat* on Broadway. Before the show, my family and I wandered the streets near the theater. I stared awestruck at skyscrapers with seemingly bottomless foundations, dodged horn-blasting yellow taxis, and watched shady street-magic from even shadier magicians. I'll always remember standing on the sidewalk in front of the theater, taking in the bright lights above the entrance with the names of each cast member blazing, thinking, "I want my name up there someday."

M::A::T::T::H::E::W::K::R::U::S::E

Perfect.

Broadway never panned out for me, but I did find a vocation that has me speaking on a stage for a living. And I still dig the idea of my name being in lights.

Which brings me to a long, ugly, rambling confession.

I want to pastor a big church. Big. I want to be known as the guy who successfully planted and grew a big church in an impossibly tough zip code. I want people to recruit me to sit on panels about how to plant a big church like that. I want to be able to tell stories about how we outgrew this space, then that space, and then another one. I want my church to be the perpetual answer to the question "Who's got the fastest-growing church in New England?" Then I want to tweet "I do" and drop it in huge font on the landing page of our website. I want my podcast to hit some top ten list, somewhere, for something, anything. I want my church to be so big we could lose two hundred people in a weekend and brush it off like it's nothing. I want to be asked questions about how we grew so fast and so big. And I'll say, "It's all about Jesus. I'm just a jar of clay," all while positioning the jar at just the right angle for the cameras.

I want my name in lights.

Every pastor does, in one way or another. But Jesus will have none of it. The New Testament is clear: there is room for only one name to be blazed across the life of a church, because there is only one name to be blazed across eternity, one name above all names, unrivaled: *Jesus*. And the pursuit of every sinner saved by grace, pastors included, must never be our names in lights, but His.

. . .

THIS IS WHY WE'VE SOUGHT TO build a church that refuses the pyramid schemes prevalent in American church culture. I know how these schemes work because I was raised in one. At the top is the pastor and his wife, and everyone else in the church scrambles to ascend to their spiritual, marital, financial, and professional heights. Ninety-nine out of one hundred times they can't get there, so they settle into living vicariously through those at the top. Everything in the church's life hinges on and flows from the gifting, charisma, and all-around awesomeness of these two leaders atop the pyramid.

A very specific recipe is required to bake this cake.

RECIPE FOR THE PERFECT PYRAMID SCHEME CAKE

Ingredients
- 1 Rock Star Pastor: witty, articulate, thin, likable
- 1 Rock Star Pastor's Wife: witty, articulate, thin, likable, fashion-conscious
- 1-2 (no more) trouble-free, photogenic children
- 1 large home in ritziest zip code near church building

- 1-3 foreign luxury vehicles
- 1-2 signs in front of church with pastor's name prominently displayed
- 1 robust social media presence, carefully curated

Instructions
- Ensure pastor and wife look great, sound great, perform great all the time.
- Encourage pastor to refer to wife as "hot" and "my better half" as often as possible.
- Disallow any admission of sin, doubt, weakness, failure, or struggle from pastor or wife (speeding tickets exempted).
- Schedule pastor to preach on all high-attendance Sundays.
- Surround pastor with yes-men in all positions of ecclesiological authority.
- Chase off any congregants with dissenting opinions.

That's the recipe, and the American church loves to bake that cake. We do it unapologetically because of its pragmatic appeal: it works. For a while, anyway. The church grows, the money flows, the mission goes. Celebrity culture is not renounced but embraced. Self-importance is baptized. Self-promotion is sanctified. Building and hyping the pastor-centric brand becomes crucial to ministry success. We replace *Wall Street* villain Gordon Gekko's cry that "greed is right" with our own: "Vanity is right!"

None of us is exempt from this temptation.

ONE OF THE CHURCH-PLANTING NETWORKS WE run with is called Acts 29. It is impossible to overstate how meaningful it was for us to get connected to this network twelve years ago. The theology, the missiology, the relationships, and the training all helped us dramatically in clarifying who we were and why we were doing what we were doing in starting Seven

Mile Road. Yes, parachurch organizations and church-planting networks are expendable institutions with expiration dates stamped on them by the Spirit, but they serve a beautiful and helpful role in the advance of the gospel when they strengthen the mission of the local church, which is what Acts 29 does. For years, we have loved the brothers and sisters in Acts 29 and invested significantly in the network in the hope of it thriving. We wouldn't be where we are without it.

In the early days of the network's existence, Acts 29 was lumped into what was dubbed the "Young, Restless, and Reformed" movement. There was a lot to like about that description, but the dark side of our youth was our immaturity and pride. We were a bunch of entrepreneurs dissatisfied with the status quo of church and wanted to make a name for Jesus among the people we loved. But even the slightest success easily morphed into making a name for ourselves and our churches. The rapid growth of some of our larger churches and the meteoric rise of the internet provided a sudden and staggering platform for national notoriety: we nobodies were becoming somebodies, fast. We quickly developed a brand identity and began to care excessively about how we looked and sounded. Tattoos, facial hair, Affliction T-shirts, black-rimmed glasses, curse words in sermons, constant references to drinking alcohol and smoking pipes, and a dozen other "tells" set us apart from other churches.

The allure of the lights was real.

In 2010, at the height of Acts 29's influence and fame, you couldn't find an American Christian (even here in Boston) who didn't have a strong opinion one way or the other about Mark Driscoll, Mars Hill, and Acts 29. I was on a team tasked with planning Acts 29's Northeast Regional Conference. I was asked what I thought the theme for the day should be, and I didn't hesitate: vanity and envy. Whenever the Lord blesses a movement of churches as He had ours, celebrity culture inevitably creeps in. Somebody's name has to be in the lights. Somebody has to be nudged toward the top of the pyramid. The two sins that accompany any move toward celebrities and lights and pyramids are vanity and envy: some of the pastors get elevated, and everyone else gets frustrated that it wasn't him. Knowing this, and knowing the wiles of my own heart, I said: "Let's zero in on the church planter's soul and address the twin sins of vanity and envy. If not, they'll kill us."

The conference went well but, being held in New England, had a limited impact on the network. Not long after, my fears materialized when we got word that one of our brothers, in a session with his elders, berated everyone in the room with these words: "I am the brand!"

I went behind closed doors and mourned the day I heard that report, but not in judgment. I mourned in repentance. I may never have yelled those exact words (probably because of how ridiculous they'd sound coming from the pastor of a hundred-person church), but I'd nurtured the premise in my heart. I'd love it if brand management were central to our church growth strategy, especially if the brand was me.

All of us trend in that direction.

But Jesus has something better for us.

. . .

THE SELF-UNDERSTANDING THAT JESUS'S apostle Paul brought to gospel ministry did not come out of Madison Avenue's playbook. He did not have lights or pyramids in mind when he planted his churches. In fact, there are four titles he took on himself, and none were remotely close to "The Brand."

1. CHIEF OF SINNERS

In 1 Timothy 1:15, Paul writes, "The saying is trustworthy and deserving of full acceptance, that Christ Jesus came into the world to save sinners, of whom I am the foremost."

If sin were a boxing match, Paul would have worn the heavyweight belt. If lawbreaking were organized crime, Paul would have been a mob boss. If holiness were a pyramid, Paul would have known where he belonged: level one, bottom floor, living in the basement apartment.

If someone lined up every soul in your church, side by side, and asked you to point out the worst sinner of the lot, where would your finger be headed? The serial adulterer? The once-a-month attender? The brash, rebellious, gossipy drama queen? The fifty-year-old Trader Joe's clerk who pays for virtual sex? No. As pastors we must—without hesitation—tap that finger to our own chests. "Right here. No one has a darker heart in this family. The whole reason I get to lead is so that everyone knows: if this guy can be rebuilt through the grace of the gospel, there is hope for anybody."

2. LEAST OF THE APOSTLES

In 1 Corinthians, where Paul is defending the historicity of the gospel events, he lists off everyone who saw and touched and ate with the risen Christ, and then he writes these words: "Last of all, as to one untimely born, he appeared also to me. For I am the least of the apostles, unworthy to be called an apostle, because I persecuted the church of God" (1 Cor. 15:8-9).

Paul could have easily defended why he was the premier apostle. He had the most training, knew his Bible the best, and had the most church-planting success. He covered more miles, preached more sermons, debated more opponents, wrote more letters, shaped more leaders, and endured more suffering than any of them. But what does he say? "I am the least of the apostles." If there were an Apostolic League Draft, Paul would be Mr. Irrelevant. If apostleship were a horror movie, he'd be dead in the first twenty minutes. If apostles were presidents, he'd be Benjamin Harrison.

Wait, who?

Exactly.

3. SERVANTS

In his First Letter to the Corinthians, Paul was dealing with rivalry in the church. (Nope, *Outreach Magazine* didn't invent the Top 100 Pastors list, and celebrity church culture did not start with Andy Stanley and Ed Young.) Sunday mornings in Corinth resembled Friday night at Comic-Con, aisles filled with fans donning the colorful shirt of their favorite apostle. "I'm with Apollos! Peter is my guy! Paul for me!"

Seeking to put a bullet in the head of this superhero stupidity, Paul posed an important (if rhetorical) question: "What then is Apollos? What is Paul?" (1 Cor. 3:5).

We know how the Corinthians would have responded. They would have gone for a moniker that captured the essentiality and irreplaceability and superiority of their guy, something like Apostle or Super Apostle or The Lord's Anointed or MVP (Most Valuable Pastor) or the kind of flamboyant title that an African president might christen himself with.[14] They would have headed straight for the top of the pyramid in search of a fitting answer.

That's not the direction Paul goes in. He doesn't ride the elevator north to some fancy-pants ecclesiastical penthouse suite in search of the right label. He doesn't scour *Harvard Business Review* for the latest and greatest in Silicon Valley nomenclature. He walks down to the scullery, in the back of the kitchen, and chooses the most ordinary, dingy, forgettable, commonplace designation in the lexicon of his day. It's a title that appears more than one thousand times in the Bible, worn by men and women, boys and girls, those of good repute, ill repute, and no repute at all: servants.

"What then is Apollos? What is Paul? Servants …"[15]

My first job was as an afterschool janitor of an early childhood center in Revere. I smelled some things in that job I will never un-smell. There was zero sexy to that work, and that's what a servant is. Lowly, invisible, unpretentious, and easily replaceable. The guy who carries your bags to your hotel room, the woman who replaces your toilet paper and puts the mint on your pillow, the kid who vacuums the dirt off the bottom of the pool.

Nobodies. That's us.

4. JAR OF CLAY

In 2 Corinthians 4, Paul is stretching the limits of language to convey to his readers the unrivaled glory of Christ. In verse 7, he juxtaposes Jesus with Jesus's gospel ministers and says, "We have this treasure [Christ] in jars of clay [us, gospel ministers], to show that the surpassing power belongs to God and not to us."

Eighty percent of my Instagram feed is filled with people posting pictures of food. (I get it. You had dinner tonight. Congratulations.) The one thing every one of those pictures has in common is that there is food on the plates. Colorful, textured, and usually environmentally friendly. What I've never seen is someone post an image of an empty place setting. I've never driven away from a delicious meal with friends and been like, "Wow, those plates though! They were something else. Did you see the pattern on those bowls?"

The plate is not the point.

Neither is the jar of clay.

Being thirty minutes from a historically evangelical seminary has its perks. We get a good flow of young men and women serious about completing their heady theological education with some real-life, boots-on-the-ground gospel ministry in one of the least Christian regions of the country. But a downside is the constant stream of requests for a "brief conversation" about church planting to fulfill some class requirements. One time I was completing a seemingly endless survey on the phone, and the interviewer asked me, "Who do you consider to be the top church planters in the New England area?" In my head, I went, *Who cares?* Then I paused, gathered myself, and, with Paul's words ringing in my soul, said: "Jesus, and a sorry collection of clay pots."

If Paul's choice of titles signals anything to us, it's that it is antithetical to the gospel for pastors and church planters to traffic in the world of brands and lights and pyramids and survey questions about who the best church planters are.

• • •

THIS IS WHY I LOVE THAT near the beginning of his speech, where Paul strings together three adjectives describing his time among the Ephesians, he places humility first on the list: "You yourselves know how I lived among you … , serving the Lord with all humility …" (Acts 20:18-19).

Paul is not demeaning the glory of his apostolic calling or the dignity of the office of elder by choosing the lowliest adjective available. He's communicating not only what must be true but also what inevitably becomes true for anyone who resolves to live and lead as Christ did.

In order to qualify and equip us for the work, Jesus humbles us.

That Paul could write these words with integrity was a minor miracle, a fascinating work of the Spirit. Paul's upbringing makes our American concept of "white privilege" pale in comparison. He had Jewish blood, invested parents, a brilliant mind, a world-class education, a relentless work ethic, dual citizenship, religious zeal, and a biting wit. Everything was in place for him to scale the heights of whatever profession he pursued.

But then Jesus knocked him off his horse. Literally.[16] In the middle of the day. With everyone watching. Had YouTube existed, that video would have gone viral overnight. Half-blinded by the brilliance of Jesus's appearance, he had to be led, by the hand, to Damascus. He fasted and prayed for three nights, but Jesus didn't say a word to him. Instead, Jesus required that Paul submit to the ministry of Ananias. Then He appointed him Apostle to the [filthy, dirty, disgusting] Gentiles, which was the least desirable assignment in the early church. And if that wasn't enough, he allowed a "thorn" to be embedded permanently in his flesh. We obsess over what the thorn was (God only knows), but we do know why it was: "To keep me from becoming conceited" (2 Cor. 12:7).

It was a broken, humble man that showed up to do gospel ministry in Ephesus.

The same must be, and will be, true for us.

...

MY JOURNEY IN PLANTING AND PASTORING Seven Mile Road has been less like the scaling of some great mountain and more like Jesus taking me on a long hike straight down the side of a pyramid. Bad sermons, misreading of people's character, false conversions, failed strategic initiatives, devastating transience, defiant teenagers, a difficult marriage: Christ has used them all to walk me and my ego to the basement apartment, that I might be finally useful to Him and His people.

Recently as I was brushing my teeth, I noticed that staring back at me wasn't the fast-talking, slam-dunking, gel-in-the-hair church-planting prodigy I fancifully remember. It was a middle-aged guy with rosacea, melanoma, zero hair, and a chip in his front tooth.

I saw the grace of God in that mirror, and Jesus's name in the lights above.

– BLUEPRINTS –

1. Refuse to elevate—and whenever possible, to differentiate—yourself from others on your team, in your congregation, or in your context.

Make sure the profile page for staff on your website doesn't communicate a Varsity-versus-JV feel. When someone else is preaching on a Sunday morning, don't wander around the back of the room; sit and listen like everyone else. Don't put your name on the sign in front of the church, please. Periodically clean some toilets and set up some chairs. Take the worst bed on overnights. Order your food last at the counter. Preach Jesus while wearing the same outfit every week. For me, this is black Vans my daughter picked out, blue jeans, and a black button-down. For you, it might be something different, but the point is to communicate clearly that you are not wanting to be noticed. (I know, I know, there is a danger here of a reverse-vanity in which your refusal to obsess over your appearance becomes a point of pride. If that happens, change it up.) Whatever it is, discipline yourself toward the kind of humility that makes outsiders unable to decipher you from others. Better yet, let your relentless service to others be what stands out.

2. Look at your hands.

Each Sunday, we finish our liturgy with a benediction and sing the Doxology. Like everyone else, I stand and sing. Every time we get to the second line ("Praise Him all creatures here below") I take a long look at my hands. Doing so reminds me of my fragility, my mortality. After all these years of pastoring, my hands have gotten older, wrinkled, and worn. No one with those dying hands can strut out of the worship service proud.

3. Get down on your knee when you talk with children.

Hanging out after the service at Seven Mile Road is like being at Chuck E. Cheese on All-You-Can-Eat-Fun-Dip Day. Dozens of toddlers, hyped up on fruit punch and Goldfish, pinball from wall to wall in our sanctuary. I love these children. (Many of them think that the church is my house and get terribly confused when they see me somewhere else in the city.) Whenever one of them comes up to me to show me something or tell me something, I always get down on one knee so I can look them in the eye and listen carefully. If I am above talking with a child, I am above entering the kingdom of God.

06 | TEARS

Church can be heartbreaking.
On investing ourselves emotionally in the work.

With tears ... —Acts 20:19

SO, I AM NOT A FOODIE. I know this is a cardinal sin against American culture right now. Sue me. Maybe it's because my wife Grace is a wonderfully fantastical Italian super chef who regularly serves up meals that would win contests on the Food Network. Maybe it's because the sleepover menu at my grandmother's in Queens included White Castle hamburgers and Oscar Mayer prepackaged bologna on white Wonder Bread. Maybe there is something biologically wrong with my palate.

Whatever it is, I don't really care about the latest ingredients, the sexy new vegetable, or the cool new restaurant that just opened. My culinary thought process is elementary: I'm hungry, there's food, I'm good.

This has caused some major relational conflicts within our pastoral team, because the guys I serve with are foodies. One of our pastors glared at me in disgust when I brought a peanut butter and jelly sandwich to a lunch meeting. When I later admitted I didn't know there were different kinds of vinegar for salads, we almost came to blows.

Another time we were in southern California at a church event, and Dan Ko, planter of our Malden congregation, said, "Hey, do you guys want to get some Korean BBQ in Koreatown for lunch?" He asked with vigor and enthusiasm. I replied with nonchalance, "Yeah, whatever." Startled and offended by my response, he was either looking for me to fight him on it—"No way, man. I don't do Korean BBQ"—or to begin weeping—"Yes, I've always wanted to eat Korean BBQ in Koreatown! Green tea! Kimchi!" He wanted one extreme or the other, not "Yeah, whatever."

Instead, I basically shrugged my shoulders.

Shrugged shoulders are a sign of disinterest, of emotional detachment. Of not being invested in a situation or an outcome.

They are the physical display of a heart that says "Yeah, whatever, doesn't really matter."

We are all like this with many things. I am like this with food, animals (I don't think your dog is cute. I didn't cry when Bambi died. I didn't panic when they shot that gorilla in the zoo. I don't swoon over the exhibits at the aquarium where they delineate how there are only nineteen fuzzy horned seals left in the Pacific Ocean), cars, fashion, political conventions, celebrities, soccer, Hallmark holidays, and *Game of Thrones*. None of these moves me.

...

WHEN I WAS 9, I WATCHED my first Super Bowl. It was the Redskins versus the Dolphins. I was a rabid Dolphins fan at the time, not because I had ever been to Florida or liked gray sea mammals or was drawn to any marketable superstars (this was before Dan Marino), but because my cousin Stephen loved the Dolphins, and that was good enough for me.

On game day, I sat in our basement, as excited as a grammar-school kid could be, ready for the big game. It never crossed my nine-year-old mind that my team could lose, but then John Riggins ran forty-three yards over a left tackle to pay dirt, and the Dolphins lost. At the end of the game, I didn't just go "Yeah, whatever," shrug my shoulders, and go play *Asteroids* on the Atari 2600. I wept. One of those long, sloppy, mom-can't-even-console-you cries.

I cried like a nine-year-old kid whose team just lost the Super Bowl.

Why the tears?

Because I was invested.

Tears are the language of "this matters." Tears can come from happiness, or they can come from sadness, but they cannot flow from disinterest or detachment. Tears only accompany investment. This is why we cry when we're accepted into college, and it's why we cry when we're not. It's why we cry at weddings and at divorces. We cry when we hit the lottery, and we cry when we lose our jobs. We cry when the stick turns blue, and we cry when the doctor tells us we've miscarried. We cry when Dad comes home from war, and we cry when he doesn't.

What binds all of these tears together?

That something really matters to us.

. . .

IT'S INSTRUCTIVE THAT OVER AND OVER again in Scripture we see God's people moved to tears. Although many things in life are fine for you to not be into, the life and mission of the church is not one of them. The Spirit makes plain to us that we are to be emotionally invested in our life together as Jesus's people because that work matters. Every good pastor ever, and every true saint ever, has been devoted to that reality with tears.

Take Nehemiah. When he hears that Jerusalem is in shambles and her saints are in disgrace and doing terribly,[17] what does Nehemiah do? Does he shrug his shoulders and move on? No: "As soon as I heard these words I sat down and wept and mourned for days" (Neh. 1:4). Nehemiah was rightly invested in the glory of the city of God and in the good of her people. Jerusalem mattered to him.

Take the psalmist of Psalm 119. He is waxing (and waxing and waxing and waxing) poetic about his love for the truth and beauty and brilliance of God's words. Then, in verse 136, he says something profound. It comes to his mind how sometimes God's people don't love and live by God's words. And what does he say when he remembers this? "My eyes shed streams of tears, because people do not keep your law." Whoa. This man was invested in seeing the law of God cherished, honored, embraced, and kept. When the people of God disregarded the words of God, he didn't just shrug his shoulders and move on. He was moved to tears. That failure of obedience mattered to him.

Take Jesus's apostle John. Have you ever read his letters? They get uncomfortable at times because he is so emotionally invested in his people. (After reading John's letters you feel like your grandfather just gave you one of those sloppy, wet, scratchy, old-man-breath kisses.) As John writes to his beloved children, he says things like "I have no greater joy than to hear that my children are walking in the truth" (3 John 4). Whoa. Maybe John was a foodie. Maybe he got big joy from kale salad and bubble tea. Maybe not. Maybe he had a German shepherd, maybe not. But I am telling you that if John lined up all his passions, everything he was invested in, first in line with no rivals in sight was this: the people of God. The work of the gospel. The health of the church. Gospel doctrine (truth) and gospel culture (their walking in it). That was everything to John. So, when he would hear that Jesus's people were thriving? Tears of joy.

Take the apostle Peter. In his epistle to pastors and elders and (through them) to all of us, he says, "Shepherd the flock of God that is among you, ... not under compulsion, but willingly ... eagerly" (1 Pet. 5:2). You could translate that "Love the church, not with shrugged shoulders, but with tears."

And then take the apostle Paul.

He articulates this idea of emotional investment in his Acts 20 speech to the Ephesian elders with these two emotionally charged words: *with tears*. Twice in this speech, Paul uses the phrase *with tears* to communicate the pathos of his gospel ministry.

First, we see *with tears* is the middle of a triad of pillars on which his ministry among them was built. He engaged them "with all humility and with tears and with trials." Paul was humble. Paul drew conflict. And Paul was emotionally invested.

I love that. He says, "Brothers, here is one of the ways you know my ministry among you was genuine. You saw me cry. A lot. I shed tears. Right in front of you. With you. For you." And not just once in a great sentimental while. Paul wept often enough that they would have known it as a mark of his ministry. He went through some serious Kleenex with these people. He was moved to tears frequently. This work mattered to him.

The phrase *with tears* then appears a second time, toward the end of his speech, as Paul reminds them of the relentless urgency he brought to his warning, pleading, and admonishing of them. He says, "I admonished everyone with tears." In other words, "I wasn't going through the motions with you. I wasn't speaking at the front of the class with a Charlie-Brown-esque monotone, waiting for the bell to ring and summer break to start. I wasn't distracted by other pursuits, playing *Fruit Ninja* half the time. I was not punching a clock with you. I was invested. It mattered to me that you listened and believed and obeyed."

Have you ever seen bad dads or moms at the playground? There's a giant slide, but they issue the briefest, most checked-out warnings to their child while staring at a cell phone. "Don't get hurt, honey." Then when the child falls and cuts his head open and there is blood everywhere, what do they say? "I told you not to walk up the slide." Well, they did, but they didn't. Not with the specificity or the urgency that was called for. They weren't invested in their child's safety.

Have you ever seen a good dad or mom giving a teenager keys to the car for the first time—or the first fifty times? For months, the parents plead with them, "You have to put your seatbelt on. You have to stay off Route 1 at all costs. And for the love of God do not text while you are driving!" What happens when junior pulls out onto the road for the first time? Tears. Why? Is it because they know there's only an 11 percent chance the car returns in the same condition in which it left? Maybe. But it's mostly because they are invested in their child.

That is how Paul pastored people: from the deepest part of his soul. And that is how we are called to do our gospel work together. The stakes are too high; God's glory too important; His people too precious; and his mission too meaningful to shrug our way through it.

. . .

DECEMBER 30, 2007.

The dreaded Sunday that always lands between Christmas and New Year's was upon us. The Sunday when attendance drops like a stone on Jupiter. The Sunday nobody—not even a skinny twenty-three-year-old seminary student with two semesters of Greek under his belt—wants to preach. The Sunday where hopefully written sermons go to die.

That Sunday was coming.

Ajay and I were only a few months into preaching together at Seven Mile Road, and neither of us wanted any part of that sermon. So, we asked the one guy we thought might say yes: an American missionary we had connected with who had spent the previous seven years in Egypt.

Here is a rough transcript of my conversation with the missionary who was going to preach on post-Christmas graveyard Sunday:

> ME: Brother, thanks so much for being willing to share with us this Sunday. I love that you've spent the last seven years living in Egypt loving ungospeled people night and day. Here are two things I need you to do: One—tell us how the Spirit worked on your heart to move you and your family overseas for the sake of the gospel. Two—share some anecdotes of what it has looked like, felt like, sounded like to be a Christian in Egypt. Our people need to know what missional living entails. To summarize: give us your story plus a few other stories from the field, all framed with Scripture. You've got 30 minutes.
>
> HIM: Yes, you got it pastor, no problem.

Have you ever witnessed a car spinning out in the snow, or someone stumbling down a flight of stairs, or a child falling from his or her high chair? Everything slows down. You know something awful is about to happen, but there is nothing you can do to stop it. All you can do is cover your eyes and hope for the best.

That was this sermon.

I sat in the front row as an act of humility and a means of encouragement. Three minutes in, I went, "Oh, no. Please, no." My friend had decided to preach—for an hour, with a 40-slide PowerPoint with size 10 font, quoting from the KJV—a theological treatise on the doctrine of God. I love the doctrine of God. But not on graveyard Sunday. I had nowhere to run, nowhere to hide. By the time he was done, my face had turned as red as Curt Shilling's right sock. When he finally (finally!) finished, I stood and was surprised to see a smattering of folks still around.

I mumbled through the close of our liturgy, bolted out the side door right into a driving winter rain, and walked.

I don't remember crossing any streets, or checking for oncoming cars, or noticing any other pedestrians, or feeling my Sunday shoes flood with water. I cried. I vented to God. I stomped in puddles. I quit ninety-seven times. Once I looked up and realized I was in Medford Square, three miles from our church, I sulked all the way back. Only a handful of folks and my wife were still around. I must have looked like a mile of bad road.

My wife asked me, "What's wrong with you?"

"This work really matters to me. And I led poorly today. And our people suffered because of it."

Now, some folks would hear that story and say, "You need some help. That was over the top. Unhealthy. Perhaps even pathological. It was just one sermon. You tried to be clear. It was merely a miscommunication." And there probably would be some truth to that. I am not contending for unnecessary drama or for running at some emotional pitch that will burn everyone out.

What I am saying is be careful of such counsel, lest it keep you from ever shedding any tears at all. Be careful when you are told we should not get too emotionally involved in the church—that people will hurt you; let you down; be irrational, unpredictable, unreliable, passive-aggressive, or worse; and so the best thing for you and your family is to guard your hearts. Such advice sounds so pious and reasonable (and there is a time and a place for it), but the clear teaching of Scripture is that we throw our hearts into the fray of the work of the gospel with tears.

If there is any temptation for American churches, it is to not be overly invested. Our temptation, what appeals to us, is the opposite. What we would do, what we tend to do, is to go through the motions of church and ministry. To shrug our way through the gospel life. Boring, quasi-heretical sermon gets preached? Meh. No one has been baptized since the Spice Girls were a thing? Meh. Gossip and slander have become the norm in church discourse? Meh. My gospel community hasn't loved anyone for a year? Meh.

That's our danger. It's always been the primary danger in Jesus's church. Spend ten minutes in a church history class, and you will read about all the times this has happened in Christendom. It is called *professionalism* in the clergy and *nominalism* in the pews. It happened in the 1500s on continental Europe, and men like John Calvin pleaded, through tears, for change. It happened in the 1800s in England, and men like Richard Baxter pleaded, through tears, for change. It happened in the 1900s in this country and men like John Piper pleaded, through tears, for change.

And it could happen with us.

We do not belong to Jesus's church the way we belong to Costco or Planet Fitness. We are not working a tollbooth here. We are loving and serving and leading the blood-bought saints of Jesus Christ, and we are to be invested in the work.

When we do this, you and I (and Nehemiah and John and Peter and Paul) are just taking our cue from Jesus.

• • •

NO ONE HAS EVER BEEN MORE emotionally invested in his or her work than Jesus of Nazareth. Read the Gospels. Jesus's emotions were moved, constantly. He was warmed by the centurion's faith, frustrated by the disciples' unbelief, angered at the desecration of His Dad's house, and delighted by Zacchaeus's humble repentance.

And, don't miss it: Jesus wept.

In Luke 19, we see Jesus about to enter Jerusalem, the city of God, for the final time. He pauses on Mount Olivet, then weeps. Luke writes,

> And when he drew near and saw the city, he wept over it, saying, "Would that you, even you, had known on this day the things that make for peace! But now they are hidden from your eyes. For the days will come upon you, when your enemies will set up a barricade around you and surround you and hem you in on every side and tear you down to the ground, you and your children within you. And they will not leave one stone upon another in you, because you did not know the time of your visitation." (Luke 19:41-44)

Jerusalem mattered to Jesus. The city was supposed to be receiving and crowning Him as Lord that week, but instead they would betray and murder Him, and then be overrun thirty years later by the Romans. The city of peace was rejecting the means of her peace. Jesus did not shrug his shoulders. He shed tears over the city.

Do we ever cry like that over our churches or our cities?

Early on in the planting of Seven Mile Road, when I was coming to grips with what the Lord had called us to do, I parked just outside of Linden School one morning, and I just started weeping. I was waiting for the crossing guard to come over and be like, "First day of kindergarten for your little girl, huh, buddy? She'll be all right." And I would have said, "No, man. We are planting a church because this is a city filled with people who need to meet Jesus. Do you know him?"

One year before, a friend came to plant a church in Somerville, and as I was praying with him, he began to weep—uncontrollably. I knew immediately that the church was in good hands.

Jesus cried like that over a city.

And not just over a city, but over individuals within that city. Our tears cannot be reserved for feelings of general, wistful, nebulous conviction. Real names and real faces and real stories should bring us to tears.

I think immediately of the story of Lazarus. The headline of the story, of course, is Lazarus's resurrection from the dead. It is John's seventh and final "sign," the clearest possible forerunner to the wild surprise of Jesus's own resurrection. But don't miss the tears in the story. Three times John tells us about Jesus's love for the family. He loved Mary. He loved Martha. And he loved Lazarus.

Think about that. Jesus did not just robotically accomplish redemption. He didn't do ministry the way Kawhi Leonard does basketball, efficient but disaffected. He didn't just check the boxes: perfect life, atoning death, vindicating resurrection, check, check, check. He was invested, emotionally, with people. And not in "humanity in general" or in "Jerusalem as a whole." Specific people. Pragmatic, dutiful, distracted (and probably annoying) Martha. Dreamy Mary. Young Lazarus. Jesus loved them personally. He was invested in them, foibles and all.

We see this when Jesus arrived at the tomb and surveyed the scene. Lazarus, his friend, was dead. Sin's curse had borne its ugliest fruit. Mary and Martha were distraught and helpless. This little family in this little village became a microcosm of all the brokenness sin had ravaged on every family in every city in all of history. Jesus took it in, and he felt the weight of it with tears.

"Jesus wept" is not merely the right answer to the Bible-geek trivia question, "What is the shortest verse in the Bible?" Those words are a window into how we are to live among our people. Aristotle was totally and terribly mistaken. God—Father, Son, and Spirit—is not an unmoved mover. He is a deeply, eternally, personally, emotionally moved mover. The people we are sent to, the Marthas and Marys and Lazaruses, matter to the heart of God.

They must matter to ours, too.

. . .

WHEN PEOPLE ASK ME ABOUT WHAT we're doing at Seven Mile Road, I never get more than a couple of sentences in without saying something like "We really love the people who live just north of Boston." And then I start crying. I just did this during a lunch with a new couple at our local Whole Foods and made everyone shift in their seats. I cry because it matters to me that when the people of these cities stand before Christ, they are able to say, "Yeah, there was a witness, clear and compelling, to your gospel, because there were some people who cared enough to plant churches. It cost them money, time, energy, reputation, blood, sweat, and tears, but they were invested in the work."

Let's live like that.

Let's cry when we baptize new believers. Let's cry when folks who have repented and been baptized disappear overnight, careening headlong back into lives of sin. Let's cry when we hear stories of couples who weather storms with us and are still devoted to each other and to Christ. Let's cry when folks we are discipling leave what we thought was a solid meeting only to send us angry, accusatory texts two hours later. Let's cry when our kids go prodigal, and let's cry when they return.

Church can be a place where we cry glad tears like that because the gospel work we have been called to matters so much to us.

– BLUEPRINTS –

1. Risk your heart.

My dad is a car guy. His garage is home to a 1945 Ford and a 1956 Chevy. Friends and curious neighbors often peek into the garage to ogle these pristine relics. They'll sit in the driver's seat, adjust the rearview mirror, spin the steering wheel around, tap on the speedometer, and ask where the seatbelts are. But they can't drive them. The cars rarely come out of the garage, which is too bad, because '56 Chevys were not made to sit idle in garages. They were made to tear down asphalt highways, taunt speed limits, thrill girls, and sometimes get wrecked.

It's the same with our hearts. God gave them to us so they might love and cherish and swoon and thrill and hope and sometimes break. Risk your heart. The handful of times I've really been hurt by people are insignificant compared to the countless joys I've received by throwing my full self into relationships with people.

2. Let your people see you cry.

In 2019, my wife was diagnosed with stage one-and-a-half breast cancer. It was an early diagnosis with a strong prognosis, but her treatment plan required two surgeries, three months of chemotherapy, and another three months of radiation. Although there were so many sweet mercies from our Father that buoyed us in that season, the tears are what I remember the most—our four children's tears when we sat and told them (they thought we were surprising them with a trip to Miami). My wife's tears when she and our daughters closed the downstairs bathroom door to shave her head. Our tears when liver counts prohibited her from keeping pace with the infusions. My tears when I told the church how we were doing. Their tears as they listened. Church is meant to be a place where these kinds of tears are shared, not hidden.

3. Kleenex.

If you are going to live this way together, make sure you have some in every room of the church. Trust me on this.

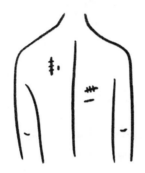

07 | SCARS

Church can be resilient.
On not avoiding opposition.

With trials that happened to me through the plots of the Jews ...
—*Acts 20:19*

MY OLDEST SON IS WAY TOUGHER than I ever was.

Mind you, I am not saying I was a wuss. I played power forward at Dom Savio High School in East Boston, a school known for the ruggedness of its athletics programs. (Our school size should have prevented us from playing in Division II, but we refused to play down in Division III as a point of pride.) I took my share of charges. I was always the first one on the ground after a loose ball. I could run eleven consecutive suicides and not cry about it. My junior year I committed more fouls than I scored points.

But my version of tough is nothing like my oldest son's.

He is 155 pounds drenched, but he plays gunner on the varsity rugby team at Malden Catholic.

Do you know what rugby is? Think football, just without the pads. These kids strap on the thinnest of fabric helmets, pull on a pair of short shorts, and grab a mouthpiece, and then they collide with each other in full sprints for ninety minutes. Ray Lewis might not have lasted until halftime in this sport.

If someone is on a rugby squad, you know it. They don't get cute stickers on their helmets for good performance. They wear badges in their flesh: Cuts. Scrapes. Giant purple bruises that look like Picasso got drunk and painted a pastrami on their hamstrings. Sometimes a tooth is missing.

If you play rugby, your body will show it.

His sophomore year, my son played a match against Catholic Memorial, and toward the end of the match, he was sprinting down the left sideline when a kid hit him late and drove him off the soft turf and onto the rock-hard track, giving him a terrible concussion. We helped him limp to the car and drove him to pediatrics at Winchester Hospital. They situated him in a layback chair. His elbows and knees were all cut up. His hair was matted down to his forehead with dried sweat. He smelled like a sixteen-year-old athlete. Grass and blood stained his rugby short shorts. His eyes looked a little glazed over. He couldn't remember the play he'd been hurt on. There was no mistaking he had played rugby that day. No mistaking he was a gunner. No mistaking he was engaged on the pitch.

Playing rugby comes with some scars.

The same holds true for every faithful church, and every lover and follower of Jesus. If we are going to believe and live the gospel, aligning ourselves with the grace and truth of Jesus, saying out loud not only what God provides but also what He requires, speaking truth to sinful people, we will have marks to show for it.

. . .

THE THIRD EVIDENCE OF GOSPEL FAITHFULNESS Paul gives in his speech stops me in my tracks: "[W]ith all humility and with tears and with trials ..."

Humility I aspire to. Tears I'm built for. But I want nothing to do with trials.

What's worse is that Paul specifies them as "trials that came upon me through the plots of the Jews."

"Trials" (*peirasmos*) is a common word in Scripture, meaning being put to the test or enduring a hard time, a conflict, a calamity, or a struggle. Trials come at us on many fronts. We can be tried by physical illness, injury, bad weather, failures in career or business, a really hard class, or just an old-fashioned doubt. So it's helpful that Paul clarifies what trials Jesus's people should anticipate: trials born of the insidious work of enemies of the gospel. These enemies did not share Paul's love for Jesus, so they set themselves squarely against his message. This opposition left scars.

In other words, Paul is saying, "One way you know my ministry was true, faithful, solid, legit, and Christlike is because not everybody liked me. Some people wanted me marginalized; some wanted me silenced; and some wanted me dead."

Dead is not an exaggeration.

...

WERE YOU TO READ THE BOOK of Acts straight through, one thing you'd observe about Paul is this: lots of people loved him, but lots of people hated him. And not just I-hope-he-gets-a-flat-tire hate, or I-hope-his-March-Madness-bracket-gets-busted-by-the-Sweet-Sixteen hate. Paul's haters wanted him dead, and they were willing to make it happen.

In fact, at three different times, people responded to Paul's ministry by plotting to kill him.

In Damascus, he had to be hustled out of town at night to save his throat: "When many days had passed, the Jews plotted to kill him, but their plot became known to Saul. They were watching the gates day and night to kill him, but his disciples took him by night and let him down through an opening in the wall, lowering him in a basket" (Acts 9:23-25).

In Greece, he also had to improvise exit plans to avoid death. After he spent three months there, "a plot was made against him by the Jews as he was about to set sail for Syria, [so] he decided to return through Macedonia" (Acts 20:3-4).

In Jerusalem, he needed a young informant to spare him from assassination: "When it was day, the Jews made a plot and bound themselves by an oath neither to eat nor drink till they had killed Paul" (Acts 23:12). More than forty people were in on this conspiracy. This whole "We're not eating until we find you and kill you" is Liam Neeson territory.

So, to be clear, when Paul says that a mark of his ministry was trials, he doesn't mean flat tires or bad tacos. He means trials in the fiercest sense of the word. He means a trashed reputation, a beaten body, and sabotaged church plants. He means literally running for his life.

We suburban, postmodern, Starbucks-sipping, *Ellen*-enjoying, you-stay-off-my-lawn-and-I'll-stay-off-yours Americans struggle with this. We have no enemies (other than that raccoon who keeps getting in our trash). We read these passages and our brows furrow. We immediately think, "Well, Paul must have had issues. He was obviously doing something wrong. Why didn't the early church send him to a PR class? Or to some sensitivity training? Or a yoga retreat? Or have him read Dale Carnegie's *How to Win Friends and Influence People?* Isn't an above-reproach minister of the gospel supposed to be thought well of by outsiders? Why all these controversies and trials?"

· · ·

IF YOU WERE TO GATHER A collection of American pastors on a random January 1st and say "Be perfectly honest with me and make a list of things a good year in ministry would entail for you," it would read something like this:

- No conflicts
- No accusations
- No picket signs
- No bad attitudes toward my preaching

- No letters to the editor
- No heated member forums
- No having to escape town in a basket
- No rogue entities swearing off food until the church is taken out
- No scars

We are convinced that a skilled and properly toned pastor executing a winsome and balanced ministry would ensure the absence of any ugliness. We're sure that a genuinely Christian church (gospel-centered and working for the good of the city) enjoys a controversy-free existence. We believe that everyone around us should always and only[18] have good things to say about us and our churches. If we do this right, they will appreciate us, not attack us.

But Paul did not say that he lived among them with humility, tears ... and a good reputation.

He said he lived with trials.

• • •

THE CLEAR TEACHING OF SCRIPTURE, from Abel through Moses to Paul, is that the faithful will endure opposition. It's actually the absence of trials and scars that should concern us. Trials are evidence of faithfulness.

Do not miss this in the text. When Paul completes his opening triad with the word "trials," he is not being apologetic or regretful or rueful or embarrassed. He's not admitting failure. He is putting forward as evidence of the legitimacy of his ministry the hatred and opposition he frequently faced.

In fact, Paul does this often.

In his second letter to the Corinthians, when Paul finds himself in the awful place of having to defend the bona fides of his apostleship, he says, "Are they servants of Christ? I am a better one—I am talking like a madman—with far greater labors …" (2 Cor. 11:23). In other words, "This is ridiculous that I have to defend myself before you. I shouldn't have to do this. You should know better. But here we go."

What Paul then trots out to show the sincerity of his apostleship is fascinating. Is it how many people go to his church? How many sellout crowds have come to hear him speak? Book sales statistics for the quarter? Awards he received from the chamber of commerce? Latest approval ratings from Gallup? His ranking on *Outreach Magazine's* Top 100 Fastest Growing Churches?

No.

He points to his trials: "… with far greater labors, far more imprisonments, with countless beatings, and often near death. Five times I received at the hands of the Jews the forty lashes less one. Three times I was beaten with rods. Once I was stoned" (2 Cor. 11:23-25).

A visual list might help us:

- Labors: a great many
- Imprisonments: far more
- Beatings: countless
  - forty lashes, less one: 5x (i.e., 195 total lashes)
  - beaten with rods: 3x
  - stoned: 1x

That's a lot of trials, and Paul is not apologizing for any of them. His trials were his credentials. His scars were his bona fides. His sufferings were his badge.

In his letter to the Galatians, Paul does the same thing. He's been slandered and assailed and hammered by the enemies of Christ for his promulgation of the doctrine of justification by faith alone. In his letter, he presents a variety of defenses for his apostolic genuineness. At the end, he mentions one final evidence: his body.

What Paul does is penetrating. Troubling. Macabre, even. The average American pastor might have had to leave the room at this moment. He lifts his shirt and exposes bare flesh. He leans down, then right, and points across to his back, besieged by scars. And he says, "From now on let no one cause me trouble, for I bear on my body the marks of Jesus" (Gal. 6:17). In other words, "Look at them. Go ahead. See those scars? There is your proof that I am a true teacher. I have taken a beating for the sake of Jesus's gospel." Not even a skillful surgeon like his buddy Dr. Luke could have remedied the terribly disfigured body of this apostle.

The word "marks" is the Greek word *stigmata*. We think instantly, and rightly, of the wounds in Jesus's hands, feet, and side when we see this word. We think of the physical marks of the sufferings of Christ at the hands of an unbelieving world, marks that speak of His love of sinners for eternity. Paul points to similar marks etched in his own flesh. Each was the result of his being hated, assaulted, and scandalized, not as signs that he wasn't loving enough, or that he was too judgmental, or that he was lacking in compassion, but that he was faithful. A true apostle is never above his Christ; a good servant is never above his master. Sometimes being faithful means being wounded, shamed, cut, hurt, marked, maimed.

• • •

THIS IS ALL PRETTY BAD NEWS for the next American pastors and our churches. We love our comforts. We *love* our comforts. Has any culture in world history had more comforts than we do, or valued them more than we do? We have heated seats in our cars. We talk to our fridges. We choose among Chinese, Italian, and Thai takeout. We have reclining love seats with beer holders and eighty-inch flat-screen TVs. We sleep in mattresses set to our exact specifications. We have central air conditioning. All of this seduces us into thinking we can proclaim Christ and maintain comfort. After all, it was the Protestant work ethic that made these comforts possible. We've made it our great ambition to never bear any marks.

• • •

MY BACK LOOKS LIKE A NEWBORN baby's bottom compared to Paul's back. Some of this is due to the providence of God, but much is due to my unwillingness to bear the marks of Jesus.

I've noticed at least two strategies of unwillingness in my own life:

1. NICENESS

I am convinced that if I just smile wide enough, lift my eyebrows high enough, and engage in enough banter about the weather and the Sox, everybody will like me. The force of my niceness will not only give me a platform for the gospel but also earn me a pass on opposition.

This may surprise you, but niceness is not a biblical virtue. I dare you to read the Gospels and find the word "nice" being used to describe Jesus. Jesus was holy, gentle, pure, approachable, and genuine, but he wasn't nice. It's staggering what mainline denominational church culture has done to Jesus in the past fifty years. We've defanged the Lion of Judah. We've taken the whip out of His hands and put a sash around His neck and mousse in His hair. Jesus was the most masculine man who has ever lived (taking responsibility for all that the Father has assigned to Him). But most Americans now assume He was the original Mr. Rogers, flitting about Judea telling folksy stories, welcoming toddlers, and petting sheep. You don't get crucified for spinning religious yarns, or loving preschoolers, or showing kindness to barnyard animals. You get crucified for calling the world to repentance, for fearlessly speaking truth to powers who don't want to hear it, for upholding the glory of God's law.

Not only is trying to "nice" our way out of trials unbiblical, but it's also not going to work. Several years ago, perhaps the nicest man in all of American evangelicalism—a guy who wears scarves and runs events where college kids get together to sing songs to Jesus—was pressured to withdraw from praying at the US presidential inauguration because he held to a common-sense and biblically orthodox understanding of sexuality. You can't be a nicer guy, but he got scarred up anyway.[19]

2. EQUIVOCATION

Equivocate is a word I had to learn, because, as it turns out, I'm a master of it.

It comes from a Latin word meaning "to call by the same name." It means to use ambiguous language so as to conceal the truth or avoid committing oneself. To say something in a way that you don't have to own it. We Americans have PhDs in equivocation.

Here's how this works:

> WE SAY: Hey, you guys should come over sometime.
> WE MEAN: Although I am not totally opposed to the idea of you coming over, I am leaving this open-ended, so I don't actually have to commit to anything right now.

WE SAY:	I'll get you back next time.
WE MEAN:	Not.

WE SAY:	That dress looks great on you!
WE MEAN:	I wouldn't be caught dead in it.

WE SAY:	It's a fetus.
WE MEAN:	I know it's a baby. I just want to be allowed to kill it.

WE SAY:	I'm fighting for gender equality in the church.
WE MEAN:	I don't care how clearly the Spirit said the opposite: we *will* allow women to teach and exercise authority over men.

WE SAY:	We're figuring some things out financially.
WE MEAN:	Heck no, I'm not tithing.

WE SAY:	We are a new kind of Christian.
WE MEAN:	We're not Christians at all. In fact, we are going to methodically subvert every tenet of orthodox Christianity over the next ten years and see if anyone notices.

It's crucial that every planter and pastor resolve to fight this temptation of avoiding trials by way of equivocation. It dishonors Christ, hurts His people, and confuses those we are sent to.

Because I have a black belt in equivocation, every time I prepare to preach, I pray for the same four things:

Humility
Energy
Accuracy
Clarity

That last one is so important for me. I beg the Spirit to give me the courage to speak clearly, to say what I mean. My primary concern is not that our people would like what I say, but that they would understand. That they'd leave every sermon thinking, "I'm working on whether I agree or disagree, but at least that preacher guy gave it to me straight." Deciphering meaning is not supposed to be the real work of hearing a sermon. Wrestling with response is. I know I'm succeeding when some in the congregation are nodding and weeping, and others are gritting their teeth and slowly shaking their head from side to side.

• • •

THE BOTTOM LINE IS THIS: TRIALS, and the scars that result from them, are not to be avoided, but to be received by faith. If we are going to be faithful witnesses to Christ in the coming years, trials will come. We can't nice our way out of it. We can't equivocate our way out of it. No amount of good work in the community or mercy ministry will temper the enmity between heaven and hell. We are going to find ourselves embroiled in some controversy or another. Unseemly headlines will run. Hit pieces will be published. Angry emails will be sent. Approval ratings will dive. Straightforward gospel preaching always causes the godless to set their hair on fire, and then come after our churches and ministries, torches in hand.

The point is not to rack up as many beatings as possible. God is sovereign over the ins and outs of our sufferings. We're not looking for fights. We're just trying to settle our souls in the truth that Jesus always has and always will trigger strong responses, for and against. People either adored or despised Him, and the same will be—should be—true of us.

– BLUEPRINTS –

1. When people endure trials for the sake of the gospel, don't shame or blame them. Stand with them.

There are so many people I can't wait to talk with in the age to come. I want to know how Nehemiah pulled that guy's beard out. I want to know what Euodia and Syntyche were fighting about, and if they made up. I want to know whether Eutychus was really dead. And I want to give Onesiphorus the biggest hug and say "Thank you, brother. Thank you." When Paul was in chains, bearing marks for Jesus, Onesiphorus didn't shame, blame, question, or abandon him. He stood with him. This is beautiful. And unusual. Teach your people to never be ashamed of the gospel or those who suffer for it.

2. Pray for your enemies.

I pray two things for the most vocal and influential opponents of God's law and gospel where we live. One is that God would frustrate their unjust, immoral work. The second is that, in His kindness, He would bring them to repentance and new life through the gospel.

3. Use biblical language.

It's a discipline to not trade-in God's words for ones that are more socially acceptable. Memorize and use God's words. Stand in the mirror and practice if you have to. For our generation these are biblical words like *sin, narrow road, wrath, judgment, repentance, degrading passions, natural relations, shameless acts, due penalty, male and female, husbands, wives, love, respect, submit, understanding, weaker vessel, predestined, I do not permit, you shall not, act like men,* et al.

This is also why it is so important to read Scripture out loud on Sunday mornings and in gospel communities: it helps us not to be ashamed of anything the Lord has spoken. (Of course, it's important to help people with context and not just hit them with sharp words they have no frame of reference for, like reading Psalm 137:9[3] as a call to worship or something.)

08 | GUTS

Church can be bold.
On having hard conversations.

I did not shrink from declaring ... —Acts 20:20, 27

IF YOU WERE EXPLORING CAREER OPTIONS with a teenager, and he or she said to you, "I don't do basements. I'm not good with wrenches. And I hate having the smell of poop on my hands," what would you say? "OK. Plumbing is out."

If you were making plans for a Friday, and your friend mentioned his or her disdain for Mark Wahlberg movies, what would you say? "I guess we are not going over to Kruse's house for movie night, because that's all he watches. I've seen that man pull off a Marky Mark trifecta—*Shooter, The Fighter,* and *The Departed*—all in one night."

If a neighbor of yours was thinking about where to move but was adamant he or she did not want to live in a pretentious city without a dedicated water supply, with ubiquitous traffic, and with more dogs than kids, what would you say? "So, L.A. is out."

And if an aspiring pastor or church planter said to you, "I don't do hard conversations. I really hate having to say hard things," what would you say?

"Please. Please. Find another vocation."

Faithful gospel ministry requires having hard conversations. You will need to correct and be corrected. You will need to prod and be prodded. You will need to forgive and be forgiven. You will have to say no and be told no. And every one of those requires saying—and hearing—hard things.

Truth be told, almost none of us does hard conversations well. One of the most helpful grids we work through with future leaders at Seven Mile Road is the "Five Conflict Styles When You Don't Agree" matrix, which could just as easily be titled "Four Bad Ways of Coming at Hard Conversations." Concern for relationships plots along one axis, concern for outcomes along the other. Each one of us tends to land in one of the four quadrants.

1. WINNERS

For the winner, outcome trumps relationships every time. We'll say the hard thing, the easy thing, or really anything if it ensures that we come out on top and our objectives are met.

You know you're dealing with a winner if he sounds like this:

> YOU: Hey, how's church planting going?
> WINNER: Awesome.
> YOU: Sweet. What've you got? Conversions, some baptisms, some real gospel wakefulness happening?
> WINNER: Nah, man, but we put five people under discipline this month.
> YOU: Isn't that like a third of your congregation?
> WINNER: Yeah. And I have to rebuke the drummer next. He's just not bringing enough energy.

If you're the winner, you're fine with hard conversations, which is good. Except that you'll end up with no one around to have them with.

2. WALKERS

Walkers are low on relationships, low on outcomes, and high on studio apartments and deserted islands. If they sense a hard conversation seven miles away, they check out. Immediately.

A typical conversation with a walker goes like this:

YOU: Listen, there is something I needed to talk with you about. ... Hey, wait, hold on, where are you going? Come back.

Not many walkers plant churches or assume leadership roles, because they would not last ten minutes before saying "Forget these people. Forget our goals. There's too much tension here. I'm out."

3. YIELDERS

Relationships are hugely important to yielders, but outcomes are not. Yielders will have the hard conversation, but they'll ride shotgun. They'll never initiate one or lean in and say the hard thing. Yielders just let the other person drive, and as long as everyone is BFFs at the end, they're good.

Here's how you know a yielder:

YOU: Hey, do you think we could work through a few things I've got concerns on?
YIELDER: Yes, absolutely.
YOU: So, there's ...
YIELDER: Fine, you're right, I'm sorry, no big deal, what do you want to do?
YOU: Wait, I didn't even get to ...
YIELDER: No, seriously. Don't worry about it. I'm good with whatever.
YOU: I know, but I just wanted to talk about ...
YIELDER: OK, so we're good then? Great. Let me know if anything else comes up. How about we get some ice cream. I'm buying.

Yielders are beloved, but while they might have a thousand Facebook friends, they struggle to move the mission of a church forward because they lack the courage to exhort, admonish, or say no.

4. COMPROMISERS

For compromisers, relationships matter, but so do outcomes. They don't want to give up on either. They genuinely love people, and they genuinely want to accomplish great things for Christ. So, compromisers will have the hard conversation, and even say the hard thing, but they won't engage in the costlier work of mining and resolving the root cause of conflict.

While this may sound on the surface like the optimal approach, it falls woefully short of what the gospel calls—better yet, propels—us to. Yet I would bet that the compromiser is where most church planters and pastors land: willing to (quickly) say the hard thing, but less interested in giving it the time and attention it really needs.

· · ·

LAST SPRING, WE HAD A RODENT problem in the Kruse house. The New England ground thawed, and a mischief of mice appeared overnight. We had a total *Ratatouille*-thing going on in the crawlspace of our basement. Remy. Emile. They were all there. So, we bought some sticky traps, dropped some Teddy's peanut butter in the center, and tucked them in the corners of the kitchen. For a month, all we did was catch mice.

I am not a big animal guy. We don't have any pets. I don't watch nature documentaries. I didn't even like *Seabiscuit* or *Free Willy*. And I don't do mice. But as the family's early riser, I'd be the first in the kitchen every morning, and there to greet me was another mouse—half dead, still fidgeting. So, I'd hesitantly tug the edge of the trap, the mouse would wriggle, and I would shrink back. Then it would turn its little head to look at me, with those giant brown eyes, as if to say, "Please, mister, don't make me starve to death in your trash can." After shrinking back five or six times, I would eventually lean in as fast as I could, without looking, then quickly lift and drop the trap in the trash, just to get it done.

That is how compromisers approach and deal with difficult conversations. We say something quickly because it needs to be said, establish the frailest agreement, and then move on.

Here is the problem with compromisers: whenever we shrink back from saying the hard thing, we fail to love our people well, and we fail to open the door to the work the Spirit wants to accomplish in our churches. So, if you are going to do this work of gospel ministry, you have to resolve to not shrink back from difficult conversations.

. . .

THIS, OF COURSE, IS EXACTLY HOW Jesus's apostle Paul was with His people.

He writes in Acts 20: "I did not shrink from declaring to you anything that was profitable. … I did not shrink from declaring to you the whole counsel of God."

In other words, Paul insists that one mark of his faithfulness was his willingness to say hard things.

"I did not shrink" translates from the Greek word *hupostello*. It means to draw back, or hold back, to stow away, suppress, conceal. It invokes the image of something that should be shown or said, but it's hidden away. And Paul says, "I didn't do that. I did not shrink back, hold back, keep back, pull back. I leaned in."

And he doesn't say it once, but twice.

He says he did not shrink back from saying "anything that was profitable." Whatever word, no matter how hard, he said it. Paul pulled no punches.

He also says he did not shrink back from declaring "the whole counsel of God." Paul didn't put his people in a little red wagon and pull them around the cul-de-sac of coffee-mug Christianity. He took them off-road in a Jeep Cherokee into the theological wild. He didn't preach the 2.5 most palatable of the Ten Commandments. He preached them all. He tabled no doctrines, not even the ones with the sharpest of edges.

For Paul to insist on this fact twice in such a short speech communicates something important: the opportunity and the tendency—more explicitly, the temptation—to shrink back was real. He could have, but he resolved not to. I never burn with the urge to tell my wife, "Hey, I watched some NBA highlights this morning, and then I grabbed a sub from New Deal for lunch." Why? Because those are easy and enjoyable tasks. But I do tell her things like, "Hey, I took down the recycling. And I sat and talked schoolwork and attitude and gospel with our teenager. And I didn't mess with the laundry on our bed." Why? Because the temptation for me not to do those things is strong. When I knock them out, it's worth telling her. It's the same thing in Acts 20. Paul sees his steadfastness to say hard words as double noteworthy. The temptation—Paul's, the Ephesian elders', and ours—is to shrink back.

Why? I'm sure you have your list. Here's mine:

1. IF I SAY THE HARD THING, THEY MIGHT NOT LIKE ME ANYMORE.

Isn't it fascinating how desperately we want people to like us? Nothing drives the American pastor more than this desire. We want our Amazon reviews to be 5s across the board. We love when someone says, "Oh, I met so-and-so, and they said you were just the best guy." We are up at night troubled by the thought that someone out there might not sign up for our fan club if we had one. And so that's how we pastor: always and only nice words, soft words, easy conversations. If we must say something hard to someone, we make it a compliment sandwich: ten minutes of how awesome you are, seven seconds of correction, ten minutes of how much I love you, and you still like me, right? We struggle with being direct. We wrestle with saying that hard thing and leaving it out there for more than a split second, because it jeopardizes our approval ratings.

So, we shrink back.

2. IF I SAY THE HARD THING, I MIGHT GET HURT.

A few months ago, I had a Woburn cop take a swing at me. Not on the street, but during a pickup basketball game. This guy played like it was the Final Four tournament. I boxed him out and our arms got tangled, and I lifted my arms to get untangled, and he hammered me and shouted, "Don't ever throw an elbow at me again." Being a good Bostonian pastor, I yelled back, "Are you out of your mind? I'm forty-five years old. I'm fifty pounds lighter than you. I got four kids and two jobs. I am not throwing elbows, you psycho."

I did not box that dude out the rest of the night. I shrank back.

That's exactly how I get with difficult conversations or sermons. Shrinking back doesn't feel like cowardice; it feels like self-preservation. "Yes, I know we need to address his anger issues. I know we need to talk about her impossible schedule. I know the Bible is explicitly clear that there are only two sexes. I know it's a dangerous mix for this guy to come to the Table while halfheartedly following Jesus. But I am not in the mood to take punches to the head right now."

So, we shrink back.

3. IF I SAY THE HARD THING, I MIGHT BE HERE A WHILE.

I am not a big Netflix or Hulu kind of guy, because I won't give it the time. I didn't even finish the first season of *Breaking Bad*. (Don't judge me.) When my thirteen-year-old daughter said to me the other day, "Dad, will you watch *Titanic* with me?" I said, "I don't know, babe, that's a commitment. They don't even hit the iceberg until like two hours in."

Hard conversations can be that way. Sometimes they even have sequels. Some wounds can't be healed lightly. I sat in a booth at the Border Café one time for four hours working to resolve a conflict in our church. These things take time, and we don't want to do the work.

So, we shrink back.

4. IF I SAY THE HARD THING, THEY'LL LEAVE.

I don't know if your church is big, but ours isn't. In fact, the church I lead is half the size it once was because we have given so many people away to transience and to church planting. It's easy to grow terrified about more people leaving.

Last year, we had a Village Church pastor from the Dallas Northway Campus spend some time with us. He sat in on a pastors' meeting, and we talked about the one hundred adults total who were committed to the life of the church. You can fit all their names on one side of an 8.5-by-11-inch sheet of paper. The whole church, on one sheet of paper.

He said to me, "Matt, I have no frame of reference for this conversation. We have 3,500 people at the Dallas Campus. Each weekend 200 people come, and 200 people go." I said, "Man, I would be dropping truth bombs like Kim Jong-un if my church were that big! Go ahead and leave, I got 3,499 people left!" But when three families make up 20 percent of your giving base, you may want to let that hard word go.

So, we shrink back.

5. IF I SAY THE HARD THING, I MIGHT GET IT WRONG.

I don't have the gift of discernment.

Have you met someone who does? They see a new person, first day, from across the room, and they say, "We're going to love having them be here." And six months later they're right.

Discernment like that is a beautiful gift, but not having it has paralyzed me. "What if I lean in and say something hard, and then I am wrong about it? I'll just embarrass myself and do them wrong. Maybe I'll let someone else do this work." We want to delegate difficult conversations to someone else. Let someone more gifted, more patient, more articulate, more qualified do that work.

Someone else.

Anyone else.

So, we shrink back.

Whatever else may be on your list, I hope you feel that under all these pathologies and excuses is fear. We hide. We "shrink from declaring." I so love these words of Scripture. They throw open a whole new vista for me: "Wait. It is actually possible to *not* shrink back from saying the hard things. By the grace and the power of the Spirit, someone else has done this, and I can too."

• • •

IF YOU HIGHLIGHTED EVERY difficult thing Paul said in his letters to the saints, your Bible would look like the Miami Beach Art Deco District when you were done.

To the Romans, he wrote, "Do you suppose, O Man—you who judge those who practice such things and yet do them yourself—that you will escape the judgment of God?" (Rom. 2:3).

To the Corinthians, "I fed you with milk, not solid food, for you were not ready for it. And even now you are not yet ready, for you are still of the flesh" (1 Cor. 3:2).

To the Galatians, "But when Cephas came to Antioch, I opposed him to his face, because he stood condemned" (Gal. 2:11). (Paul said a difficult thing to Peter.)

To the Ephesians, "For you may be sure of this, that everyone who is sexually immoral or impure, or who is covetous (that is, an idolater), has no inheritance in the kingdom of Christ and God" (Eph. 5:5).

To the Colossians, "Wives, submit to your husbands, as is fitting in the Lord" (Col. 3:18).

To the Philippians, "I entreat Euodia and I entreat Syntyche to agree in the Lord" (Phil. 4:2). (Yes, the man stepped into the middle of two women fighting, called for peace, and lived to tell about it.)[20]

To the Thessalonians, "If anyone is not willing to work, let him not eat" (2 Thess. 3:10).

To Timothy, "I do not permit a woman to teach or to exercise authority over a man" (1 Tim. 2:12).

To Titus, "One of the Cretans, a prophet of their own, said, 'Cretans are always liars, evil beasts, lazy gluttons.' This testimony is true. Therefore rebuke them sharply, that they may be sound in the faith" (Titus 1:12-13). (You know that Titus was doing gospel work on the island of Crete among Cretans, right?)

To Philemon: Actually, the whole letter is a hard conversation, with Paul basically telling his brother that he needs him to take back a servant who stole from and abandoned him.

Paul said the hard thing. Over and over and over again.

Why did he do it? What drove Paul to risk relational fallout and loss of time and bodily harm by saying hard things? Was he looking to get an invite to speak on successful conflict management techniques at the next regional conference? Did he have a death wish? What was driving Paul?

He loved those he wrote to. He knew that every hard word or conversation was an opportunity for profound gospel formation to happen. He was all-in on their holiness and maturity and joy, and he would do anything and say anything to help get them there. And nothing drives forward holiness and maturity and joy in a soul or in a community more than saying and hearing the hard thing.

...

ALL OF US WOULD SAY, WITHOUT hesitation, that the hardest conversations people have had with us have also been the most helpful. I have never felt more loved, or more served, than when the people of Seven Mile Road have leaned in and said hard things to me.

A sampling:

I was riding shotgun in Brent's car one time on Highland Ave. in Malden. Danny from Dorchester was on WEEI ranting about the Red Sox's refusal to trade for a bat at the deadline. Apparently, Brent was saying something, too. Brent suddenly turned and looked at me and said, point-blank, "Matt, you don't listen to people. They are talking, but you're already miles down the road. And it makes them feel like dirt." That was hard to hear, but that helped me. I started praying that the Spirit would help me listen while others talked rather than using that time to formulate my next point.

I spoke once at a big, hipster-cool church in Boston, and I had an attitude about it because I am the opposite of hipster-cool. I am also a punk. Before I began speaking, I made some snarky, offhand comment about the bright lights. A friend called me that week and said, "Matt, you cannot step into someone else's pulpit and slam on their setup. What's wrong with you?" That was hard to hear, but that helped me. I called the pastor and asked for his forgiveness.

Kevin stopped me short one time in the middle of a conversation about my marriage at Panera and said, "Wait, wait. I am not sure if we are talking about you having sex or about you loving your wife. Which is it?" That was hard to hear, but that helped me.

We were working on a podcast with some of the women at our church. After a fitful first take, one of them said to me, "Well, that was fine, except you were preaching at the beginning. And that's not what we are going for, Matt." She wasn't being sassy. Or disrespectful. She was being helpful. And I am sure it was hard to say.

Last month, I was in a coaching session with Justin, our executive pastor. He's like our resident John Wooden. So I had to listen when he said to me, "Matt, you're never happy. You only see losses, never wins. Getting you to celebrate something is like getting the Browns to cover. And it is weighing on the team."

I could keep going. Every one of those hard words led to a hard conversation that profited me, so I've worked to return the gospel favor to others.

. . .

THE NUMBER OF HARD CONVERSATIONS I'VE had in my years as a pastor is now approaching triple digits. A few lines from them:

"Listen, you cannot leave the church that way. You have to come meet with us again."

"If you don't start dealing with this gay porn issue, it will kill you. Not handicap you or hurt you. It will kill you."

"No, we are not starting a youth group right now."

"You are preaching too long. I know you love the Bible and have a lot to say, but you need to edit things down if you are going to help people."

"You really hurt her. No, hang on, listen to me. You hurt her."

"Um, so, you can't be a brand new mom, work full time in the city, have a one-hour commute, teach Pilates three times a week, go to every baby shower, bridal shower, christening, and bachelorette party that every friend you have ever had ever has, and also have a strong marriage and be invested in the mission of the church. Someone is going to suffer here—probably your husband and son."

"I know your dad is being impossible and crazy, but the Spirit meant it when He said we must honor our father and mother. I need you to set your heart to do that. It's a good command. You're going to have to trust me on that."

"I know you want to plant a church, but we just don't see it happening. Here's why."

"You are not qualified to be a pastor right now."

"I am so sorry. We messed that up bad. Will you forgive us?"

If you love your people, if you want to be helpful, you will not shrink back from those conversations. You'll lean in. Church can be a place where everyone is bold enough to go there.

- BLUEPRINTS -

1a. Know the truths your people need to hear most and say those the most.

When I text our folks who attend church a third of the time and gospel community even less, I reference the story about Mary and Martha, and I write about the difference between good things and gospel things. When I talk with our folks who barely give, I give the Sermon on the Mount and draw lines on napkins with Christ on one side and dollar signs on the other. When I talk with young men, I talk about self-control. (That's pretty much it.) When I meet with husbands and wives who noticeably sit across the room from each other, I press on the oneness embedded in the marriage covenant. When I sit with people with tender consciences, I make them look me in the eye, and I gospel them hard with Romans 8. When I sit with people who are cavalier about their sin and presumptuous about God's forgiveness, I go hard on Romans 1 or Hebrews 6. None of that is easy. All of it is helpful.

1b. Identify the truths your culture opposes most vehemently and then preach on those.

Penned by novelist Elizabeth Rundle Charles more than one hundred years ago, these words still ring true: "If I profess, with the loudest voice and the clearest exposition, every portion of the truth of God except precisely that little point which the world and the devil are at that moment attacking, I am not confessing Christ, however boldly I may be professing Christianity. Where the battle rages the loyalty of the soldier is proved."

Seven Mile Road has been sent by Jesus to postmodern, secular, academic, humanistic, decadent, blue-state Massachusetts. And we have preached sermon series on the doctrines of Scripture, man, sexuality, substitutionary atonement, the resurrection, and the church. Yes, I've had to preface nearly every sermon with some version of "So, it's gonna get a little spicy in here today." And I don't want to finish my forty years able to say only that "I declared to you *most* of the counsel of God."

2. Never say hard things over email or text.

Hard conversations are sacred. Respecting the dignity of the other person means creating as safe an environment as possible for him or her to hear hard words, being surrounded by the most obvious and tenderest care. Doing so requires presence and some other basics things like cold water, tissues, a room where you can hear the person, etc.). So, our rule of thumb is this: If it's easy (positive or neutral), text it. If it's hard (difficult or pointed), wait for an in-person conversation.

3a. Memorize helpful phrases.

I am a coward, and I literally need to memorize verbal cues like these that allow me to break the plane of a hard conversation:

> Hey, I need you to talk to me about [blank].
> Will you help me to understand [blank]?
> Can you walk me through [blank]?
> No. (The hardest word of all.)

3b. If those phrases fit with Scripture, all the better.

I was sitting with a couple, and they had set up this schedule that only newly converted Bostonians would think was possible to maintain. He was working full time; she was working full time; they had a baby; he was running a business on the side; they were landlords of two tenants; he was training for a marathon. Seriously. Marathon. So, I needed to say the hard thing: "You are anxious and troubled about many things, but one thing is really necessary, and you've left it out completely." We had a young guy once, and he was so self-interested and narcissistic. I had to make sure to look at him and tell him this road ends badly. Here's how I said it: "Do you see a man who is wise in his own eyes? There is more hope for a fool than for him." And if I had a dollar for every time I've said, "Live with your wife in an understanding way," I'd own a condo in Bermuda.

09 | THUNDER

Church can be anchored.
On loving and leading from the words of Scripture.

Teaching you in public and from house to house ... —Acts 20:20

Remember the words of the Lord Jesus. —Acts 20:35

IT WOULD BE IMPOSSIBLE TO WRITE about the work the Spirit has accomplished at Seven Mile Road without calling attention to the centrality of the Bible in the life of our church. When you walk into our sanctuary, staring back at you, dead center, is the pulpit. That placement is no accident. The Scriptures are at the center of all we do. And not just central, but everywhere. The Bible is always coming at you. This is the way Jesus intended His church to work.

...

IF YOU CAME OVER TO THE Kruse home and spent some time with us, you would encounter some things happening constantly. Ubiquitously. Non-stop, drive-you-crazy, all-the-time.

1. DRIBBLING

A basketball is always being dribbled at our home. Inside. Outside. Front porch. Back steps. Summertime. Wintertime. Crossovers. Inside-outs. Behind-the-backs. Hesitations. *Boom, ba-doom, ba-doom* is our house's soundtrack. (It's also my love language. When Grace and I were dating, I used to take her to empty basketball courts and run through drills with her. Romantic.)

2. LAUNDRY

The six humans in my home somehow generate more laundry than a beachfront hotel in Miami. We live in a four-season city, so we own an irresponsibly enormous amount of clothing: hats, gloves, scarves, swim trunks, raincoats, thermals, hoodies, jeans, sweats, jorts (mine). We have enough socks to outfit a small nation. And let's not talk about towels, school uniforms, gymnastics leotards, Rugby short shorts, or Dad's Rondo jersey he sweats up every Friday playing old-man ball at the Y. The result is a washing machine and dryer perpetually grinding. There are always clothes to be washed, or folded, or put away.

3. EXAGGERATION

Bostonians have PhDs in exaggeration, and my wife is a tenured professor. Listen:

> "Brandon, that kid who was covering you was two foot two."
> "Suzanne texted me 150 million times today."
> "Julia has thirty hours of homework."
> "You never listen."

Our kids are not far behind:

> "I'm starving."
> "No one else on planet Earth has to share a room with their ten-year-old sister."
> "That sermon was eight hours long."

If you spend a day in my home, you'll notice exaggeration flavors everything. And if you spend a month at Seven Mile Road, you'll notice Scripture flavors everything.

Every gathering, setting, situation, and rhythm encounter the words of Scripture read, heard, believed, loved, and obeyed. Sunday mornings, gospel communities, staff meetings, baby dedications, leadership development tracks, planning retreats, membership interviews, conflict resolutions, and yes, even business meetings: all begin with Scripture. Hearing from, thinking on, marveling at, and submitting to the canon is the norm. Our songs, sermons, classes, podcasts, liturgies, prayers, and random conversations are always referencing, quoting, and bringing Scripture to bear.

Whenever I hear someone condescendingly refer to Christians as being "people of the book,"[21] three comebacks flash through my forehead:

1. You mean "people of the library."

Our word *Bible* comes from the Koine Greek word *tà biblía*, which means "the books." The Bible is not a book but a collection or library of books, each unique in its content and style and genre, and all of them cohering beautifully together and revealing truth and pointing us to the person and redemptive work of Christ on behalf of sinners. We're people of those (sixty-six) books, plural.

2. So? Every community that's ever existed is a "people of the book."

Every culture ascribes to some collection of words, teachings, dogma, or doctrine. Maybe those words have not been written and curated and bound neatly under one cover, but we all live according to the authoritative words of somebody. We all have apostles and prophets whose teachings define for us what is good and beautiful and true. If you are a Christian, it's Moses, David, Miriam, Isaiah, Matthew, Mark, Luke, Lemuel's mother, John, Peter, James, Paul, and the twenty-plus other inspired authors of Scripture. If you're not, it might be Billy Joel, Whitney Houston, Tupac, Johnny Cash, Taylor Swift, Steve Jobs, Mark Zuckerberg, Bill Gates, Mark Cuban, Carl Sagan, Sigmund Freud, William Shakespeare, Margaret Sanger, Betty Friedan, Gloria Steinem, Muhammad, Buddha, Deepak Chopra, Jordan Peterson, or someone else. But all of us live by somebody's words.

3. Yes! 100 percent, absolutely, no doubt, no embarrassment, no hesitation, with gladness and energy and abandon, we are people of the book!

Orthodox theology is one of the five non-negotiable essentials that flies like a banner over everything we do, and by it we mean that we are committed to Scripture being the first voice and final authority for all our faith and practice. Latin may be a dead language (except on hipster Christian T-shirts), but the words *sola scriptura* are alive and well and will be forever. God's words are eternally true. He has spoken on the pages of Scripture, and we are convinced that our deepest joy intersects with our clearest comprehension of what He has said to be true about who He is, what He has done for us, and how He calls us to live. We want all of our thoughts about God and ourselves to be shaped by the words of Scripture.

We say it like this: If you love your Bible, you'll love Seven Mile Road.

We receive this Psalm 119-esque devotion to Scripture from Jesus, of course. He loved His Bible as no one ever has. Quoting Scripture was His signature move. "It is written" served as the mixtape of His life. "Let the Scriptures be fulfilled" drove His self-understanding. "Have you not read" was His sharpest dig. When throwing down with the devil in the desert, His weapons of choice were Deuteronomy 8, Psalm 91, and Deuteronomy 6. How Jesus came to a self-awareness of His messiahship is one of the mysteries of the Incarnation, but when He was ready to burst onto the scene, He did so quoting Isaiah 61. When everyone from his hometown rejected him at Nazareth, He processed the pain through 1 Kings 17. When He made His dialectical method of choice (parables), His decision was informed by Isaiah 6. When He defended His Sabbath healings, He referenced 1 Samuel 21. When He was pressed on God's intentions for marriage and sexuality, He went immediately to Genesis 1 and 2. When the Pharisees demanded signs, He responded with Scriptures. When His table-flipping, temple-cleansing tirade was complete, He explained Himself with Isaiah 56 and Jeremiah 7. When He wanted to flummox His opponents, He riddled them with Psalm 110. When He prepared His disciples on the Mount of Olives for their imminent desertion, He quoted Zechariah 3. When He was falsely tried in the middle of the night by the envious and corrupt Sanhedrin, He affirmed His identity by marshaling Daniel 7. When He was minutes from death, at the bleakest moment of His life, with all the weight of every sin the elect have ever committed driven through His hands and feet, Psalm 22 burst from His soul and lips, giving voice to His suffering. When He walked the seven-mile road from Jerusalem to Emmaus and explained to His downcast disciples the necessity of the cross and resurrection, He unpacked Scripture.

The blood that ran through Jesus's veins was 100-proof Bible.

. . .

SO IT'S NO SURPRISE THAT IN Acts 20, when Paul references his central activity in planting Jesus's church in Ephesus, we're hit in rapid-fire fashion with references to the ministry of God's word. He reminds the Ephesians constantly that teaching the glorious truths of the Bible is the ground their church was built on. In fact, preaching and teaching were so foundational to Paul's ministry that he mentions it four different times in four different ways.

1. TEACHING

In verse 20, Paul says he came "teaching you in public and from house to house."

When the Ephesian Christians got together at their meeting place on the Lord's Day, there was Paul, Scriptures open, teaching. When the doorbell rang, there was Paul, Scriptures open, teaching. Workshop. Coffeeshop. Mountaintop. Wherever you encountered the life of this church in action, the Scriptures were open, and Paul was teaching.

2. TESTIFYING

In verse 21, he says it like this: "testifying both to Jews and to Greeks about repentance toward God and of faith in our Lord Jesus Christ."

Jews. Greeks. Tentmakers, soldiers, magicians, carpenters, jailers, fathers, mothers, butchers, bakers, and candlestick makers—it didn't matter. Whoever Paul was working with, the word of the gospel was in the mix.

3. DECLARING

In verse 27, Paul says, "I did not shrink from declaring to you the whole counsel of God."

I love the object of this sentence: the whole counsel of God. All of it. No skips. Paul was in Scripture so often with these people that he didn't miss a chapter, verse, truth, or implication. He worked his way through all the words, all the stories, all the doctrines. Whatever the issue, question, circumstance, objection, or controversy, he declared what God had said about it in the word.

4. ADMONISHING

And in verse 31, he reminds them, "For three years I did not cease night or day to admonish every one …"

Jack Bauer took more bathroom breaks than Paul did. Night and day for a thousand days, Paul never paused from proclaiming gospel truth from the pages of Scripture. Yes, Paul's rhetoric is hyperbolic here, but he's making an important point. The one thing he always did—relentlessly, tirelessly, ruthlessly—was go to the word. Teaching. Testifying. Declaring. Admonishing. Paul believed, down in his bones, that the one true and living God worked through words to accomplish His purposes in the souls of His people, and so Paul piled up the gospel-saturated, Bible-birthed words. He was convinced the words of Scripture held the power to change hearts and minds.

...

EVERY NOW AND THEN I WILL grab a children's fiction book at the library just to keep up on what is being pushed out there for kids in our culture. The last one I sampled was *The Witch's Boy*, by Kelly Barnhill. The story is about a boy whose mom has a jar with magic in it. Some bad guys are about to steal the jar, but instead of allowing itself to be stolen, the magic sneaks under the boy's skin. The boy ends up with a nonstop stream of words running up and down his arms and legs and shoulders just waiting to come out of his mouth and be put together in the right spells so that magic will happen.

In describing this, Barnhill writes a sentence I love: "A word, after all, is a kind of magic. It locks the substance of a thing in sound or symbol, and affixes it to the ear, or paper, or stone. Words call the world into being."

I don't know if she is a Christian, but Barnhill is actually getting at something beautifully biblical right here. In a mysterious but real sense, God has chosen for this world to work in such a way that words have a power to get things done. We see this in the Bible's first pages, when God speaks the created order into existence. First, words: "Let there be light." Boom, the universe lights up like Pats fans on Super Bowl Sunday. God is speaking—authoritatively, forcefully, effectively—from the first moments of time, and He never stops. He calls all of creation into being. He commands and converses with Adam and Eve. He sends prophets, speaking His word. He etches His ten definitive commands on tablets of stone. When the Son comes, in the fullness of time, He begins His ministry with His mouth open, voice raised: "Repent, for the kingdom of heaven is at hand" (Matt. 4:17). And for three years He never stops talking.[22] Then he sends His apostles, commanding them to herald the gospel and teach obedience. The early believers devoted themselves to the apostles' words. Two thousand years later, we still do the same because God works through words.

And those words work.

. . .

ONE SUPER HOT SUMMER, WHEN THE boys were six and eight, all the Kruse men went up to New Hampshire for a one-night stay at a campsite. When I say campsite, I don't mean patch of dirt in the middle of the woods with no shelter or bathrooms or running water in sight. We're not masochists. I mean retreat center with cabins and kitchens and hot showers. We stayed in the oldest cabin, a Swedish original, situated less than five feet from the lake. About 4 p.m., a storm rushed off Mount Monadnock and hovered directly over the lake. What was normally a serene body of water safe for canoeing, swimming, or turtle-watching suddenly became a tempest. Have you ever seen waves on a lake? You could've surfed on this thing. The floating dock was leaping out of the water.

Then the thunder started.

I grew up playing a game where we'd watch for a lightning bolt and then count until we heard the thunder. *One—two—three.* Every second corresponded to a mile between us and the lightning, or so we thought.[23] Having this knowledge assuaged any fear in us that we'd be struck. In this storm, there were no seconds between bolt and thunder. It was simultaneously *flash/boom.* And the boom wasn't a gentle rumble. It sounded like ten thousand drum sets being hurled to the ground from the skywalk on the Prudential Tower.

Thunder. This is what the word of God is like. This is the force, the aggression, the power we are talking about when we talk about gospel words. We don't analyze or consider or tinker with or seek insights from the words of Scripture. These words descend on us with all the fury of a summer storm.

Psalm 29:3-6 is one of the many beautiful places where Scripture attests to its own nature:

> The voice of the LORD is over the waters;
> the God of glory thunders,
> the LORD, over many waters.
> The voice of the LORD is powerful;
> the voice of the LORD is full of majesty.
> The voice of the LORD breaks the cedars;
> the LORD breaks the cedars of Lebanon.
> He makes Lebanon to skip like a calf,
> and Sirion like a young wild ox.

I've tried to cut wood in my backyard with a manual woodcutter before. Throwing all the power my 210-pound frame can muster into it, I can barely split a 10-inch log. But the voice of the Lord snaps cedars in two—Lebanon-grown cedars. (Lebanon was to trees like Kane's is to donuts: the biggest, baddest version there ever was.) God speaks and whole forests snap to attention. Or in half. Opening the word of God is like lighting a wick on dynamite. Like lifting the velociraptor cage in Jurassic Park. Like standing barefoot in a puddle while grasping a metal flagpole in the middle of a June thunderstorm. I have always felt that all Bibles should be sold with bright yellow warning labels on the cover. They should be stored behind the counter with the cigarettes. You should have to show ID to buy a Bible. They should come with hardhats and safety goggles.

09 | THUNDER

People sometimes call me animated when I preach. (I've literally had newer folks ask if I was signing while preaching.) I punch my chest. I widen my eyes. I let out *whoosh*es and *whoa*s and the occasional *What the ...?* I pause and appear as if I am about to buckle over. Some of this, I'm sure, is due to growing up around an expressive father and Hispanic mom, but mostly I am just trying to help our people to feel the weight and the glory and the power and the explosiveness of the words of Scripture and the gospel they contain. A good preacher is not there to cajole or flatter or make some suggestions or chat or tell anecdotes or share his opinions, ideas, perspectives, insights, or feelings. He is there to thunder the word of God—to illuminate with clarity and love. When pastor and church give themselves to this as the primary rhythm of their ministry, everyone benefits.

• • •

I WAS BORN AGAIN IN A hyper-experiential, theologically sketchy church, so the idea of Scripture centrality was brand new to me when we started planting Seven Mile Road. My dad was a hippie who was saved in Vietnam, my mom the daughter of a Pentecostal, so they naturally gravitated toward the wildest church in town for our family to attend. I was taught there that, while the word is great and important, what we are really shooting for, what people really need, are emotionally charged, Holy Ghost experiences. So, we'd open the Bible to begin our services, but everyone understood that a good service didn't center on or end with the word taught and applied. A successful service culminated in us running and jumping and shouting and crying and feeling. A good pastor was not necessarily one with a deep, abiding, soul-crushing love for the words of Scripture, or with a disciplined, careful, meticulous study of the text, or with a purposeful, accurate, skilled ability to connect the text with his particular context and people group. A good pastor was one who could leverage any text at all and frenzy the crowd. I can remember being a teenager and loving the fleeting moments in sermons when we were actually digging into, coming to grips with, and being confronted with the word itself. I was hungry for that, but I was mostly fed more emotionalism. We lived from and for the experience, not the words of Scripture.

When Grace and I graduated from college and got married, we determined not to do the TBN church thing. So, we went anti-all-we-ever-knew and began attending a ninety-person, hymn-singing, plate-passing, pew-sitting New England congregational church. The pastor was a holy, Dana Carvey doppelganger. He would preach each week, for twenty minutes, directly from his Bible, which he held directly in front of his face. No drums, no choirs, no smoke, and no lasers were used, but I experienced more Holy Ghost power (explosive, soul-stirring, sin-convicting, affections-moving, heart-changing power) in those three years than I had in the prior ten. No one in the room could hear it, but thunder was roaring in my chest. The voice of the Lord was over the waters of my soul. Breaking cedars. Shattering deep-seated sin. Overwhelming lies I had believed. Exploding idols. Washing away guilt and shame.

I will rejoice forever in the faithfulness of my pastor of those years. He was doing exactly what he was called to do. He was doing exactly what I needed him to do. He was doing what Jesus and Paul did before him. He brought the explosive power of the gospel to bear on me. He loved and led from the words of Scripture.

Church can be a place where we do the same.

– BLUEPRINTS –

1. Love and get familiar with your Bible.

This has to start with you. If you don't love the word yourself, if you are not weekly being wrecked, corrected, moved, enlivened, inspired, and changed by it, there is no way you can lead your church toward these things. If you can't say with the psalmist "The law of your mouth is better to me than thousands of gold and silver pieces," or "My soul is consumed with longing for your rules at all times," or "At midnight I rise to praise you, because of your righteous rules," you've got trouble. The Spirit gets His work done through the word, and we are dead without it.

We run something called Ox Track for our young men who aspire to pastoral ministry. Every time we are together for a couple of hours, we open our souls, confess sin, and often deal with deep, ugly stuff. I've given and heard a lot of troubling, dangerous, potentially ministry-handicapping confessions in those times: struggles with porn, anger toward children, deceit in marriage, unbelief in the power of the gospel—you name it. But the most frightening confession I've heard may have been this one: "I haven't opened my Bible in weeks." This scared me not because of some arbitrary standard we've set on acceptable Bible reading frequency. It scared me because, as he spoke, you could tell that his heart was not there yet. He was not sold on how essential time in the Scriptures with the Spirit is. He aspired to pastoral ministry sans a devotion to God's word. He was destined to fail.

2. Preach and teach the words themselves.

Don't be in the vicinity of the words. Don't start in Scripture but end in some galaxy far, far away. Don't read a text and then quickly vault from there to what you really want to say. Say the text. Point to the text. Highlight the text. Don't let there be more than one degree of separation from what you say and what the text says. The words themselves are where the power lies, what the Spirit uses, what your people need. Give them the words.

A Pastor's Sketches: Conversations with Anxious Inquirers Respecting the Way of Salvation is a wonderfully helpful book written by Ichabod Spencer, a pastor in early 1800s Massachusetts and New Jersey. The book is basically his journal of sitting one-on-one with lost people or people in need of gospel care. Spencer couldn't recount a single conversation in which he did not marshal the words of God. He was sitting with a woman once and, in the course of their conversation, he referenced twenty-two different texts. At one point she timidly but hopefully said to him, "Is that in God's word?" I read that and remember thinking, "There it is! There it is! Old Ichabod did his job. He brought God's words—not his—to bear on her soul, and she could feel the difference." Then I thought, "Has anyone I've met with ever had to ask me that question?" They should.

3. Remember that the "gospel word" and the "words of Scripture" work in tandem. Press them both.

Don't miss that in Paul's speech he cites two distinct but complementary elements of word ministry, both of which must be present in our churches.

The first time he uses the word "word" (Greek: *logos*) in the singular: "And now I commend you to God and to the word of his grace, which is able to build you up and to give you the inheritance among all those who are sanctified" (Acts 20:32). There is a "word" that Paul commends them to stick with and to live from and go back to over and over and over again. It is the "word of His grace," or what we call the gospel word. This is the word preached, declared, announced, thundered. This is the spoken unsearchable riches of God's love and work for us in Christ. God saves sinners and strengthens saints through repeated exposure to this word, so we should devote ourselves to it.

Then Paul uses "word" a second time (again *logos*), only this time in the plural: "Remember the words of the Lord Jesus" (Acts 20:35). The "words of the Lord Jesus" are, of course, in one sense, the "red-letter" words scholars have highlighted as coming from His mouth during His ministry. But an orthodox understanding of the inspiration of Scripture intimates that all the words of Scripture—from בְּרֵאשִׁית ("In the beginning") to Ἀμήν ("Amen!")—are the words of Jesus. In other words, we don't just love preaching: we love the words of our Bibles. We don't forget them, fade from them, work around them, or find substitutes for them. Let's give ourselves to the study and exposition of Genesis to Revelation, in public and from house to house. A dusty Bible on a shelf is a travesty. It should be an impossibility. We are to remember the words of the Father, Son, and Spirit.

Both of Paul's uses of "word" dovetail in the apostle's mind. For example, in 2 Timothy 3:16, he writes, "All Scripture is breathed out by God and profitable for teaching." He is referring to the "plural" words of Scripture. But then he immediately launches into an urgent plea that Timothy "Preach the word!" As Kevin DeYoung says in his killer book on the doctrine of Scripture, *Taking God at His Word*, "Only the word of God can save. Only in Scripture do we encounter the fullness of God's self-disclosure." We are to love and lead from both the words of Scripture and the word of the gospel that emerges from them.

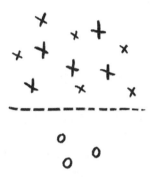

10 | OUTSIDERS

Church can be outward.
On moving toward folks who aren't there yet.

Both to Jews and to Greeks … —Acts 20:21

ONE OF THE MANY BEAUTIFUL SCANDALS about Jesus of Nazareth was that He earned the cutting nickname "friend of sinners." Gladly for us, the slander was apt. Christ's coming to seek and save grimy, unlovable, lost sinners, and not just moral, likable, highly functional people is central to the good news of the gospel. So, it should be central to our identity and practice. Yet oddly, as Tim Keller puts it (quoting John Stott), "There has always been a strong tendency for Christians to 'withdraw into a kind of closed, evangelical, monastic community.'"[24] Fighting that tendency is one of the hardest tasks before us.

. . .

THE ORIGINAL SEVEN MILE ROAD GATHERS in a suburb a few miles north of the Zakim Bridge, a scenic new suspension bridge running due north from downtown Boston. Hop on the Orange Line at North Station, take it five stops straight up, and you've arrived. We are the 1920s brick church building with 180 seats, four big sanctuary windows, a cool gray matte sign, and zero parking spots.[25]

The church scene in Melrose mirrors the championship parade scene in Cincinnati or the skateboarding scene in Port St. Lucie: not much going on. There are twelve "churches"[26] in town, none of which sees more than 150 adults on a Sunday. Most draw fewer than 50. Out of the 30,000 Bostonians living in our city, fewer than 3 percent would identify as evangelical, and that number dwindles with every obituary. Melrose—and America, increasingly—is so post-Christian it's pre-Christian. Biblical literacy is at historic lows, caricatures are all anyone knows about Jesus or the Christian faith, and the aftershocks of the pedophile priest scandals that plagued the Roman Catholic Church continue to reverberate. More people go to the dog park, the nail salon, or the Y than to church on any given Sunday. If you built a pie chart of Melrose with blue being outsiders to gospel grace and brown being insiders, it'd look like an ocean with a super skinny rowboat in it.

Call us strange, but we find this energizing.

In fact, our city resembles, in many ways, the Ephesus that Paul spent three years evangelizing. (No, it's not apples to apples. Yes, there are significant differences.) Ephesus was a first-century Melrose: rich, pretentious, cosmopolitan, sexually decadent, idolatrous. Jesus has called us to plant the gospel in this particular soil, and we're not going to cry about it. The gospel is the power of God for salvation of first-century Ephesians, third-century Alexandrians, sixteenth-century Genevans, eighteenth-century Mohican Indians, and twenty-first-century Bostonians. Christ won for Himself a bride on the cross, and some included in that corporate identity live in the 02176 zip code right this second. They just need a bold, hospitable, contextualized church to move toward them in love and call them to it. When the Jesus of the definite atonement bids a man come, he comes. Gondor (without Aragorn) stood a better chance against Mordor than Hell's gates do of holding back the advance of Jesus's gospel, but this only happens as the church embraces her missional identity and positions herself rightly toward outsiders.

· · ·

HOW TO RELATE TO OUTSIDERS IS not a uniquely ecclesiological question. It's actually a question every community with specific parameters has for membership.[27] Every nation, school, business, family, condo association, golf club, and political party must decide: "How do those of us who are 'in' feel about, think about, speak about, and engage with those who are 'out'?"

As we've talked with our people about their posture toward friends and neighbors who are unchurched and ungospeled, we've discerned a variety of default responses.

1. IGNORE THEM

This one's easy. Anyone who is not a Christian, or part of the church community, isn't even a pale green blip on our radar.

One of my great skills is coming home on Friday afternoons, which is trash day on our block, and walking past empty garbage cans like they aren't even there. This drives my wife crazy because she swears I do it on purpose. I try to tell her that's not the case. I just don't see them. My mind is occupied with getting into the house, putting on my LeBron 11s, shooting some hoops in the backyard, showering, and reading a book. She replies, "But how can you walk right by them and not even pay any attention to them? They are right in your face!"

That is how Jesus's church lives sometimes: technically located in a city, but doing our own thing, oblivious to anyone outside our doors, rolls, or rhythms. Sure, once a year at the city-wide fair we throw up a booth and hand out some trifolds, but if the Black Death tore through and 90 percent of our city's residents dropped dead, we might not know for a month.

2. AVOID THEM

This is less "Oh, I was so occupied with insiders that I didn't see you there" than "Oh, no, I saw you there. And I shimmied right away."

I hate traffic. I've lived just north of Boston for thirty-five years, and I have mastered the art of avoiding lights. To get to my day job, I need to drive through four cities: Melrose, Malden, Everett, and Revere. According to Google Maps it should take me sixteen minutes. It takes me eleven, if I'm not speeding. The route includes several parking lots, a gas station cut-through, and multiple rights on red, but it works. You know how Google Maps gives you a no-tolls option? I've seriously thought of going on *Shark Tank* with a map app for greater Boston that gives you a no-traffic-lights option. Avoiding 100 percent of the lights would be the dream.

That too is how Jesus's church lives sometimes. Outsiders are to be avoided at all costs. Of course, moments occur when we are called to avoid participation with sinners in sin or in situations where we would be required to celebrate sin. Some locations, events, parades, celebrations, etc., we must abstain from—similar to Daniel and his friends' response to the king's feasts. But those are the exceptions to the rule. The rule is that we be fully engaged in the lives, rhythms, events, ebbs, and flows of the cities we are sent to. We're not to section ourselves into Christian ghettos, being careful never to engage with anyone or anything that doesn't have the adjective *Christian* before it. Our spirit is never to be "Tell me you're a Christian, and then we can hang out. If not, you get off my lawn and I'll stay off yours."

3. BLEND WITH THEM

I don't tell this story often, but in April 1994 I accompanied a friend to Boots & Diamonds Saloon in Tulsa, Oklahoma, for a night of line dancing. Every male in the joint had on tight Wranglers, a tucked-in shirt with tassels, boots with spurs, and a ten-gallon hat. I was wearing baggy jeans, an untucked shirt, Air Jordans, and a Celtics visor. I lasted about two and a half minutes of a George Strait song and headed straight for my car.

I did not blend.

Now, pretend with me that upon reaching my car, I sped over to Drysdale's, spent two hundred dollars, changed, came back, and jumped in line. (I know, that would never happen. Pretend.) That's what Christians and their churches do sometimes: "If we just look and act like everybody else, they'll like us, and accept us, and maybe even approve of us." I am not referring to fitting in a context like a good missionary, or humbly embracing neutral, external, cultural commonalities in order to love and engage people. I am talking about betraying the distinctiveness of Christ. Trading the burly doctrines of grace for a pair of postmodern skinny jeans. Going along to get along. This is what 90 percent of the churches in my city have done in the last generation: compromised, one by one, purposefully, on every and any Christian doctrine that would set them apart from outsiders, so desperate to be viewed favorably by the world that they'd leave the gospel behind, crumpled on the floor of a dressing room. Instead of being a city on a hill, the church becomes just another face in the crowd, indistinct, unrecognizable, superfluous. And once the blending is complete, the church disappears altogether.

4. VILLAINIZE THEM

There are villains to be opposed. John refers to them as antichrists. Jesus's apostle Paul prefers the label "dogs." Jesus called them hypocrites, whitewashed tombs, blind guides, fools, foxes, and vipers. We encounter enemies of the gospel who take a formal and public stand against Christ, His law, and His church. Although we are to stand and fight, sometimes our view of specific outsiders colors our view of every outsider, as if anyone outside the four walls of the church community is a bloodthirsty orc to be hewn down.

Hillary Clinton helpfully modeled this tendency for us in her failed 2016 presidential campaign when, in one sentence, she demonized the 60 million Americans who were outsiders to her convictions, labeling all of them "deplorables."[28] This was classic villainization: insisting that anyone and everyone who does not believe the way she did was of one stripe, and that stripe needed to be eliminated.

When trying to decide where my oldest son would attend high school, someone mentioned the possibility of him going to Bishop Fenwick High School in Peabody because several young men from our town attended there to play basketball. I was succinct in my response: "Never. I don't care if they gave him a full scholarship and escorted him to school in a limo every day. No Kruse kid is ever going to Fenwick." As a Savio kid, anyone who ever attended or taught at or coached at Fenwick was, in my mind, deplorable.

We humans are great at this. If you are inside with us—our race, our sex, our worldview, our culture—you're good. If you are outside, we're not out to love you or win you, but to end you.

. . .

THEN WE COME TO SCRIPTURE AND something else is going on entirely. Jesus's people—insiders to grace by grace—don't avoid or ignore or blend or villainize outsiders, but they move toward outsiders in gospel love. They build churches that say "We see you. You matter. We love you. And we've got the best news you'll ever hear."

That this needs to be our default posture is the clear teaching of all of Scripture, and it leaps out at us in a simple conjunction in Paul's speech. In reminding them of what kept him occupied for three years on the ground in Ephesus, Paul says he was "testifying both to Jews and to Greeks of repentance toward God and of faith in our Lord Jesus Christ" (Acts 20:21).

The word *testify* in this verse is that big, lively, urgent, intense action verb for moving toward outsiders, letting them know about their desperate need for a savior, and about Christ's unrivaled qualifications and unquestioned willingness to meet their need. Paul was able to say to outsiders in Ephesus, with a clear conscience, "I saw you, I loved you, and I pointed you to the reality of Jesus in every way I could."

At Seven Mile Road, we say our big dream is "Every Bostonian Jesus gives us being loved and gospeled well." Or, as the Presbyterians say it, "The church's power is ministerial and declarative." Or, as the Baptists say it, "The Church is God's plan to reach the nations with the hope of the gospel." However you say it, the big idea is that every church needs to look in the mirror and ask, "Are we built to love and gospel outsiders together?"

We've sought to embody two missiological truths from this text in how we relate to outsiders:

1. OUTSIDERS ARE ON OUR RADAR

The early church gave their prayer, time, money, and energy to connect with people (Jews and Greeks) who were not yet part of their community.

One of the fun things we used to do in our new member classes was talk about how a church is best organized and governed. *Polity* is the word for this, and, depending on the backgrounds of the attendees, the conversation could last one hour or five. We'd group a few people together, hand them a large sheet of paper and a Sharpie, and ask them to sketch their best understanding of biblical polity. Although we'd end up with a variety of diagrams, littered with boxes, circles, arrows, and gaunt-looking stick figures, there would always be two constituents who never made it onto any of the org charts.

The first missing entity was always Christ Himself. "Uh, where is Jesus on here?" was always met with sheepish chuckles and an "Oh, right, we assumed that, of course. Didn't have to write His name on there."

The second was outsiders. Not yet Christians. Lost people. "Ungospeled, all-set Bostonians," as we lovingly refer to them. No one ever included the four million or so of them, ever, anywhere on the page. This always led to engaging conversation about the missional identity of the church. By the end of the night, we'd flip the org chart sideways and write "Bostonians" in bright red letters down the right margin, emphasizing the surprising and beautiful truth that the church is the only institution that exists in a pronounced way for those who are not yet members.

When Southwest Airlines came into existence, only about 15 percent of the US population actually flew. Air travel was too expensive and too complicated for the common man. So everyone in the airline industry was competing for a share of the insiders. Every marketing campaign and strategic shift was based on giving the existing pool of flyers a reason to choose their company's airline. Enter Southwest, which stood the industry on its head. Southwest's mentality was "We're not going for that 15 percent of the population who already flies. We're going for the other 85 percent not yet flying." When asked who their fiercest competition was, Southwest executives would not answer "American" or "Delta," but rather "the car" and "the bus." Their mission was to see to it that the common man and woman were finally "free to fly about the country."

That is how our churches need to think and behave. We exist—not exclusively, but pronouncedly—to help outsiders become insiders.

The multiplication of our original church into several churches was built on this conviction. We were not going only for people who were already insiders to gospel grace and simply needed a good church. One church can do that work just fine. We were purposefully, intentionally, happily going for the 99 percent of Bostonians who were not insiders to gospel grace yet. We were planting the gospel among these distinct people groups and hoping churches emerged. To avoid or ignore them was not an option. Outsiders needed to be on our radar.

2. ANYONE CAN GET IN ON GOSPEL GRACE

Here's the gospel in a nutshell: we are all complete idiots and unhinged rebels by nature and by choice, but our future is super bright because of Jesus, and anybody can get in on this.[29]

And by anybody, we mean anybody.

When the Spirit delineates both Jews and Greeks in this text, it's code for everybody. Clean people and not-clean people. Put-together people and not-put-together people. People born into the covenant and people not born into the covenant. Everyone is valuable, and everyone is broken, and everyone is redeemable. Everyone is called to repent and believe, and Christ will turn nobody away who does that. The force of it is this: there are no outsiders who cannot become insiders.

This truth was central to the apostle Paul's ministry. Jesus commissioned Paul specifically to open the floodgates for non-Jews to storm in. Every ethnic and cultural barrier to their entry was bulldozed: circumcision, dietary restrictions, hairstyles, holidays, all of it. Gone. All that was required was repentance and faith, evinced by a pursuit of personal holiness in accord with God's moral law. Although the prophets explicitly prophesied this global altar call, it was a scary, confusing, uncomfortable, humbling culture shift for the Jewish Christians. The makeup of the people of God was no longer mostly Jews and a handful of Greeks. It was both Jews and Greeks, as many of either as would come. And come they did. By the tens of thousands.

This is the glorious scandal of grace that drives the universality of the church's mission. God's acceptance of us is not contingent on our ethnicity, last name, religious ceremonies, or good works. No one merits adoption into the family. No one climbs the ladder, passes the test, or checks the boxes. Jesus sweeps in and saves each and every one of us the same way. No other community on earth is like this. All pigmentations, all intellects, all heights and weights, both sexes. Degree and no degree. Wealthy and broke. The church has one qualification to become an insider: you are a sinner, ready to be done with your sin, ready to fly to Jesus. So rather than avoid or ignore or blend or villainize, let's move toward outsiders in gospel love.

• • •

IN JONATHAN EDWARDS'S FAREWELL SERMON TO his Northampton congregation, he paints a picture (as only he can) of the Day of the Lord when the countless masses will gather before the judgment seat of Christ. On that day, Jesus will judge all things in perfect justice. In his sermon, Edwards emphasizes for his people that on that coming day every one of them will stand before Christ and give account for how they handled themselves in the ecclesiological controversy that resulted in his dismissal.

I've often thought about that day in terms of the Bostonians Jesus has sent us to. Will we have engaged in the gospel mission with such fervency, such prayerfulness, such boldness, such relentlessness, that all those living just north of Boston will have to admit to Jesus, "You did send us a clear and compelling witness. Seven Mile Road Church loved and gospeled us for years. They sacrificed time and energy and money for us, they opened their homes and lives to us, they were diligent about understanding and articulating and declaring and defending gospel truth to us in language we could understand. There wasn't one more thing they could have done to give me an opportunity to repent and believe the gospel."

May that be said that day of all our churches by all the outsiders.

– BLUEPRINTS –

1. Teach your people to pray for outsiders.

We encourage our folks to pray regularly for specific friends, neighbors, and local communities (i.e., running club, school PTO, class at school, or any other group they belong to). It's amazing how the Lord can soften our hearts and ready us for opportunities if we are diligently seeking Him.

Here are the four things we encourage our people to pray for outsiders:

> Pray for dissatisfaction with the status quo of their lives.
> Pray for conviction of sin.
> Pray for opportunities to love and gospel them.
> Pray for gospel wakefulness.

2. Articulate missional distinctives that you are committed to, and make sense of them in your context.

Mission fades like Randy Moss, so it's crucial we champion an outward focus with our people. Although every church is called to engage in the mission of God, not every church will strategize toward this end similarly. Think on your context and what missional distinctives make sense for you, then phrase them as succinctly and clearly as possible and keep them before your people constantly.

Here are the four missional distinctives we have embraced at Seven Mile Road. They drive our decisions about time and energy investment and hold us accountable to keep outsiders central to the rhythms of our church life.

1. BOLDNESS

We are not going to live scared. The gospel is the power of God for salvation for all who believe, so let's hype the grace and truth of Christ boldly.

2. HOSPITALITY

We want every Bostonian we meet, in every context we meet them, to feel like Seven Mile Road was specifically built with them in mind.

3. CREATIVITY

Bostonians don't tend to seek out a Sunday service or church community, so let's be thoughtful and entrepreneurial about ways to move toward them.

4. LONG GAME

Leading Bostonians to Jesus takes time—consistent, unrushed exposures to gospel truth in multiple contexts. Overnight success is not our measure.

3. Be in relationship with outsiders yourself.

Regardless of your personality, your spiritual gifting, or your schedule, there are no excuses for not being in relationship with people outside the ecosystem of the church. "My" outsiders are the dozens of people I am on a first-name basis with at my day job, the old guys I play pickup with at the Y on Fridays, and the twelve or so families who live closest to our home. If your list begins and ends with your mailman, it might be time to rethink some things.

11 | X-FACTORS

Church can be daring.
On taking big risks.

Not knowing what will happen to me ... —Acts 20:22

JOIE THOMPSON, BROTHER AND best friend of mine in ministry, planted and pastors Restoration Road Church a mile and a half north of the original Seven Mile Road. It's a church successfully making a distinct group of Bostonians into disciples. Had he not taken five big gospel risks, though, his church would still be a dream.

RISK 1: THE PHONE CALL

Joie had been leading worship at an earnest but not-so-healthy, actually-a-little-bit-shady church in Saugus that's now defunct. One week he grew so troubled and frustrated by what was happening at the church that he resigned on a Monday, and he started his own church the following Sunday. He would happily tell you today this was probably not the wisest timing. The church, called The Father's House, was born with no funding, no training, no team, no strategic plan, no children's program, no website, no affiliations, no polity, and no statement of faith. It was just Joie, a Bible, a guitar, and some folding chairs. A few years into the work, things got stuck, both missionally for the church and personally for Joie. We had met each other on the diamond of an overly competitive church softball game, so he decided to call me to talk about where he was at. That phone call was a big risk. Joie had no track record of relationship with me or Seven Mile Road, no guarantees of how he would be received, and no certainty about how the conversation would unfold. The continuum of possible outcomes ranged from "I'll make a solid connection with a faithful brother" to "I'll get shamed and hustled off the phone," but Joie took the risk.

RISK 2: THE INVITE

We talked that day (I remember exactly where I was standing) for an hour about life, theology, ecclesiology, lost people, and the Celtics. I loved every second of the conversation and immediately talked with our team and then our church about it. Ox

Track is the leadership development community we run annually for men who want to explore the call to doing pastoral ministry in the life of our church. Normally we know a ton about a man before inviting him into the track, but in Joie's case, all we knew was he was a great centerfielder, loved Jesus and family, and had some guts. I raised the question anyway: "What do we think of inviting an outsider into the Ox Track this year?" I knew it would be a risk. Ox Track is a serious investment in someone, but we felt like it was the right thing to do. So, we invited Joie in, not sure if he'd even make it through the first month.

RISK 3: THE BIG ASK

We spent the entire year together, and it was immediately apparent that Joie was called, gifted, and qualified to pastor and plant a church. But it was just as apparent to Kevin and me (leading the track) that the current iteration of Joie's church could not be reworked on the fly. The best case for long-term gospel advancement in and through Joie's life would be to shut his plant down and have him come live and pastor with us to get healthy, equipped, and prepared to try again. In other words, we were going to counsel Joie to hit the reset button. Only this was not a video game. This was Joie's entire life's work. I remember looking at Kev and asking, "So are you going to say it, or am I going to say it?" I drew the short stick and slowly laid out the case for what we thought was best. This was a huge risk. Joie could have responded in a thousand ways, from fired-up to flummoxed to furious to felonious, but we made the big ask.

RISK 4: THE RESET BUTTON

Then came the biggest risk of all: Joie saying yes. Everything he had worked at, every relationship he had fostered, and every vision he had cast would be placed in jeopardy with a yes. He would have to table all of it and trust that in the long run, somehow, someway, somewhere, things would still work out. There was real potential for good, but also for loss, hurt, and disappointment. His dream might die and stay dead forever. Joie took some time, came back to us, and, in the quietest of voices, said, "OK. If this is the Spirit's way forward for us, I'm in. I don't know how this is going to go exactly, but I trust God." Risk taken, we closed down The Father's House, and Joie literally crashed, emotionally and physically. If you've ever seen a marathoner at the end of the race crumple to the ground after exerting every ounce of energy, you know what Joie's first month at Seven Mile Road was like. At one point he was so weak he needed medical treatment. I sat with him at Melrose-Wakefield Hospital, an IV in his arm, and thought, "That's an exhausted but courageous man right there. If Jesus's modus operandi really is to break us down to make us useful, in a few years Joie might be the most useful church planter and pastor in Massachusetts."

RISK 5: RUN IT BACK

The Lord then graced us with three formative and fruitful years of Joie healing, learning, and serving beautifully as a pastor at Seven Mile Road. Then came a fifth and final risk: we were going to run it back. I remember sitting in what used to be one of the reading rooms in the Christian Science church building we had purchased and refurbished. I said to Joie, "Listen, man. We are planting a church with you. The light is green. Let's do this." Seven Mile Road risked financial support, some current giving, twenty-five adults along with their kids, and a great pastor of ours. We said, "We don't know how this is going to go, but we trust God." Today there is another gospel-centered church thriving in a place that needs hundreds of them.[30]

• • •

THE CAUSE OF THE GOSPEL HAS always advanced because Jesus's people are good with taking risks—a "risk" being any action that exposes you to the possibility of loss or injury or failure,[31] like these:

- a loss of money, like betting against the Patriots making it to the Super Bowl.
- a loss of reputation, like when Roy Cruz challenged me to a game of one-on-one in my own backyard.
- a loss of privilege, like breaking curfew only to come home to find your dad sitting on your bed.
- a loss of relationship, like when a godly couple in our church abstained from celebrating an unlawful "marriage" that a niece of theirs was entering.
- a loss of health, like when you eat that Chinese food that's been at the back of the fridge since New Year's Eve.
- a loss of life, like when a firefighter rushes into a flaming building.

Although nobody enjoys losing something of value, all of us have different dispositions when it comes to taking—or not taking—risks.

Some of us are big risk takers. Thrill-seekers. Daredevils. Kenny Rogers is our soundtrack. We view risk the way I view Rocky movies: the more, the merrier. The rabbit hole of "fail videos" on YouTube wouldn't exist if not for us. We think, "Hmm, let's see what happens if I jump off my roof onto a Slip 'N Slide. This will go great!" Our common-sense meter is busted. We don't plan; we just figure things out as we go. We go to Vegas and we are either rich or broke in fifteen minutes, cruising the strip in a Jacuzzi limo or hitchhiking back to Massachusetts.

If there were a box, we'd live way outside of it.

Others among us are risk avoiders. Nervous Nellies. Control freaks. (We prefer the terms *cautious*, *judicious*, or *prudent*.) We do not like taking risks. We do not jump right into the deep end. We love certainty. We really love guarantees. A sure thing makes our day. We always have a plan, and our big win is everything going according to that plan. We vacation with a color-coded agenda for every potential activity. We meet suggested deviations from the day's plan with death stares. We've never been to Vegas.

If there were a box, we'd live squarely inside of it.

Neither of these extremes is morally evil in and of itself. Marriages, families, churches, and businesses thrive when populated with folks who land all along the chaos-control continuum and learn to appreciate and work with each other. We have both optimists and realists (and maybe even a few pessimists) on every ministry team at Seven Mile Road, and while this makes for some tense conversations, more and healthier gospel work is accomplished because of it. But both extremes do present serious dangers.

Despite what John Eldredge says in *Wild at Heart*, recklessness is not a virtue. Sometimes flamboyant risk-taking Christians and churches do more harm than good in the name of "going all out for Jesus." Putting your seatbelt on is not a sign of cowardice. Passing on the greenish mayonnaise is not playing scared. Not patronizing the portable bungee jump at the county fair does not make you a chicken.

But the remedy for recklessness is not the elimination of, or even minimization of, risk. Yet this is exactly where churches tend to gravitate. Many churches in Massachusetts have not taken a missional or financial risk in decades. I met a deacon from a church two miles east of us that was as dead as Martha's Vineyard in mid-February. The church's Sunday attendance had been on the decline for twenty years. Their children's programming was suspended for lack of need. They hadn't seen a visitor since Ray Flynn was mayor (so, the 1980s). But when he cataloged the church's assets for me, I was shocked. They owned a church building and a fellowship hall (both debt- and tax-free), they had enough recurring income to hire a full-time pastor, and they were sitting on $1.1 million in the bank! Envy, then horror, gripped my soul. This church was squatting on millions of dollars of Jesus's money, burying it in the dirt like the third and unfaithful steward in His parable, unwilling to risk a penny of it. I asked my friend how he felt about the state of the church, and his answer made perfect sense: "Oh, we're fine. Everyone loves each other, and we pay our bills on time."

This is not Jesus's call for His church.

We cannot be risk-averse and follow Jesus. We cannot play it safe and inherit the kingdom of God. Yes, good financial stewardship is a virtue; reducing unnecessary liability is wise, and cost-benefit analyses are important. But none of us has the first or final voice in the life and mission of our churches. We must be ready to take gospel-centered risks together.

・・・

A WILLINGNESS TO TAKE SOME BIG risks is definitive of every man and woman who has ever loved, obeyed, and accomplished great things for God.

Noah risked building an ark in the middle of a desert. Abraham risked uprooting himself from Ur and striking out for lands unknown; he risked granting Lot the fertile land of the valley; and he risked his son's neck on the altar. Joseph risked displeasing Potiphar's wife. Moses risked making stuttered demands of the most powerful man in Egypt. Rahab risked housing the spies. Joshua risked marching around Jericho before making his assault. David risked fighting Goliath to the death, and then risked letting Saul live. Ruth risked a night at the foot of Boaz's bed. Daniel risked a night in the lions' den. Elijah risked drenching the altar with water. Nehemiah risked rebuilding the walls of Zion. Esther risked making herself known to the king. Nathan risked confronting David; Abigail risked approaching him. John the Baptist risked calling Herod out on his sexual sin. The bleeding woman risked touching Jesus's robe. John risked standing by Jesus's cross. Nicodemus risked asking for Jesus's body. Ananias risked walking into a room with Saul the assassin, then Barnabas risked befriending him, then the apostles risked giving him the right hand of fellowship. And then he—-Saul who became Paul, Apostle to the Gentiles—-never stopped taking risks that might advance the cause of the gospel.

. . .

PAUL'S RISK-TAKING JUMPS OUT AT US not only through bold missionary exploits but also in the text of his speech to the Ephesian elders. Paul gave this farewell in the port city of Miletus. This would be like grabbing lunch with someone at South Station or Logan Airport two hours before the person's train or plane departs. In other words, he was going somewhere. He says it like this: "And now, behold, I am going to Jerusalem, constrained by the Spirit ..." (Acts 20:22a).

So, Paul was headed to Jerusalem not on a whim, but from gospel conviction. He and his team had been collecting money from Gentile Christians to give to poor Jewish Christians in Jerusalem. This generosity was a visible display of the mystical unity they all now shared in Christ. By sending financial support, the Gentiles were making the bold statement: "Because of Christ and His grace, we who used to be enemies are now family. You have a need. We have an ability to meet that need. So, we are sending help." You can imagine how dear this trip was to Paul's heart. He was the Apostle to the Gentiles. The bottom line of his ministry was seeing the Gentiles grafted into the people of God. Delivering this benevolence money to Jerusalem would not only affirm the legitimacy of his commission but also adorn the gospel and strengthen the church, so Paul knew it had to happen: "I am going."

Then he adds something fascinating: "... not knowing what will happen to me there, except that the Holy Spirit testifies to me in every city that imprisonment and afflictions await me" (Acts 20:22b-23). Real risk was involved in Paul saying yes to this Jerusalem trip. He did not know the details of what would happen, or what the exact outcome would be. Arrest and affliction were certain, but then what? Rejection? Imprisonment? Execution? This trip was filled with many x-factors, but Paul went anyway.

Gladly, we are not left to wonder at his motivations. Paul clearly states exactly what was driving his willingness to step into the unknown, and what the grounds of all our risk-taking should be: to testify to the gospel of the grace of God. In other words, "What's most important is not that I don't fail. It's not that all my relationships are maintained"—in fact, he knew that going to Jerusalem meant he'd never see these brothers again—"or that my nest egg remains solvent, or that my reputation remains pristine, or that I remain safe, or free, or even alive. What matters most is that the gospel of the grace of God is testified through my life. If taking this risk is going to advance the cause of the gospel, I'm in."

A few cities later this conversation circled back to Paul. He was with another church, and the context of Acts 21 suggests he told them something similar. A prophet named Agabus walked up to Paul, took Paul's belt, and bound his own hands and feet with it, essentially saying, "But I do know. Listen to me, Paul. If you go to Jerusalem, here's what is going to happen" (my interpretation). When the believers saw this, many of the control freaks among them balked. "Uh, Paul, you can't take that risk. There are way too many x-factors involved here. If they get their hands on you, who knows what they'll do next." Acts 21 says that they "urged Paul not to go up to Jerusalem," but Paul would have none of it. He answered directly, "What are you doing, weeping and breaking my heart? For I am ready not only to be imprisoned but even to die in Jerusalem for the name of the Lord Jesus" (Acts 21:13). There it is again, the ground of all our risk-taking: love for the name and the fame of Jesus. Prioritizing gospel advancement over the desire for certainty or control.

...

THIS MAY SURPRISE YOU, COMING FROM a church planter and all, but I am not a big risk-taker. I don't get amped by invitations to whitewater rafting or skydiving. I've never invested a nickel in a penny stock or hedge fund. Although I have gone on all the insane thrill rides Six Flags has to offer, it's primarily out of love for my kids (who want Dad to go with them) and protection of my ego (I don't want anyone to think I am scared). The truth is that I close my eyes and hope for the ride to be over as soon as the harness clicks in. It's no wonder that for the past fifteen years my tentmaking position has been as a CFO, another word for *controller*, meaning "the guy who makes sure we don't run out of money, chooses the most reliable vendors to do business with, and keeps a bottom drawer stocked for a rainy day." I like my ducks, and I like them waddling predictably in a nice, neat row.

From the outset of planting Seven Mile Road, Jesus took this tendency of mine and lovingly placed it in an incinerator. Our church started by taking the big risk of hiring me to plant it. When Grace and I said yes, they handed a $26,000 paycheck to an unemployed man and his eight-months pregnant wife. And it's never stopped.

Some risks have worked out swimmingly since then, like these:

1. ASKING JOHN FREDERICK TO PLAY LEAD GUITAR

We needed a lead guitarist for our worship team, so in the first week of our church's life, I asked John to join the band. I had taught John in high school, and he was the only person in my Rolodex whom I both liked and knew could play the guitar.[32] I offered him $50 a week to come sing and strum three chords for an hour. As broke college students tend to do when cash is involved, he said yes. For three years we loved and gospeled John, seemingly to no avail. But then, while traveling with his band in Georgia, John was born again in a van in a Barnes & Noble parking lot. He called me at midnight to explain what had happened. The next week we sat in a local pizza place, and he talked non-stop for an hour. I remember him saying, "So what I am saying is, you don't need to apologize to anybody for me anymore. I'm in, with Jesus." John, who now pastors an Anglican church in Australia, was the first of many all-set, ungospeled Bostonians we have seen come to new life in Christ through our willingness to risk inviting them into community with us.

2. CALLING AJAY THOMAS TO PASTOR AT TWENTY-FOUR YEARS OLD

When we first called Ajay to pastor at Seven Mile Road, he was greener than Kermit the Frog. But we were in desperate need of growing our pastoral team and taking some of the preaching load off me, so we put every guardrail we knew in place and went for it. For a year's worth of pastor meetings, he would sit quietly and nod at whatever I said. But he served us well, grew like a weed, and has now planted the healthiest and most beautifully multiethnic church you've ever seen in Philly.

3. LAUNCHING KALOS TRACK

Our church started a year-long discipleship community built to help the women in our church believe the gospel, adorn it through a happy embrace of their femininity, and partner with our pastors in doing gospel work. The first year of the Kalos

Track entailed myself and six women at our church getting together monthly to sit in a circle, open our Bibles, and talk freely about things like equality, distinction, headship, submission, strength, weakness, freedoms, boundaries, and masculine and feminine glories, to name a few things. I was scared to death, but it's ended up being one of the most life-giving, mission-advancing, church-strengthening things we have ever done. We now have a dozen women serving on a diaconal team committed to ensuring that every woman Jesus gives us is loved and gospeled well at Seven Mile Road.

Other risks have sunk to the bottom of the pool and torn a hole in the lining, like these:

1. EXPERIMENTING WITH MULTISITE

When we bought our space in Melrose in 2011, it was two miles from where the church was currently meeting in Malden. Rather than uprooting our entire church, we decided to go "multisite." Although we had some highlights during that time, like me seeing how fast I could make the drive between sermons on a Sunday, multisite ministry was not a fit with our theological, philosophical, or missiological convictions. We lost nearly two years of potential momentum and tens of thousands of dollars spinning our wheels in two places before consolidating and then replanting the Malden church from scratch as an autonomous mission.

2. PREACHING ABOUT CHURCH FATHERS AND MOTHERS

It was summer, and we had just finished preaching through the older covenant typologically, marveling at how Christ perfectly recapitulated the ministries of forerunners like Joseph, Moses, Joshua, David, Jehu,[33] and Jonah. Rather than launch into a new series when half the church would be traveling, we flipped the script and looked at how the life of Christ informed some of the saints of church history, such as Augustine, Perpetua, Polycarp, Calvin, and Knox. Many of our people were confused as to why we would get away from preaching the inspired text of Scripture, even for a handful of Sundays. They were right. The series was disjointed, the texts were cherry-picked, and we vowed never to do it again.

3. HAVING A DEEJAY SCRATCH TURNTABLES DURING CHRISTMAS EVE SERVICE

No further comment.

...

ALTHOUGH SOME RISKS LEAD TO BIG wins for the gospel in our lives and churches, and some lead to loss or injury or failure, the truth is that no risk taken in obedience to God or in love for God and His glory is ever ultimately a failure.

For one thing, God is working all things out in real time for His glory and our good, even our failures. You may start a church and see it fail, only to discover that failure was the greatest thing to ever happen for your soul and marriage and ministry. You may lose a bunch of money on a risky move for the sake of the gospel only to find out that God was removing an idol in your life that would have killed you. You may lose a relationship but realize you've gained hundreds of others. Jesus works redemptively in everything in our lives, even our so-called failures.

The day of Jesus is coming, when every word you have said, and every deed you have done, and every risk you have taken (and not taken) will be exposed for what it was in the light of Christ's perfect justice. On that day Jesus will not say to us, "What were you thinking? You shouldn't have taken that risk for my glory and the advance of the gospel and the good of the church."

He is going to say, "Well done, good and faithful [and risk-taking] servant."

- BLUEPRINTS -

1. Pray for and platform visionaries.

When I say "pray for," I don't mean pray that they'd come down to earth with the rest of us. I mean pray that Jesus would send them to you. When I say "platform," I don't mean put them on stage so everyone can look at them. I mean let their voices be heard, especially on teams driving strategic decision-making that impacts the mission of the church. Churches quickly slide into "control" mode, doing this year what we did last year because "that's how we do things around here." We are perpetually in need of having our eyes lifted to see potentials that easily escape our view. Not everything we throw at the wall will stick, but we will make sure the church doesn't get stuck.

2. Don't be afraid to say "We risked and failed."

Really, it's OK.

3. Don't go a year without taking a risk, however calculated it might be, especially if you favor control over chaos.

I don't mean to radically reinvent your ministry model every twelve months. Your people can't handle that kind of volatility, and they'll bail on you the same way you'd bail on that ride that spins so fast you stick to the wall. I mean make sure there are ministry and mission initiatives happening where success or failure is an open question, where risk is involved, and where new avenues of engagement and discipleship are being explored. If you are clear in communicating the "why" behind the risks, your people will get on board.

12 | GLANCES

Church can be content.
On embracing our callings and capacities.

My course and the ministry that I received ... —Acts 20:24

THE GEORGE WASHINGTON BRIDGE neatly scissors the Hudson River from Jersey to the Bronx. If you've ever driven over the "GW," you know it's one of those bridges that, no matter what time you cross, holds unholy amounts of traffic. Eight in the morning? Two in the afternoon? Midnight on Christmas Eve? The bridge does not care. A thousand brake lights and "I♥NY" bumper stickers await you.

If you're coming north on I-95, a few miles before the bridge, there's a fork in the road. There you have to make a choice: express or local. If you want to get out of Jersey[34] and home to Boston as fast as possible, what do you do? You choose the express lane, of course.

A few years ago, we were driving home from visiting our church plant in Philly. We hit the 95 fork, and I veered left to go "express." Fifty yards after the split, red lights lit up my windshield. The express lane was at a standstill, but the local lane was free and clear. Cars whizzed past us. Eighteen-wheelers flew by. A Prius bombed through my peripheral vision doing forty-five miles per hour. An elderly woman in the breakdown lane buzzed by on her motorized scooter with the shopping cart accessory.

One of two things was going to grip my heart: either a God-centered gladness in all the grace of the weekend we'd just had, or a cranky, miserable, ugly discontent.

Gratitude should have been the play. Think of all the things I could have been thankful for comfortably:

My wife, Grace, was beside me. Although she was forcing me to listen to Michael Bublé for six hours, she was still there, committed to our marriage and energetic about the mission of our church.

All four of our children were with us, alive, healthy, growing fast, playing punch buggy, and asking if we were there yet.

We'd just finished worshiping with Ajay and the people of Seven Mile Philly, and they were doing great: three years in, thriving in many ways, still figuring some things out, and celebrating unexpected surprises. One surprise was that an established church that Seven Mile Philly had been renting space from had sold a two-million-dollar property to our new church plant for one dollar, because the old church believed our new church was worth investing in.

I had much to be thankful for, but I'm a serious work in progress, so envy became my play.

I wished I were somewhere else.

The local lane would have been good. A warm bed in Boston would have been better. White Castle in Queens on the other side of the bridge: the best. Anywhere but where I was.

I wished I were driving something else.

A monster truck. A tank. The Batmobile. Anything but a minivan.

I wished I were someone else.

A pilot sounded nice. Or governor of New Jersey. Or Inspector Gadget. Anything but a pastor with four loud kids, taking six-hundred-mile road trips that included crossing the GW, to visit churches his church had planted.

Then I noticed something. For the hour it took us to go those two miles, my head kept glancing sideways, over the Jersey barriers, to the local lane, toward a reality that wasn't mine.

That's envy: a sideways glance of the soul. A tilt of the head that says, "I wish my life were that one over there, and not the one I have right here."

...

THE MID-NINETIES FOR ME HELD A simple daily routine: eat, sleep, go to school, play pickup, and listen to hip-hop. You've probably never heard of Skee-Lo, but he was a diminutive nineties rapper whose biggest (only?) hit was a song called "I Wish."

It started like this:

> I wish I was a little bit taller.
> I wish I was a baller.
> I wish I had a girl who looked good, I would call her.
> I wish I had a rabbit in a hat with a bat and
> A six four Impala.
> I wish I was like six foot nine.

I could quote the rest of the lyrics from memory, but you get the idea. "Confessions of Rapper Envy" would have been a fitting title to the song, and it's a tune all too familiar to pastors and church planters. If we had a dollar for every time we've said "I wish," or for every sideways glance we've taken, we'd all be living on the north coast of Kauai.

The list of ways we envy others is as ugly as it is long:

1. I WISH I HAD DIFFERENT GIFTS. LIKE HIS.

I remember the first Acts 29 regional conference I attended in Troy, New York, with Ed Marcelle. Ed is a pastor and missiologist who has spent decades engaging post-Christian culture in the upstate New York capital region. Although he's a Yankees fan, Ed sports a magnetic personality, a 1600-on-the-SAT-level

IQ, and elite communication skills. Ed spoke that day, strikingly, for an hour, without ever misspeaking, or looking down. I preach with my eyes on a manuscript.

Paul McPheeters, pastor of the small church that planted the original Seven Mile Road, is a soul whisperer. When I sit with someone, one on one, for an hour, it routinely makes things worse. But Paul is with somebody for seven minutes, and he beautifully draws out of the person all he or she needs to express, and he wisely speaks what he or she needs to hear. I sat with him once and observed him. "Ohh. *That's* how this works," I thought. "You listen to people. I thought you just yelled Bible verses at them."

Joie Thompson, one of our church planters, has evangelized and baptized his entire social network. I know one kid from high school who might be sort of interested in coming by the church someday.

Matt Chandler is Matt Chandler.

I wish I were any of these gentlemen.

2. I WISH I WERE CALLED TO A DIFFERENT CITY.

I am so glad that, in His providence, God allowed Al Gore to invent the internet, because it's been a force for so much gospel advancement across the globe. It is breathtaking to think of the global access to clear gospel witness and solid, orthodox resources. But the net has also become a dangerous culprit in pulling my glance to the side. Having immediate and relentless access to the stories and successes of ministries across the country is often a trigger for discontent instead of joy.

I read once about a church planter's launch service in Missouri. His basic story was, "I took these two sticks, and I crossed them, and boom, there were 450 people there." Whoa—450 people! My church-planting fantasies don't have 450 people in them. Where is Missouri again? How much are homes there?

I scrolled through some Easter Sunday updates once from Acts 29 and realized many of my brothers had baptized more people in one day than we had in ten years. Their attendance figures on Resurrection Sunday dwarfed ours. "We had 797 people on Easter!" "We had 3,936!" "We rented out Quest Field!!" I thought, "Maybe if we could get all of Seven Mile Road together, we could fill up the visiting dugout at Fenway. Can we do our Easter service there next year?"

Interestingly, this cuts both ways. We're in Boston, so I can delineate dozens of the negatives when compared to other cities: cost of living is brutal, climate is borderline masochistic, people are generally angry, no road runs straight for more than a mile, non-Democrats don't even bother running for office, Sunday is the new Saturday, we tax you when you make money and tax you when you spend it. I could go on. But this works opposite, too. I've had conversations with guys from the Bible Belt, and in explaining to them our context, I've seen their glance tilt in my direction. "Man, I wish I were where you are. I am dealing with hypocritical nominalism, goofy Christian subculture, the Jesus inoculation. I'd give anything to just know the people with me are with me for good, gospel reasons. I wish I had a bunch of straightforward, no-nonsense, all-in people. That would be so much easier."

Envy is an equal-opportunity destroyer. Wherever you are called, it will crane your neck somewhere else.

3. I WISH I HAD A DIFFERENT HUSBAND OR WIFE.

Any church, whatever the size, is filled with people, many married. If you're married, but not 100 percent locked into your husband or your wife, you'll glance sideways.

"Look at the way he gives emotional support to his wife. My husband doesn't hold my hand like that. He doesn't speak to me like that. He bought her purple and white tulips! He got her tickets to Bruno Mars at the Garden! My husband never does anything like that."

"Look at how she's so bubbly and joyful. My wife is so quiet and somber and serious. Why can't she be more bubbly like her?"

"Look at how serious and mature she is. My wife is so giggly and bubbly and girly. Why can't she be more serious like her?"

"Look at her. She reads theology. She signed up for the summer study in the Minor Prophets. She's working through that book by Jonathan Edwards's wife. She's on a Bible-reading plan. My wife watched the Country Music Awards last night."

"All my wife does is read theology. Every day UPS bounds up the stoop with another Piper book. And how many journals can one woman keep? No, I don't know whether I am pre-mill, amill, or post-mill—stop asking. Why can't we just watch the Country Music Awards?"

We think that adultery begins with the lust of the eyes, but it is just as likely to begin with envy in the heart.

4. I WISH I HAD A DIFFERENT UPBRINGING IN THE FAITH.

I was born again into an unhealthy church. I am so thankful God in His grace caused my eyes to see my sin and His Son's cross at that church, but I was discipled in a legalistic, works-based, Jesus-saved-me-then-but-now-I-have-to-pay-him-back theology that crushed me for years. It wasn't until I was twenty-four that I learned about the doctrines of grace, of justification by faith alone, and of the God-centered gospel. Sometimes I meet twenty-four-year-old men and women who have been raised around sound doctrine. They love the church. They know the five solas. They've memorized the catechism. I think, "If that were me, think of the time I would have saved and the pain I would have avoided."

If you weren't a pastor's kid, it's easy to wish you had been. Imagine having a father who loved the gospel, was conversant in Scripture, and was committed to his children's thriving in the knowledge of the truth. Plus, a parking spot close to the church! But then you talk with pastors' kids and the blood rushes from their faces as they stammer, "Uh, no you don't. There were days when I would rather have been an orphan on the streets of Rio than a pastor's kid."

God is sovereign, even over our childhoods. But it takes great faith to not hold it against Him, to not wish somebody else were our dad or mom.

5. I WISH I WERE WORKING AT SOMETHING ELSE.

Pastors call this "Milk Truck Monday" syndrome. Every Monday at 9 a.m., we wish we were alone in the cab of a truck, listening to WEEI, quietly doing our deliveries before clocking out for the night. No flock, no stress, no emails, no bad giving reports, no flaky volunteers to manage, no grumpy neighbors to assuage. We joke about this, but it's not funny. When you are longingly gazing at the milkman, wishing you spent your days delivering Garelick Farms 2% across New England, serious issues abound in your soul.

I wish I had a different body type.

I wish I wasn't tall and bald with rosacea and a chipped tooth and a giant scar on my head.

I wish I could sing like her. Think like him. Organize like her. Fundraise like him.

I wish I had blue eyes. Brown eyes. Straight hair. Curly hair.

I wish, I wish, I wish ...

This is the natural disposition of our hearts. We are perpetually dissatisfied with the providences of God in our lives; we're discontent with the sex and capacities and callings and personalities and eye color He has assigned to us. Dangerously, all of American culture exists to flame these fires of envy. Social media, academia, and Hollywood pour kerosene on envy's embers. The drum beats daily: what we have is never enough; who we are is never enough. Someone else out there has it a little better than we do.

If we submit to this sin, to the sideways glances of the soul, we'll never be the joyful, unified, prolific planters and pastors Jesus intends us to be.

• • •

THE DELETERIOUS EFFECTS OF ENVY ON gospel ministry are innumerable.

Envy robs joy.[35] Envy casts dissatisfaction's dark shadow over our workdays. Envy makes us grumpy, moody, cranky, mirthless. I've walked into important meetings already irritable, before a single word was spoken, because of envy.

Envy suffocates usefulness. Envy steals the energy, the fire, and the focus we need to give ourselves fully to the work before us. If we look over there, we are not looking right *here*, at what God has put in front of us. Envy distracts. Envy paralyzes. Envy zombifies.

Envy cripples our ability to enjoy others' successes. If we wish we were them, we will spite their success, because we want it for ourselves.

We planted the original Seven Mile Road in an old elementary school on the west side of Malden. As the church grew, we spent two years searching for a suitable space to house it. One of the facilities we found was a nonprofit arts studio in Medford called Springstep, a perfect spot to plant a church: beautiful open floorplan, seats a buck fifty, parking lot free on Sundays—the works. So, I called the executive director, and she treated me the way former Bruins manager Harry Sinden treated general managers phoning to inquire about a trade for Cam Neely: "No way, not happening, never going to rent on Sundays to a church. Have a nice life." One year later a guy named Tanner Turley from Kentucky rolled in to plant a church in our backyard.[36] I sought to welcome this brother, and I told him that while Springstep would be the best place in Medford to plant, he could *fuggedaboutit*; I had already asked, and I was told no. Like a good church planter, he asked anyway, and a new executive director answered the phone. She loved the idea of having a church use the space, and it would cost about half of what Seven Mile Road had offered the previous executive director.

My response in moments like this one should be joy. Delight. I should be pumped! These guys love Jesus, and they've got a space to plant a church to see people I love come to see the glory of the gospel. But if that green and fickle beast of envy has his claws in me, I'm frustrated. I'm ticked. I'm down. My soul misses out on a chance to celebrate.

Even worse, envy sabotages. Envy puts rocks in our hands and bids us throw. If we allow envy to fester, we not only overlook God's grace to others—we can begin to *oppose* the work of God in others.

We see this on horrific display in the response of the Pharisees to the ministry of Christ. No one in Israel should have been more enthused about the arrival of Jesus than these men. The Pharisees knew the Scriptures, but they missed the central point and promise completely. Instead of celebrating and submitting to and partnering with and following Jesus, they opposed and vilified and crucified Him. Shrewd and ruthless Pilate intuited what was driving them. The Spirit tells us that "[Pilate] knew that it was out of envy that [the Pharisees] had delivered him up" (Matt. 27:18). Whoa. The Pharisees couldn't stand to see Jesus's ministry thriving. *They* wanted the glory, acclaim, and popularity with the people. They grew so rabid in their envy that they riled up the crowds to shout "Crucify!" And every time we allow envy to pit our souls against the work of God, we're in danger of aligning with these men whom Jesus fired His woes toward and on whom Jerusalem came crashing down.

It is not beyond you to hang your brother out to dry because you envy him. You have the capacity to do that. Envy, unchecked, will lead you there.

. . .

THIS IS WHY THE WORDS OF verse 24 in Paul's speech to the Ephesian elders have become precious to me. They picture a soul in which envy has been vaporized by the gospel. They give a snapshot of what it feels like for someone to be good with whatever the Lord has put before him or her. They offer me an invitation to straighten my gaze and be satisfied with what Jesus has given me and called me to.

First, in verses 22 and 23, Paul says, "And now, behold, I am going to Jerusalem, constrained by the Spirit, not knowing what will happen to me there, except that the Holy Spirit testifies to me in every city that imprisonment and afflictions await me."

These words stop me in my tracks. This is one hundred thousand times harder than being stuck in the express lane on the Jersey Turnpike. This is much worse than what most of us face on Monday morning, or any morning. Imagine the Spirit telling Paul, "So, two things I have lined up for you, Paul: jail and beatings. There may be others, but those are definitely in your lane." The door's been opened wide for Paul's sideways glance of envy: "Jerusalem, imprisonment, and afflictions? How about Bermuda, sandy beaches, and Coronas? Or at least Ephesus? Why are you putting this before me, Jesus? I've been in jail already. I've been beaten, flogged, and whipped. You are giving this to me again? There is a whole ungospeled world out there. Why back to Jerusalem?"

If this were me in this text, the next thing we'd expect to read is how we shrugged our shoulders, shook our heads, gazed longingly down the road *not* headed to Jerusalem, and then shuffled forward, slow and frustrated, thinking, "I wish I weren't going."

Instead, Paul says, "I do not account my life of any value nor as precious to myself, if only I may finish my course and the ministry that I received from the Lord Jesus."

This is a holy and grown man owning what the Lord has assigned him.

Don't miss the first-person pronouns: *My* course. The ministry *I* received. There is no pining for another's course. No envying another's ministry. He has a calling, and all that matters is that he does well with it. Nothing to the left matters. Nothing to the right matters. "I trust Jesus. He has not made a mistake with what He has given me. He's put a course and a ministry before me, and nothing else is on my radar. Just let me finish that course; let me discharge that ministry, and I'm good."

No, the Spirit is not saying that we should not have ambition to go for big things. We should and we are. The Spirit is not saying there is never a time to revisit our course, our plans, in prayer and in community. We do. The Spirit is saying—shouting, really—that it is possible for us to be energetically, enthusiastically, resolvedly content with whom Jesus has made us, how Jesus has wired us, where Jesus has sent us, and what Jesus has placed before us.

. . .

WHEN I FIRST MEMORIZED ACTS 20, I did so through tears.

Every time we open Scripture, we should be seeking to understand, believe, and live its words before us. But sometimes the Spirit will accelerate one of these pursuits. Sometimes He may give us the grace to understand a truth with a clarity we lacked before, and our souls will soar. Sometimes He may bring to mind opportunities to obey things we need to obey immediately, and we leap to follow through. Sometimes He births in us a conviction we did not have before about His truth and goodness toward us, and we believe more deeply, and we weep for his grace to allow it.

That was my experience with this verse. Our raggedy church plant had somehow become viable, but as a perfectionist, I still had a million complaints. Most revolved around my pretentious pursuit of vain glories. As I memorized verse 24, the Spirit brought me to a fork in the road, where I needed to either continue straight or exit. If I wanted to exit and shake myself free of all the mundane and glamourless realities in pastoring a church, I could do that. But if I was to stay straight, my envious sideways glances needed to die. Whatever was on the road before me—successes, failures, false conversions, difficult people, minimal results, financial difficulties, whatever—I had to be good with it.

Another way to say it is the Spirit personalized these words to me: "There's a lot more work for you to do, and it's not going to go the way you want. In giving a continued 'yes' to this road, you're saying 'no' to hundreds of others. Are you in or not?"

I pleaded with Him: "Yes. Forgive me. Have mercy on me. But I'm in. I do not account my life of any value or as precious to myself, if only I may finish my course and the ministry that You have for me. It's a good course. It's a noble ministry. It's from You."

Something changed, permanently, in my soul that day. I handed envy a pink slip. Yes, I still bristle at times when I realize my life's work is never going to show up in any hall of fame or book of world records or Top 50 list. But the glances are gone, mostly, and I'm better for it.

Church can be a place where that becomes true for everyone.

- BLUEPRINTS -

1. Be the first and the loudest to celebrate the success of others.

I've been embroiled several times in heated arguments over whether cheerleading is a sport. Whatever it is, we should set our hearts to be the loudest cheerleaders of gospel advancement in our churches and cities. Seven Mile Road has planted seven churches, and each of them paced differently out of the gate. What has been crucial is that all eight churches celebrate whatever progress is made. Tweet and retweet any good news other local churches publish. Offer a "Congratulations. This is awesome. I love this!" when another church has good news. If you have an inner critic, silence him when necessary. "Whoever is not against us is for us" is actually true. Be glad in it.

2. Beware the internet.

Don't assume that the only sin the web can trigger is lust. It's just as effective with church envy. If you find yourself longingly surfing other churches' websites, or downing a gallon of mint chocolate chip while glumly scrolling through other churches' Instagram accounts, or skeptically obsessing over other churches' baptism statistics, turn it off, call a brother, and confess as quickly as if you were viewing pornographic images.

3. Grow familiar with Psalm 73.

If your head tilts left and right, nothing will straighten it out like Psalm 73. It's a brutally honest confession and a helpful roadmap for how to move from envy to contentment.

13 | LOVE LETTERS

Church can be warm.
On stirring our affections for Jesus's people.

Care for the church of God, which he obtained with his own blood. —Acts 20:28

THE MAILBOX AT THE END OF my driveway was jammed. Not, per usual, with supermarket flyers, gutter-cleaning offers, or coupons to Billy's Roast Beef. A pile of real letters kept the lid from closing, and my name was on all of them. They were thank-you cards. One by one I opened them, and a deluge of appreciation, affirmation, and love poured out. Every word was carefully penned, free of the fake sentiment of a Hallmark machine. Each letter delineated specific ways my pastoral work had moved, shaped, or inspired the writer.

I stood there, on the sidewalk, and cried.

Over the years I've read and heard lots of horror stories about what sometimes happens in churches between pastors and their people. It's an ugly list: misunderstandings, unfair presumptions, confused expectations, slanders, betrayals, etc. This has not been my lot. The Father has almost exclusively sent me brothers and sisters who are *for* me. Tangibly, actively, unmistakably *for* me. Seven Mile Road is packed with men and women who obey the Spirit's command to honor those who labor for their souls and make their work as happy as possible. Because they love their Bibles, they care—really, actually *care*—that my soul and body and marriage and fatherhood remain intact and healthy. I've always assumed this is because God knows how weak I am, how much support I need to function, and how fragile my pastoral ego tends to be. Or maybe He's just a good Father who knows what gifts we'd really appreciate, and He constantly goes over the top in giving them.

I would take a bullet for every man, woman, and child at Seven Mile Road. But that one week, my mailbox told me they would do the same for me.

This kind of mutual love between shepherd and sheep should be normative in the life of Jesus's church.

⋯

"OX TRACK" IS THE FOLK NAME of our year-long pastoral training intensive at Seven Mile Road. The name comes from the biblical allusion that being a pastor is like being an ox: head down, lifting heavy loads, working hard.

The track is built around three essentials.

The first is assessing and developing character. A pastor must be a man of the highest Christian character ("above reproach") if he is to serve as an undershepherd of Jesus. The eternal significance of Jesus's church and her mission demands nothing less. So, Ox Track strongly emphasizes gospel-centered character assessment and formation—the kind of deep, soul-level work that enables us to identify and work through any sinfulness that would potentially shipwreck a pastor and harm the church and its mission.

Second is instilling sound pastoral theology. To lead Jesus's church well necessitates having a mature grasp of His truth. If a man is to preach, teach, admonish, encourage, evangelize and lead well, he must be theologically sound. Our track emphasizes pastoral theology, mining deeply the places where biblical theology intersects with pastoral leadership in the church. Our hope here is for each man to emerge with a strong foundation of what Scripture calls pastors to and how Scripture shapes that work.

The third is fostering affection for Jesus's people. Pastoring is not an occupation; it's a vocation demanding the full engagement of the pastor's soul. It is a call to give, like Jesus, our lives for the sheep. Without such selfless, sacrificial love for the sheep, a man is unqualified to serve as their shepherd. What gets a pastor up at 6:00 a.m. to pray? What keeps him diligent in his study?

What moves him to read and respond to an 11:00 p.m. text? What convinces him to keep going? Although many answers are possible, the one compelling answer is this: he loves the people Jesus has given him.

• • •

THE APOSTLE PAUL'S LETTER TO THE young Christians in the city of Thessalonica is like one of those theme-park thrill rides. Your first thought when you look at it is, "I really, really want to experience that." Your second thought is, "Wait, there is no way I am getting on that ride. I could never handle it. It's too much."

Paul arrived in Thessalonica on his second missionary journey looking like Sylvester Stallone at the end of *Rocky I*: beaten, haggard, and unable to see out of his left eye. Somehow, he pressed on and preached the gospel in this pagan city, and the Thessalonians responded. By the grace of the Spirit, they believed what he said, and a church was born. But within a few weeks, his bloodthirsty opponents from Philippi had hunted him down and chased him out of Thessalonica. His First Epistle to the Thessalonians is the fruit of his concern for the well-being of the church, and in it, the love of a pastor for his people is on full, compelling, uncomfortable display:

> Being affectionately desirous of you, we were ready to share with you not only the gospel of God but also our own selves, because you had become very dear to us. (2:8)

> We were gentle among you, like a nursing mother taking care of her own children. (2:7)

> We endeavored the more eagerly and with great desire to see you face to face, because we wanted to come to you. (2:17)

13 | Love Letters

The first time I read 1 Thessalonians, I had to put my Bible down and walk away for a minute. Paul's relationship with these men and women was not transactional. He did not view them as customers, or patrons, or acquaintances. He saw them as family. He missed them. He tossed and turned at night with concern for them. He gave them not only the gospel but also himself, body and soul.

He loved the people Jesus had given him.

• • •

PAUL'S NON-NEGOTIABLE LOVE FOR GOD'S PEOPLE is the *bona fides* of true gospel ministry. It emerges clearly at the center of Paul's speech when he hits us with a metaphorically glorious one-two punch: "Care for the church of God, which he obtained with his own blood" (Acts 20:28).

Reading this backward has been helpful to me, as the second clause is the foundation for the first.

"Obtained with his own blood."

With these words, Paul steals our breath, communicating forcefully just how valuable the elect of every church are, no matter how raggedy, inconsequential, or expendable they seem. Every soul under our care was purchased by Christ with His own blood, and "greater love has no one than this, that someone lay down his life for his friends" (John 15:13). Jesus loves His people. The angsty, pimply teenager in the back row. The exhausted mother of three who dozes off a third of the way through every sermon. The baby boomer who keeps everyone at arm's length. The stage-cage seminary student who's foaming at the mouth to defend the legitimacy of presuppositional apologetics. The pizza delivery guy who shuffles in thirty minutes late each Sunday. The high-maintenance wife who's into everyone's business. The immature twenty-year-old who's more excited about fantasy football than the doctrines of grace. The earnest missionary couple readying to sell all they have to go overseas. And everyone in between.

Christ won them, out of love, and we must care for them like it.

"Care for the church of God."

Yes, of course. The men and women whom Jesus has given us are not pawns to be manipulated, projects to be worked on, problems to be resolved, handicaps to be dragged around, or customers to be pleased. They are the sheep to be cared for. This command cannot be obeyed mechanically. It must be carried out with love. Your mom packing a thoughtful lunch is different from the lunch lady slopping burnt macaroni and cheese on a plate. Your dad spending an afternoon changing your oil with you is different from a distracted Jiffy Lube attendant rushing your car through the line. Your mortgage company mailing you a boilerplate birthday card is not like your ten-year-old hand-crafting a ten-page booklet. Care assumes affections. To pastor is to love people, desperately. The sheep become like a family to the good shepherd.

...

NO CHAPTER OF SCRIPTURE HAS HIT me harder when it comes to assessing my own motivations for gospel ministry than John 10. In this text, Jesus, the Good Shepherd, is explicating for His disciples the kind of love He has for them and all of His redeemed. He does so by contrasting a hireling with a good shepherd. After stating matter-of-factly what we know to be true about all hirelings—that they bolt at the first sign of difficulty or danger, leaving the sheep vulnerable—Jesus drills down to the root of that cowardice: "He flees because he is a hired hand and he cares nothing for the sheep."

Those last words surprise me. I can think of many reasons any pastor would want to flee, taking the next red-eye to Maui, drowning his sorrows in Mai Tais:

- He flees because the sheep wouldn't listen to him.
- He flees because the deacon board wouldn't increase his salary.
- He flees because nobody stops the audio system's piercing feedback.
- He flees because there was a better opportunity at another church.
- He flees because he got scared, overwhelmed, embarrassed, or exhausted.

But that's not why Jesus says the hireling runs. He says he flees because he didn't care for the sheep. In other words, his abandonment was an affections problem, a heart issue. He didn't love the people Jesus had given to him. They didn't matter to him. He didn't value them for what they were. If he loved them rightly, he'd never run.

We are all susceptible to this.

• • •

I SPOKE ONE TIME TO A mostly empty room at a regional conference for church planters. (Church planting conferences in New England draw about as many people as celibacy conventions in Vegas.) At the end of the night, the speakers were asked to be on a panel. Preparing a talk is a delight for me, but sitting on a panel is a terror. Imagine being on *Jeopardy!*, and the only category is undefined: "Any Question on Earth, for $100." You are given no idea of what's coming, no background or context for any question, no insight into the motives of the questioner, and almost no time to formulate an answer. Ugh.

Someone asked the panel, "What do you do if you discover you have no love for the people in your church?" It's a fair and important question. Maintaining proper affections for Jesus's people isn't easy. Church people can be hard to deal with. They have attitudes. They run late. They text you seven minutes before an important meeting or event that they can't make it. They flake and fudge. They waffle and wander. They refuse to give. The temptation is strong to despise them, to slander them to the nearest listening ear, to whine and complain about them, and then to grow cold, doing your pastoral work in spite of them, instead of out of love for them.

After a long, barren pause, my good friend Doug Logan, president and professor of urban ministry at Grimké Seminary, with a PhD in telling it like it is, offered a one-word answer that hung in the air like a John Wasdin fastball.[37]

"Repent."

It was a "Sunday school" answer, but sometimes the Sunday school answer is the right one. Doug's insinuation was this: a lack of love for Jesus's people is not just a problem to be fixed, but a sin to be turned from, a sign that something was off in the soul of the pastor who asked it. At first, I thought, "Wow, that was a harsh, unnuanced answer." But on later reflection, I changed my mind. It's not just bad practice for a pastor to operate without love. It's sinful, because it's a denial of one of the underpinnings of our role as undershepherds: we are to love as Jesus did.

And as He still does.

...

THE CROSS WAS, IN A GLORIOUS sense, the zenith of Christ's love for His people: the parading before all powers and authorities the depth of God's love for sinners; the one act of love that defines all others. Our adoration of Christ in the age to come will center on His being "the Lamb of God," the One who substituted Himself in our place for our sins that we might be reconciled to God. We'll never stop singing about the love Christ displayed on Calvary.

But Jesus's love for His people didn't begin, or end, on that hill. Right now, this very moment, whatever time zone you are in, the Son of God continues to identify with, to intercede for, and to love His people. When Saul was harassing the first Christians, dragging men and women from their homes and imprisoning them, Jesus confronted him with the inquiry, "Why are you persecuting me?" When John received his beautifully comforting revelation on the shores of Patmos, he saw Christ standing among the lampstands. Translation: He was standing amongst His people. Among Jesus's many refrains in His seven words to the churches, He repeatedly says, "I know." Don't miss the intimacy, the concern, the love in those words. "I'm absent in body, but not in Spirit, or in concern. I know what's happening. You matter to me."

This is the love we must bring to our work: Gospel-driven, self-forgetful, other-focused love that is a fruit of the Spirit at work in us. Not the counterfeit kind of love quoted on coffee mugs, or put on posters at pride parades, or sketched on signs outside UU churches. It's costly, sacrificial, putting-the-needs-of-others-ahead-of-your-own love. Love that does all those unnatural and non-intuitive things that 1 Corinthians 13 says it does.

Church can be a place where love like that animates and motivates everything that happens.

– BLUEPRINTS –

1. Tell your people you love them.

One of the things I have set my mouth to do, no matter how awkward, is to tell our people I love them. A co-pastor does a good job counseling someone? "I love you, Justin." A Kalos team-member is working with me to disciple someone and is crying because she's been hurt? "I love you, Sara." Our worship leader punches his chest (in the good kind of zealous, masculine way) in worship? "Man, I love you, Josh." A deacon builds a gaga pit for the student ministry to use in the backyard? "I love you, Jacob." A sister loses her mom to a year-long battle with cancer? "I love you, Noelle." Yes, your life needs to back up the words, but verbalizing them establishes an unmistakable ethos: we are going to love one another.

2. Do not appoint men to the office of elder or call them as pastors if they don't live and die with the people of the church.

Because Seven Mile Road has planted a number of churches, outsiders assume we are cavalier with green-lighting prospective planters, or run our residency like a youth soccer program, or dole out church plants the way Oprah doles out new cars. Not true. We've said "No" much more often than "Go." Sometimes those negative assessments are easy to arrive at, and sometimes not, but one sure sign that a "No" is coming is recognizing a lack of affection for the people. Many times, at the end of our pastoral training, a man will thank us for the year, but freely admit, "Yeah, so, I don't really love people the way you guys do." I'm actually thankful for the honesty of those conversations, because it means we're communicating well the baselines of John 10, 1 Thessalonians, and Acts 20.

3. The starting place for your love for Jesus's people is your love for Jesus himself.

I've always loved Jesus's conversation with Peter at the end of John's gospel. The heart of Christ is on beautiful display as He restores Peter, offering three affirmations that effectively reverse Peter's three denials. Their conversation is a recommissioning of sorts, and Jesus begins each exhortation with a question:

"Do you love me?"

"Yes, you know I do."

"OK, with first and primary love established, now go, feed my sheep."

When our affections for our people wane, our immediate response should be to fan the flames of our love for Christ.

14 | WOLVES

Church can be orthodox.
On fighting heresies and those who tout them.

Fierce wolves will come in. —Acts 20:29

MY WIFE IS INCREDIBLE WITH CHILDREN. Our children, the church's children, random screaming children at the supermarket, it doesn't matter. She knows exactly how to gauge, calm, and encourage little ones. So, it's no surprise she's constantly being asked to babysit the children of friends, neighbors, and random locals she met once at the park.

One school year she watched a two-year-old boy every Friday while his mom taught school. She refused any form of payment, but at the end of the year the father thanked her and demanded she let him compensate her in some way. He was a carpenter, so she asked about building our kids a treehouse in our small side yard. He happily agreed. I thought we were going to get four planks of wood with a rope hanging down. Instead, be built a 200-square-foot villa, complete with roof and balcony. Eight to ten children can play in this treehouse at the same time. We've considered renting it out in the summer for $750 a month.

The second night we had the treehouse, sometime past midnight, a raccoon the size of a hobbit climbed in through a space in the platform but couldn't get back down. Twelve hours later, our ten-year-old daughter Julia unknowingly stepped inside and was greeted by the hangriest raccoon in Massachusetts, standing on its back haunches, baring its claws and teeth, and hissing. Julia rocketed down the stairs three at a time and ran into the woods screaming for her life. Unsure of what to do, we carefully jerry-rigged the door open, hoping the hobbit would quietly return to his home in the forest after dusk. He did, and now our kids religiously peer into the treehouse before making their entrance. What was supposed to be a safe, healthy, enjoyable place for our children had become a danger.

I told that story to some friends of ours who live down in Texas, their ten-year-old son Cole listening intently. When I finished my tale, Cole flashed a quizzical look and deadpanned, "Why didn't you just shoot him?" Is that not the perfect response from a ten-year-old Texan? I didn't have the courage to tell the boy, "Uh, not only do I not own a firearm of any sort—I have never actually fired a gun." But I did love his response. In Cole's mind, if a dangerous, sharp-toothed, woodland creature has found its way into the space where your kids hang out, and if you love your kids, there's no question.

You shoot it.

It's the same thing for the family of God. If a church is going to be safe and healthy for Jesus's people, we must be aware that wolves will find their way inside. And when they do, we can't hesitate about what to do.

Good shepherds silence wolves.

• • •

WE SPEND A LOT OF TIME at Seven Mile Road on what we call the "grammar of the gospel," frequently going over basic biblical concepts and truths. Our context is so post-Christian that there is little cultural memory, awareness, or understanding left of fundamental Christian categories. I remember more from kindergarten than most Bostonians remember about the Bible. Frankly, some have never been exposed to any Scripture at all.

One of the grammatical lessons we teach is on the realities of orthodoxy and heresy, and the interplay between them.

ORTHODOXY

We love this word.

We received it into English by cramming two Greek words together: *ortho* plus *doxy*, meaning "right" plus "belief," or "good" plus "teaching," or "sound" plus "doctrine." For

Christians, orthodoxy is any belief that aligns with and accounts for Scripture's meaning, consistency, complexity, mystery, and (most importantly) central message, which is the gospel.

God has spoken in His Word, and when what we believe is a tight fit with what He has revealed, that's orthodoxy. Orthodoxy is not the theological view that happened to win out in church history because of political gamesmanship, ecclesiastical power plays, financial manipulation, or charismatic personalities. No. Christ, by His Spirit, in love for us, has been guiding His people over time (including through some wild and dark times), cementing His truth deeper and deeper in the soul of the true Church. For thousands of years, Christians have opened the Scriptures together and worked hard to understand and embrace and codify this truth in creeds, catechisms, confessions, hymns, books, and sermons. All that the Bible has to say about who God is and what He has done, and who we are and what we are called to do is the body of work called *orthodoxy*, and it's where we want to live.

HERESY

We hate this word.

Like orthodoxy, heresy also comes from Greek. Its root reflects the idea of making a choice, specifically the choice to deviate from the teaching of Scripture in favor of one's own insights. Heresy veers away from orthodoxy on essential gospel doctrines. It's not just a minor theological error or misstep, or someone landing somewhere different than you on a secondary or tertiary doctrine. It is a decisive turn from gospel truth, and we want to stay as far from it as possible.

Putting all this together, we tell our people, "Orthodoxy gives life, but heresy kills."

We were on a men's retreat one frigid February, and the superintendent of the grounds said, "Hey, why don't you gather everyone up and meet me at the lake. I'll run my snowplow on the ice and clear you a place to play some hockey." One of our teenagers responded, "Wait, you can drive a pickup truck out on the ice?" He said, "Oh yeah, the ice near the shore is probably six feet thick by now." I remember thinking, "Man, I hope you're right, 'cause I am not wading into almost frozen water to save your drowning self."

Orthodoxy—right belief—really matters in a situation like that. Whether that man's belief about the thickness of the ice was in accord with reality or was a sharp turn away from it, was a life-or-death matter. It's the same with our theology. When we believe and live based on what is true about God and His world and our place in it, we experience freedom, peace, joy, and life. When we believe and live based on what is untrue, we reap confusion, bondage, misery, and death.

Because of this, it becomes imperative that pastors be vigilant to maintain orthodoxy in our churches. Sometimes we do this proactively (see chapter 9: "Thunder"), but sometimes reactively. It's not enough only to hype orthodoxy. We must also hammer heresy.

• • •

PAUL MAKES THIS EXPLICIT IN HIS speech when he warns the Ephesians about a clear and present danger every church faces: theological wolves, creeping into the gate of the church.

He says it like this: "I know that after my departure fierce wolves will come in among you, not sparing the flock; and from among your own selves will arise men speaking twisted things, to draw away the disciples after them" (Acts 20:29-30).

Paul is now leaving the Ephesian church for good. He won't be coming back, ever. He knows that his presence, or even just the threat of his presence, had kept the wolves at bay, but once he leaves on that midnight train to Judea, the floodgates will open. Emboldened by his absence and seeing an opportunity to platform themselves, boost their followership, and grow their brand, heretics would rush in. The mother of all heresies is selfish ambition, and when the cat's away, the ambitious mice will play. Only in this case, it's not mice, but wolves. Fierce wolves. Mice just nibble on your Nutter Butters and poop on your counter, but wolves will tear your throat out. And Paul is saying, "Beware!"

. . .

WERE WE TO GATHER EVERYONE AT Seven Mile Road around a whiteboard and work a SWOT[38] analysis together, the list of threats to the well-being of our church would be a long one:

- Rapidly secularizing culture
- General populous uninterested in Christianity
- Sunday is the new Saturday
- Growing hostility to religious freedoms
- Super high cost of living in greater Boston
- Obscene transience
- Proliferation of other gospel-centered churches nearby
- No endowment, rental income, or benefactor
- Potential changes to the tax code
- Aging lead pastor
- Zero dedicated parking spaces

While these are all legitimate threats to be noted and addressed, two major misconceptions lie behind a list like this.

First is the nature of the list. The greatest threat to the health of Jesus's church is never financial, relational, cultural, or demographical. It is always theological. It is always someone poisoning the spring of gospel truth with lies that wreak havoc downstream in the lives of the people. "To speak twisted things" in this text means "to distort; to make defective; to corrupt; to turn away; to deviate"—so, "men speaking twisted things" is simply code for "heretics touting heresies." Those are the dangers that Paul warns these pastors to be on the strictest guard against.

A better whiteboard session might begin with a list of threats that reads like this:

- Legalism
- Antinomianism
- Narcissism
- Secularism
- Modernism
- Postmodernism
- Universalism
- Feminism
- Prosperity gospel
- Therapeutic gospel
- Social gospel
- Any gospel contrary to the one we received

These are the real threats to the soul of a church, each of them, in its own twisted way, not sparing the flock.

The second problem with the first list is the location of its items. Our original SWOT analysis almost exclusively identified externalities, but the supreme threats to both the church's life and every local congregation's life always come from the inside.

Paul uses two different phrases to communicate this truth to us. First, he says "among you." This is like that raccoon sneaking up quietly through that little space between the tree and the platform. These wolves would probably be new arrivals after Paul's departure. They would creep in, slide in, blend in, fit in, receive their ordination (formal or not), and then, like Greeks dropping into Troy from a wooden horse, maim everyone in their path. Second, he says, "from among your own number." This is nasty. These are men who already had positions of power and influence in the life of the church and would now leverage that insider status to do great harm. These are rogue elders, teachers, deacons, gospel-community leaders, or student ministers. The one thing worse than a wolf in sheep's clothing is a wolf in shepherd's clothing.

In other words, the real dangers are theological, and they come from within.

AN EXERCISE:

Circle the name that poses more of a danger (real or potential) to the church:

- Madonna or Sarah Bessey?
- Jason Lewis or Joel Osteen?
- Carrot Top or John Piper?
- Richard Dawkins or Andy Stanley?
- Blake Shelton or Lecrae?
- Mark Zuckerberg or Tim Keller?
- A professor at MIT or a professor at Gordon-Conwell?

ANOTHER:

Circle the name of the media company that poses more of a danger (real or potential) to the church:

- Harvard University Press or Crossway?
- Politico or Her.meneutics?[39]
- CNN or The Gospel Coalition?

- Barstool Sports or Focus on the Family?
- Playboy Enterprises or ChristianFeminism.com?[40]

ANOTHER:

Circle the name of the person who poses more of a danger to Seven Mile Road:

- Pastor Matthew Kruse or anybody else?

If you are tracking with me, your right column should have all the circles (except the last one). I am not accusing everyone on that list of being heretics, or every publishing company of undermining the gospel. I am emphasizing the point that insiders who break bad pose more of a threat than the outsiders everybody already recognizes as heretics.

. . .

IF THIS IS ALL TRUE, IF Jesus desperately loves His sheep, and those sheep live and die with gospel truth, and that truth is always under threat of heretics arising in the church wielding false gospels, what does a healthy church do with wolves?[41]

We do not coddle them.

We do not dialogue with them.

We do not consider their perspective.

We do not invite them to join a panel.

We do not defer their ideas to a study committee.

We do not suggest or recommend or propose or intimate.

We silence the wolves.

Or, as ten-year-old Cole from Texas might put it, you shoot them.[42]

In the aforementioned book *The Witch's Boy*, Áine's father issued her this stern warning just before they moved to the woods: "Mind you. Shoot them before they rip out your throat. Never trust a wolf."

Every pastor should put that up on his mantle. Or, if not, at least this quote from Calvin: "The pastor ought to have two voices: one, for gathering the sheep; and another, for warding off and driving away wolves and thieves. The Scripture supplies him with the means of doing both."

...

SADLY, THE AMERICAN CHURCH HAS ONE voice and one voice only.

I am seventeen years into trying hard to plant strong, orthodox, gospel-centered churches in Massachusetts, and, while there are many good churches around (praise God!), hundreds have been ravaged by wolves. The people of God are lost, like me in a Bass Pro Shop. When I drive by and see these churches becoming condos, Cole's question rings in my ears: Why didn't anyone quiet the wolves? Who was in charge? Who was guarding the doctrinal gate? Where were the godly pastors and elders and Titus 2 women? Where were the Berean-esque members? Why didn't somebody say, "Enough! Gospel truth is too precious; orthodoxy is too life-giving, and the sheep are too valuable. We're not letting this happen!"?

Why doesn't anyone silence the wolves anymore?

Because it's hard, unwelcome work.

Dealing with wolves is no day at the beach, unless that day includes wading into shark-infested waters with a spear gun. In our postmodern world, the only heresy is noting that there are heresies, and the only voice to be silenced is the one who believes in voices being silenced. Every time we address a contemporary heresy from the pulpit at Seven Mile Road, all the air is sucked out of the room. The creak of every chair echoes across our 180-seat sanctuary. You could hear a snail fart. It's not that people disagree with the doctrinal instruction being given. It's that we are uncomfortable with the whole enterprise of calling a spade a spade. "Sure, we believe you. It's right there in the Bible. But do you have to say it out loud?"

Yes. Jesus requires it of all His shepherds.

Church can be a place where shepherds protect the sheep.

– BLUEPRINTS –

1. Lead in such a way that potential wolves know not to bother.

The majority of interactions we've had with wolves at Seven Mile Road have been with folks who were around for a bit, kicked our theological tires, realized they weren't going to get anywhere, and left. This does not mean beating people over the head with your theological distinctives. It means wearing orthodox theology on your sleeve, in high definition, with excitement and vigor and conviction. You want wolves thinking, "I've got a better chance of getting a room at the Boston Harbor Hotel on New Year's Eve than making headway here."

2. When you have to shoot, shoot straight and fast.

A few years into the life of Seven Mile Road, when we were cementing the gospel and orthodox theology as the foundation of our church, a woman approached excitedly with a book in hand. "Pastor Matt, we really need to use this book in our small groups." The author's big idea was that in order to reach an unchurched generation we needed to "rid ourselves of things like creeds and confessions" and "be open to new interpretations" and blah, blah, garbage, trash, nonsense. She was not humbly asking me to help her think critically through the assertions in the book. She was attempting to put some twisted things into the hands of our people. So, I simply said to her, "We are never reading this book at this church." That led to the most awkward sixty seconds ever. But the gate was guarded.

3. Take seriously the biblical criterion that pastors and elders be qualified to teach.

Among Paul's qualifications for elders, the one with the least play in our day is "able to teach." Everyone notes immediately how it's the one characteristic not necessarily connected to character, which is true, but that does not relegate it to secondary importance. It is essential that men who assume the office of pastor/elder be not only above reproach in character but also rock solid in orthodox theology. The internet has provided multiple ways to develop this quality in others, but however you go about it, be sure to train and vet men for guarding the doctrinal gate.

15 | YEARS

Church can be durable.
On marrying frequency and longevity.

For three years I did not cease night or day ... —Acts 20:31

MY GRANDMOTHER WAS THE KIND OF lady who could fly from LaGuardia to Logan (a forty-five-minute flight she'd often take to visit us from Queens) and somehow become lifelong friends with everyone in her row. There was no conversation she wouldn't have or didn't enjoy. When I was a teenager, I'd stay up talking with her until 2:00 a.m., and then she'd be at the breakfast table by 5:00 a.m., ready to go, voice chirping. Everybody loved Dotty Kruse, because she would talk to anybody.

People often assume I inherited some extrovert DNA from her because of the energy I bring to preaching, leading, and playing pickup basketball (I never stop talking on the court), but that's not true. I love to communicate in front of crowds, but I'm intimidated to be in one. Yet as a church planter and pastor, my calling many times requires me, in love, to work a room. In those moments I take a deep breath, channel my inner Dotty Kruse, and lean in.

I'm familiar with a few routine responses from Bostonians when I simply ask, "Hey, how's it going?" "Cold, man, freezing," is typical from anyone in New England from October to April. Another is "Not bad, except for ... ," followed by a petty, narcissistic, superficial complaint about their neighbors or in-laws or boss or the Republicans. Then there is the most common comeback of all, "Wicked busy," often followed by a laundry list of activities they've stuffed into their calendar. "School. Work. Travel. Kids. Family in town. Charity marathon. Kickboxing classes. Catching up on *Game of Thrones*. NBA League Pass. My cousin's wedding. Book club. Pilates." On my better days, when I am in tune with the Spirit and actually hearing the person in front of me, I've learned to pivot into a gospel conversation about time with the simple words: "So talk to me about your calendar."

Although it's possible "wicked busy" is a good thing (assuming we're busy doing things God commands and calls us to) or just a seasonal reality, it's usually something darker. Rather than it being a culturally conditioned response to an innocuous inquiry, I've come to see that "wicked busy" is often a confession of sin, betrayed by the mixture of exhaustion, frustration, regret, and despair that accompanies it. It's an admission that we Bostonians don't do time well, an acknowledgment that the lives we've set up for ourselves work against our joy and usefulness. "Wicked busy" is a plea for help.

It's also missional kryptonite. Without giving gospel, community, and mission the time required, it's impossible for our churches to be healthy, united, or fruitful. We Americans struggle to believe this. We think that a Bible verse here, a Hillsong chorus there, following Tim Keller or Matt Chandler on Twitter, and podcasting a sermon every third Sunday successfully checks the boxes for the Christian life. We're convinced that showing up at church, shaking the guy's hand next to us, reading updates the staff sends out, and attending the occasional picnic, prayer meeting, or cleaning day will suffice. But this truncated approach to our investment of time will never work. Listening, loving, confessing, affirming, sharing meals, having gospel conversations, asking hard questions, resolving conflicts—none of this happens accidentally or quickly. In a post-Christian context, nobody comes to Christ in sixty seconds or less. Gospel advancement takes time.

Lots of it.

Everyone at Seven Mile Road calendars differently. Some max out Google Calendar's possibilities; others take to pad and pen or giant calendars with cat pictures. Regardless of our eclectic congregation's preferred methods for staying organized, we talk schedule with them often, because we've learned that healthy people and a healthy church cannot exist unless we give our work the time it requires.

Here's how we say it: "We are all-in, as long as it takes."

• • •

WE GET THIS DIRECTLY FROM JESUS'S Apostle Paul. He addresses this issue of time near the end of his speech to the Ephesian elders when he says, "Be alert, remembering that for three years I did not cease night or day to admonish every one with tears" (Acts 20:31).

We tend to rush past these words, but don't miss the two explicit measures of time here. Paul clocks frequency (night and day) and longevity (years). These dual timestamps have become foundational to establishing a missional chronology for our church.

Because we planted a church not far from MIT, we have a few mathematical savants in our congregation, so we're not scared of algebra at Seven Mile Road. Here is the equation we built from this text. It is one we employ in all our conversations about time:

REPS x YEARS = GOSPEL IMPACT

Each element of this equation is worthy of some extended meditation.

1. REPS (FREQUENCY)

"I did not cease night or day" is a Jewish way of saying *frequently*. Paul and his team went at their gospel work a lot. They saw each other a lot. They engaged their city a lot. In the first century, dusk meant darkness and everything outdoors shutting down. In Jewish reckoning, evening was the "start" of their day at home with family. This was when Paul would sit in homes with believers, sharing meals and spending time in the word, prayer, and gospel conversation. When the sun rose again, everyone would go to work. For his first year or so in Ephesus, Paul would have been at his tentmaking station, laboring. But this was not gospel-free time. He would have conversed with whoever was present while making his tents, talking with them about the life, death, resurrection, and the kingdom of Jesus. In years two and three, when some funding kicked in, he would have been "reasoning daily in the hall of Tyrannus" with anyone and everyone (Acts 19:9). And of course, on the weekends, everyone would gather for word, fellowship, and evangelism in the synagogue.

Day after day, night after night, in homes, in synagogues, in the hall of Tyrannus, and in the shop, Paul engaged the people he was sent to. He knew making disciples required time together. Without those in-person reps, relationships don't grow, questions can't be asked and answered, tears can't be shed, meals can't be shared, jokes can't be told, and the gospel can't advance.

We know this to be true about anything worthwhile in life. You have to give it the reps.

...

AFTER MY (PATHETIC) JUNIOR YEAR, MY high school basketball coach handed me a written assessment of the state of my game. You would have assumed I was a wheelchair-bound ninety-five-year-old if you'd read it. I received no scores above 4 out of 10 on any metric. My shooting range was listed as "1-2 feet." The "areas for improvement" list ran off into the bottom margins. I was either going to have to quit hoops or get serious about improving.

I had not given my game the reps it needed.

Over the course of the next nine months I lived in two places: Nautilus Plus Gym and the Edith Street Courts. I lifted five days a week and balled for seven. I spent the mornings alone, pushing myself through drill after drill. Afternoons were filled with pickup game after pickup game. Evenings were pumping iron. Dribbling reps. Shooting reps. Benching reps. Thousands of them.

I showed up at tryouts 16 pounds heavier, 10 times stronger, and 100 times more skilled. I dominated two days of scrimmages. At the end of the tryouts, the coaches called me into their humid office and asked, "What in the world happened with you? You're killing people."

Answer? Reps.

You won't see gospel advancement in your own soul, or among those Jesus has sent you to, if you don't get the reps in. There is no substitute for time invested.

We're not talking here about spiraling toward burnout, or overdoing things, or setting up a scenario where all we do is church stuff. Many of us grew up in church programmatic cultures where the week looked like the following:

Sunday:	Two services in the morning, one at night
Monday:	Bible Study
Tuesday:	Soup Kitchen
Wednesday:	Midweek Meal and Service
Thursday:	Choir Practice
Friday:	Youth Group
Saturday:	Church Softball

We all have an unhealthy tipping point. Only a small handful of Jesus-Navy-Seals living in super close proximity to each other with super flexible work and family schedules could make it happen. Others can try, but they cannot keep this pace. There is something important to be said for viability, for lovingly taking into account the familial and seasonal realities our people face. A gospel-centered calendar is supposed to have the effect of filling our tanks with premium, not strapping a piano to our backs.

Frequency is less about flirting with burnout than it is committing to concentration and devotion. It's about being so serious about the work that you gladly reorient your schedule to give the gospel a chance to thrive in and through you.

If anything, we Americans underestimate the amount of time available to us. An honest assessment of most of our weeks betrays an obscene amount of time wasted. Although hundreds of solid time-management books and tools are available to help, the issue is always the heart. One corollary to the maxim "you are what you love" is "you give what you love a ton of reps." If we really long for gospel advancement in our churches and cities, we'll rebuild our schedules to give our churches and cities the time they need.

And not just enough for now. Enough for long.

2. YEARS (LONGEVITY)

In 2017, we sent one of the two pastors who were still serving our original congregation (I was the other one) to assume the pastorate at Community of Grace Church in Buffalo. Before hiring his replacement, we spent six months with our congregation revisiting the essential commitments required if we were going to thrive missionally over the next five years. This process yielded two surprises. First, we replaced a pastoral role with a ministry coordination/mission catalyst role. Second, we articulated four missional essentials we felt would best propel our mission forward. The fourth we coined "The Long Game" and explained it like this: "Leading Bostonians to Jesus takes time—consistent, unrushed exposures to gospel truth in multiple contexts. Overnight success is not our measure. We're growing oaks, not Chia Pets."

If this is true, then transience threatens the strength of a church as much as busyness does.

Paul knew this. He was committed to giving the work the time that it needed. "Years" is how he says it in the text, or, in the case of his time in Ephesus, 3 years: 12 seasons, 156 weeks, 1,000-plus days.

Paul stayed the course.

Do you think everything went great every day, 1,000 days in a row? Every conversation was pleasant? Every sermon was well received? No. He had conflicts to resolve, personalities to navigate, opposition to face. Paul lived through a riot. Literally. Any of these could have caused him to short-circuit the work and move on to greener pastures. But he stuck it out, as the Lord enabled, for as long as it took. That time created the space for deep relationships. Think of the end of this speech in Acts 20 as they weep with the realization that they're not going to see each other anymore. A commitment to longevity made it possible for them to build something beautiful together.

We intuitively grasp that good outcomes take time. Sometimes it just takes a while for some work to get done. A good meal? Can't microwave that. A good team? Doesn't happen in two practices. A good marriage? Requires "till death do us part." It's the same thing with a healthy soul and a healthy church, and that means we have to dig in for the longer haul.

This is especially tough for us at Seven Mile Road. We Americans are generally on the move, and Boston is the kind of town you patronize to get educated, work your first job, and then move on. The cost of living here is borderline criminal, like living in an airport terminal where everything is three times more expensive than it should be. The median price for a house in Melrose, Massachusetts, where our original Seven Mile Road is located, is $750,000. The same house in Dayton, Ohio, or Austin, Texas, or Broken Arrow, Oklahoma, is $240,000. We tax you here when you make your money, tax you when you spend your money, and tax you when you die and give your money to your kids. We tax you when you buy a car, drive a car, and then sell the car. It's cold here. I don't mean cute, fun, "do-you-want-to-build-a-snowman?" winter days. I mean freezing cold for 120 days. I mean the-sun-sets-at-four-o'clock-for-four-months-cold. I mean the entire state is on suicide watch by the fourth week of March. People arrive here and they love the city from what Instagram has sold them. Fenway! Citgo sign! The Freedom Trail! But two years in, they're broke, have been cut off more times than you can count, haven't met a single Christian, have no hope of ever owning a home, have burned through three pairs of boots, and are inquiring into breaking their lease. Life just north of Boston comes with an expiration date for most people.

The problem with this is that building a healthy church, with deep relationships and a faithful gospel presence, over the long haul requires someone to lock in for that long haul. Things usually don't happen super fast in the lives of churches. It may appear otherwise from the outside, but any kind of movement takes years. This is equally true of the human soul. None of us changes quickly. We take years to repent and mature. We need a church where somebody runs with us for as long as it takes.

This is what Paul and his team did. They stuck with the work long enough to see it thrive.

...

HERE IS THE GRID WE WALK our people through to help them self-assess how they are doing in giving the gospel the time it deserves and requires. When we walk through this, we are clear that we are not primarily talking about time management, but *heart* management. You are what you love, you eat what you love, you worship what you love, and you schedule what you love. Having our people plot themselves honestly and talk freely about why they land where they do has been a meaningful means of discipleship.

The Y axis is "reps." This is our frequency measure. How much time do we give to each other and our missional work?

The X axis is "years." This is our longevity measure. Are we staying with the work for long enough?

FIREWORKS	
SQUIRRELS	

⇧ REPS

YEARS ⇨

SQUIRRELS: Low frequency, low longevity.

Squirrels are folks who flit from church to church without ever investing themselves in any relationships or discipleship communities or missional endeavors. They give the gospel no opportunity to take root in their souls, and they are useless in serving, gospeling, or discipling anyone.

FIREWORKS: High frequency, low longevity.

Fireworks are folks who show up with big energy and even bigger promise. They fill out the connect card in the seatback in front on day one. After a week, they are on the welcome team *and* the setup team, and they've attended two different gospel communities. By the time week two comes around they have signed up for online giving and had two coffees and a meal with three different people. But then, before you get to know their story, their sin, their wiring, their ambitions, their issues, they are gone. Sometimes this is because they had not properly vetted their fit with the church's distinctives. Sometimes a conflict arises, and they are just not willing to do the work of forging long-term relationships. Sometimes a newer, shinier church comes to their attention. Whatever the case, gospel work and gospel mission have been short-circuited because they didn't commit to enough seasons.

CONSUMERS: Low frequency, high longevity.

Consumers are folks who come to church services for years and years. That's it. Church is in the same category as the dentist. They are convinced, whether from Scripture or tradition or personal preference, that it's important that they attend a church, so they do. They don't make waves, cause strife, or bristle (too much) at the preaching. But they are unwilling to live in the costlier rhythms of communal life. They disappear completely over the summer. They love and serve no one, year after year.

VESSELS FOR GOSPEL IMPACT: High frequency, high longevity.

This is where we want to live. This is life lived with the people of God on the mission of God, day-after-day, week-after-week: praying, reading, arguing, loving, serving, dreaming, confessing, forgiving, changing. This is where we get to see each other at our best and worst. This is where the Spirit works through the word as we give ourselves, repeatedly, to the Scriptures. This is where we get to watch one another take jobs and get married and have babies and bury dad and mom. Here—at the holy intersection of reps and years—is where gospel impact happens.

• • •

JACOB AND AMY ARE THE KIND of people God brings into your life to blur the line you thought existed between family and friend. They moved from Portland, Oregon, the land of arboretums, meadowlarks, and fir trees, to West Medford, Massachusetts, home of Italian bakeries, concrete playgrounds, and the West Medford business suit.[43] Jacob had landed his first job as a registered nurse. They both assumed they were stepping into the short-term adventure of living in an exotic place they could one day tell fanciful tales about before heading back west. They arrived at Seven Mile Road when the church was like an infant in the NICU, unsure if we were going to make it another week. Upon arrival they gave themselves to the frequency required for impact. They had our family over to their cozy second-floor apartment for dinner. Beginning with that meal, our friendship blossomed from "getting-to-know-you" to "would-take-a-bullet-for-you."

A few years into their time with us they hit that decision point that The Clash famously sang about: Should we stay or should we go? I was braced for the worst. Another of our most deeply loved, missionally minded, disciple-making families was going to move south or west. Trulia.com was going to tell me their new home was five bedrooms and three bathrooms on two acres. Christmas cards would come with pictures I'd barely recognize of their quickly growing kids. One step forward, one step back, the waltz of the Bostonian church plant.

I'll never forget hearing Jacob say the words "We're buying a house. In Saugus." I wept. They had decided NOT to leave. They knew about the angry drivers and endless winters and sticker shock when leaving the grocery store, but they bought a house in Saugus anyway, saying, "We're in, as long as it takes, however many years that is, to see Jesus do something beautiful through this church." It was a watershed moment for my soul and for our church. They were the first folks we ever had who moved from "just-passing-through" to "here-to-stay," and I will love them for it forever.

...

AS I WRITE, GRACE AND I are going on forty-plus years of living in greater Boston and almost twenty years of serving and leading the life and mission of Seven Mile Road. We have zero plans or ambitions to go anywhere else. We've felt all along that the providence of God placed us in this spot for these people, where there are so few indigenous pastors and planters. It is going to take *decades* for Seven Mile Road to do what we're called to do. We've made every sacrifice and strategic decision we know of to lock in, long term, come hell or high water. Yes, we also need to prepare to be told "Time's up, Kruse. Your years of service have been strong, and now it's time for someone else to move in: one jar of clay for another." Yes, it's possible that life circumstances, divine providence, or other gospel opportunities will move us to another zip code one day. But we're not caressing the "eject" button. We have no exit strategy. I don't know where the parachutes are, or how they work. My heart doesn't want out. We're all-in, as long as it takes, as long as God will have us.

Church can be a place where people live long-term life together.

– BLUEPRINTS –

1. Context and season matter for setting expectations of frequency.

Frequency is not a one-size-fits-all reality for any church. In the early years of launching gospel communities at Seven Mile Road, almost none of the participants had children. No one had a fixed dinnertime, bath time, story time, or bedtime to worry about, so getting together every Tuesday night from 6:00 until whenever was not only plausible but also desirable. As the church grew and aged, weekly small group nights became impossible for many families. The solution was not to bail on frequency, but to lovingly mesh new callings (i.e., fatherhood, motherhood) with intentionality. Legalism around scheduling is death, just as it is anywhere else. Keep asking, "Are you giving it the time it needs?" And keep working to help your people find ways to answer "Yes."

2. The key metric for longevity is not "Did you stay in one place forever?" but "Did you stay long enough?"

There are no set rules for "long enough." While Young, Restless, and Reformed church planters love to throw around the phrases like "We're dying in this house" or "We're here for life," long enough does not necessarily mean forever. For Paul in Ephesus, long enough meant three solid years. For Jesus, it meant the same. For James, it meant a lifetime in Jerusalem. Kevin and Bridget served us beautifully for five years before heading to Tanzania; Ajay and Shainu, four years, before planting in Philly; Joie and Natalie, three years, before going to Wakefield; Jeremiah and Ashley twenty-one months. But each was all-in for long enough to give and receive in a way that left us weeping, Miletus-like, upon their departure.

3. If the gospel is true, then some good things will have to give way to gospel things.

Saying yes to the call to plant Seven Mile Road meant giving up one of the things I loved to do more than anything on earth: coach high-school basketball. Coaching well is a year-round gig (recruiting, learning, summer camps, fall ball, regular season, tournament) with an especially grueling gauntlet in season (minimum of 3-4 hours an evening for six days a week, plus all day on Saturdays.) There was no way to do both, emotionally or practically. Something had to give. Help your people see that, on a much smaller scale, the same will be true for them. Some things they just need to say no to, either indefinitely or permanently. The goal is to be able to lay our calendars before the Lord and say, "Look, see? I was advancing the gospel, in and through my life."

16 | FRESH WHITE KICKS

Church can be simple.
On refusing materialism.

I coveted no one's silver or gold or apparel. —Acts 20:33

WHEN I WAS IN FOURTH GRADE, my brother James and I nailed a wooden backboard to the telephone pole in front of my best friend Jason's house, screwed on a shiny new rim from a sporting goods shop on Jewett Avenue, and fell in love with the game of basketball. James became the real star, eventually playing Division I for Hall of Fame coach Bill Self. I maxed out as a Catholic Central League All-Star, but my affection for the game has never waned. Our congregation has me on a strict quota of hoops-related analogies. (I am allowed bimonthly mentions of the Celtics.) Every Friday at 6:00 p.m., I strap on my heavy-duty knee braces and run full court with the over-thirty crowd. I've perused the Naismith Hall of Fame from door-opening to lights-out. Every June, I throw a party at my place to watch the NBA draft, complete with Gatorade and energy bars.

I am a hoops junkie.

This also means, by extension, that I am a sneakerhead. Tying on a pair of fresh white kicks is a euphoric experience for me. I could spend an entire paycheck (or two) in fifteen minutes at Foot Locker. My attic has trash bags filled with played-in, worn-out sneakers I refuse to throw away. (There is a pair of black Larry Bird Converse with the heel literally worn down to the sole.) The desktop picture on my MacBook is a pair of blue-on-black '86 Jordans.

Not surprisingly, the first thing I notice when showing up at the gym is who's wearing what. My eyes drop immediately to the floor in search of the latest fashions. Now that I am a father of four with a (very) limited personal apparel budget, those observations often terminate in covetousness. It seems everybody in the gym these days has fresher, whiter kicks than I do, and I wish it weren't so.[44]

As pastors and church planters, if we're not careful, a gym routine can become our 24/7. Unless we are pastoring or planting in a very distressed area, we'll perpetually be surrounded by others with more: more scratch, more security, more status, more swag. So it's essential we settle on the front end of our ministries where we are with money and the material things that come with it.

CONFESSION: I LOVE MONEY.

I don't think this was as true back when I didn't have any. When I was growing up, my dad was an electrician (non-union) and my mom was a bookkeeper. We lived in Everett, a blue-collar, gateway city that bordered the Charlestown neighborhood of Boston. We always had just enough money, but never a dollar extra. Anything exotic, like a trip to Disney or a new washer and dryer, happened thanks to the magic of plastic. In undergrad, I remember pining for pizza on Friday nights but not having the $8 to place the order. I can still see the contract I signed for my first job as a high school teacher in Lynn: $20,000.

But then, after finishing an MBA at Boston University and falling into a sweet tentmaking gig while planting Seven Mile Road, I began to be blessed by God with a solid, steady monthly income. I quickly realized, "Whoa, I like this 'having money' thing." This quickly morphed into, "Oh man, I love this 'having money' thing." A whole new vista of purchasing possibilities had opened before me, and along with it came wandering eyes. The world became my Foot Locker. If someone else had it—cars, homes, lifestyles, investment accounts—I wanted it.

• • •

THIS IS WHY PAUL'S WORDS IN Acts 20:33 stop me cold. Paul is presenting another mark of the genuineness of his ministry:

"I coveted no one's silver or gold or apparel."

Remember that Paul was a tentmaker and a pastor for part of his time in Ephesus, and a full-time pastor for the rest. Neither of those was a lucrative vocation. Meanwhile, Ephesus was rich. It was the third- or fourth-largest city in the Roman Empire, home to dozens of thriving industries. Paul would have been evangelizing and observing people who had much more wealth than he did. Regularly, he would have seen people with higher earnings, more financial security, better vacations, fancier wardrobes, and newer cars.

Yet, somehow, he was able to write these words: "I coveted no one's silver or gold or apparel."

I hate to admit it, but my first reaction when reading this verse is to doubt my beloved apostle's veracity. These words seem akin to someone studying the display case at the front of a Cheesecake Factory and then remarking, "Yeah, none of that looks any good at all." Or to having a Bostonian who watched the entirety of Super Bowl LI claim he didn't get goosebumps at least once in the second half.

I was listening to a comedian who was the hot, new comic in Hollywood. Upon moving to Los Angeles, he started making super rich comedian friends like Chris Rock, Dave Chappelle, and Martin Lawrence. He recalled the one time he was afforded an opportunity to visit Lawrence's 36-million-dollar house—complete with a pool hall, hang-gliding field, 10-car garage, movie theater with popcorn machine, and basketball courts with microfiber surfaces. He confessed that when he arrived home later that night, he was cranky and depressed. He thought, "What I am supposed to do, watch a movie on a TV? With microwave popcorn? Play basketball on concrete? How am I supposed to be happy, now that I have seen what Martin Lawrence has?"

Translation: "I coveted Lawrence's silver, gold, and apparel."

Now *that* sentence, I believe.

A few years ago, I was heading into the city to get lunch with three guys from Seven Mile Road. I stopped at an ATM, and whoever was in front of me accidentally left his receipt in the machine. I gave it a quick glance and noticed his ending balance: $365,370. I coveted someone else's "silver or gold or apparel" that day, and for several days after. I carried the receipt around with me and kept showing it to people until the ink faded. "Look at this! That's a checking account!" My mind was racing. If someone has $365,370 just in his checking account, how much other money does he have? What kind of investments? What kind of assets? What kind of vacations does he take?

I want it.

I want it all.

And yet, somehow, Paul says, "I was around a slew of Martin Lawrences, and I knew a bunch of people with $365,370 in their checking accounts, and I did not covet. I made tents and preached the gospel in an opulent city but was not moved by the material things around me."

To covet something means to really want it bad. *Covet* is a neutral verb. When someone says something like "I covet your prayers," she is not confessing sin, but rather communicating intensity. She is saying, "I really need you to pray. I am dead if the saints are not seeking the Lord with me on this thing. I desire, earnestly, your prayers." But usually, because our hearts are so twisted and dark, the word *covet* shows up in a sinful context, quickly contorting from earnest desire into an irregular, violent, impure desire. That's usually what *covet* means, and that's what it means here. Paul is saying, "I didn't have an irregular, unchecked, impure desire for material things."

The triad of *silver, gold,* and *apparel* are *metonyms,* meaning "stand-ins for something else."

When Paul says silver and gold, he's saying, "All that these precious metals afford us." As cash-loving Americans, we've coined dozens of metonyms for money: bank, Benjamins, bills, bones, bread, cabbage, cheddar, clams, c-notes, coin. And that's only the Bs and the Cs. But however you say it, you are referencing not the money itself, but what the money can do for you.

The same holds true with Paul's reference to apparel. He's not speaking primarily about an attraction to colors, materials, or fabrics, but about the status and prestige an elite wardrobe brought with it. We don't intuit this easily in our American context, because clothing is less and less of a differentiator of class or buying power in our culture. But this was not so in Ephesus. In the same way you'd know exactly which *Hunger Games* district of Panem you were in, based on the outfits you saw, any Ephesian would know immediately what crowd someone was from based on apparel.

So, here is what Paul is saying: "My heart was not moved with a desire to use my ministry among you to get my hands on money—or the status, security, and comforts it can buy." And our ability to make a similar declaration is essential if we are going to be faithful ministers of the gospel.

・・・

IT IS THE CLEAR TEACHING OF Scripture, from beginning to end, that we can either love God, or we can love money, but we cannot love both. At the bottom of our lives, where the engine exists that turns all the other gears, where the one thing that we are ultimately looking to and counting on and trusting is found, is either God and all that He is for us, or it is money and all it can do for us. There's no room for compromise. Yet when we covet, we are saying, "Having God is just not sufficient. I must also have this other thing, too."

We know this to be true, of course, from the Ten Commandments. Have you ever noticed the symmetry of the first and last?

1: You shall have no other gods before me.
10: You shall not covet your neighbor's house; you shall not covet your neighbor's wife, or his male servant, or his female servant, or his ox, or his donkey, or anything that is your neighbor's.

These are bookends, because coveting is going after another "god." It is not being wholly content with God alone, satisfied in God, good with God and whatever He has and hasn't given you. It's gazing longingly at something else or someone else. And it is sin.

This is exactly how Jesus taught it: "No one can serve two masters, for either he will hate the one and love the other, or he will be devoted to the one and despise the other. You cannot serve God and money" (Matt. 6:24).

Here is how I put this truth into "Bostonian" for our people at Seven Mile Road:

"We can either have our money, our Victorian homes, our Fidelity 401(k)s, our Herb Chambers Honda Pilots, our Jordan's Furniture sectionals, our season tickets to the Red Sox, our Cape vacations, our Amazon Echos, our fridges that talk to us, and our fresh white Adidas crow tops, or we can have God. But we cannot have both."

Here is how I say it to the Bostonian I see in the mirror each morning:

"Matt, you can either have a $600,000 house in Melrose with a fireplace and a glass backboard in the back and a raccoonless treehouse on the side and a 2019 Honda Accord and a graduate degree from Terrier U and a great day job with a pension, or you can have God. But you cannot have both."

Let me state it another way.

It's not that you can't have money, or even lots of money, or a nice vehicle, or dope apparel, or material possessions, even costly and beautiful ones. It's that *they* cannot have *you*. Christ has no rivals in your life.

. . .

ONCE WE ARE CONVINCED OF THIS truth, we need all the help we can get in ridding our souls of covetousness. The Holy Spirit meets that need for us with one simple word in verse 34: *necessities*. Every word of Scripture is breathed out by God, and we should make it our lifelong pursuit to let as many of those words as possible echo off the walls of our souls until we understand, believe, and live them. *Necessities* is one of those words. With this little word, the Spirit opens a window for us to see how we can overcome our natural disposition toward the never-ending pursuit of *more*. Paul, recounting the way he handled his income during his time as a tentmaker and pastor in Ephesus, writes, "You yourselves know that these hands ministered to my necessities." Rather than constantly looking at what others had, Paul was content with the basics.

Defining what is and isn't a necessity is, of course, a minefield we must maneuver with humility. The most recent of many fights in our home was about braces for our children. I said that braces were NOT a necessity. Grace insisted that they WERE. (Grace won.) The point is not that we have a master list somewhere of what is and is not a necessity in life. The point is we agree with the Spirit that *necessities* is a category, and if *necessities* is a category, then *luxuries* is too. We should regularly be asking the questions, "This purchase—this use of money—where is my heart in this? Coveting or content? Necessity or extravagance?"

That pastors live this way is a qualification for ministry, as Philippians 4, 1 Peter 5, and 1 Timothy 3 make clear. If we are stepping into or operating in ministry as a means of personal financial gain, something is terribly wrong in both our motivation and our basic assessment of how life works. (Hint: if it's money you're after, Christian ministry in post-Christian America is not the best choice.) But it's more than that. It's an invitation into a life free from the love—and the inevitable letdown—of money. That's the life our people need to see us living.

- BLUEPRINTS -

1. Walk in the light with men you trust about exactly how much you make, give, spend, and save.

One of the exercises we work through with our pastors and pastors-in-residence is called "Bottom Drawers." It is meant to invite others into the details of our financial lives.

We have each man complete an Excel spreadsheet delineating the following for the most recent year:

Income – all sources
Taxes – may take a while, being in Massachusetts
Giving – how much and to whom
Spending – both the total and the four largest costs (tuition, mortgage, etc.)
Savings – amount and destinations
Assets – everything you own
Liabilities – everything you owe

When they first hear we are doing this, most guys stain their boxers, but being honest about our financial lives is an exercise in gospel freedom. Any irresponsibility, greed, or covetousness is made plain, either on the screen or in conversation. In love, we forgive, instruct, challenge, and plan with each other toward being more faithful with our money. We are building a culture of contentment and generosity, which together form covetousness's kryptonite.

2. Dress humble and free.

This might sound petty, but there is pressure on pastors when it comes to apparel. The job description requires being in front of people often, for long stretches of time, with them necessarily staring at what you are wearing. We are establishing culture constantly, and our choice of apparel contributes (or detracts). Our aim should be to land somewhere holy on the continuum between "John Piper wearing the blazer he got at Savers in 1993" and "that Acts 29 guy who has worn a different shirt thirty-two Sundays in a row." I hate shopping and love simplicity, so I wear a black shirt, blue jeans, and black kicks nearly every week. The point is not to dress like me or anybody else, but to dress in a way that shows you are free from the love of the world and from worrying about the opinions of people.

3. Don't refuse God's blessings.

Being a pastor does not require taking a vow of poverty. Sometimes God blesses us financially. We shouldn't feel guilty or uncomfortable with that, but rather rejoice in His kindness and mobilize all our assets for gospel advancement. If your wife buys you a pair of fresh white kicks for your birthday, wear them. Francis Chan is a wonderful example of this: in his humble surprise at the financial boon his first book generated, he was giddy to give most of it away.

17 | HANDS

Church can be close.
On living in super tight community.

These hands ... —Acts 20:34

I WAS ON FACEBOOK FOR ONE year. One long, humbling year.

My primary motivation to join had been to give family and friends a window into my life. But I quickly realized that the "me" they saw was a sham—a highly edited, carefully crafted, patently false rendition of me.

"Fakebook Kruse," I called him.

He was thoughtful, witty, pleasant, and always tanned (even though he lived in frigid New England). He oozed consideration for his wife, patience with his children, and generosity with his money. He filled his days with successes at work, happy laughter at home, and frequent dining out, with the selfies to prove it. Sports, trivia, cooking, recycling: the man excelled at all of it.

You would have loved getting to know this guy.

Except that you would have been getting to know a ghost: a virtual version of me, brought to life thanks to the distance between me and any encounters with my audience.

This distance, of course, is a big part of Facebook's appeal. Americans and especially New Englanders prefer to live our lives at a safe distance from others. We love hiding the messy, grumpy, petulant, needy, overwhelmed, sinful-but-true versions of ourselves behind a veneer.

And we'd kindly ask others to do the same.

Facebook enables this duplicity by making it possible for us to keep up appearances without becoming entangled in a web of real-life relationships. Nobody has bad breath on Facebook. Or needs a ride to the airport. Or pees on your toilet seat. Or eats the last donut. If anyone does frustrate or annoy you, you scroll to the next person. And if things go really badly, you are one anonymous click away from ending the "friendship" entirely.

Revolving doors. No physical contact. Divine editorial powers.

This is the way of Facebook.

But it is not the way of the gospel.

. . .

EVEN A CASUAL READING OF THE New Testament shows Jesus's church marked by a beautiful, messy, holy, relational intimacy. These saints knew one another's name, story, sins, strengths, weaknesses, issues, dreams, fears, all of it. They lived in close, face-to-face community.

They were known.

When Euodia and Syntyche dug their heels into a nasty conflict, everyone knew. When Alexander abandoned the faith, everyone knew. When Trophimus was terribly sick in Miletus, everyone knew. When Archippus needed a kick in his skinny jeans, everyone knew. When the household of Stephanas first converted to Christ in Achaia, everyone knew. When Phoebe thrived in her diaconal role, everyone knew.

And because they knew—the good, the bad, and the ugly—they were able to love, serve, admonish, encourage, and disciple each other. They gospeled well. Euodia and Syntyche were encouraged to make peace. Alexander was held back from the Table. Trophimus was prayed for. Archippus was encouraged. Stephanas was celebrated. Phoebe was recognized.

Relational intimacy enables fruitful gospel ministry, and we are called to give ourselves to it.

...

THIS TRUTH EMERGES BEAUTIFULLY IN PAUL'S speech with these six simple words: "You yourselves know that these hands …"

I love this. Paul looked these men in the eye and said, without hesitation, "You yourselves know. You personally. You specifically. You. Not because somebody else told you. Not because it came across your Facebook timeline. Not because I am pitching it to you now. You yourselves know."

Know what?

"These hands."

Paul's ministry among these men was so intimate that they knew not only his theology and cadence and face but also his hands. You can know someone's reputation from what others say about him. You can learn her gait by observing her from across a room. You can pin down his personality by listening to podcasts. But knowing a person's hands? That happens only if you are close, really often. Paul was close with his people. And often.

The word *hands* in this text is especially powerful when you remember Paul's trade. Tentmaking was manual labor of the fiercest kind, and it did a number on a man's hands. Have you ever asked a pair of hands what job they would prefer their owner to not take up? *Lobsterman in Gloucester* and *tentmaker in Ephesus* would top the list.

17 | Hands

Here's how tentmaking works: Use a dangerously sharp knife to slice through stubbornly tough leather, over and over again, all day long. Paul's hands would have been constantly cut and calloused. And Paul's ministry was such that his people would have known his mangled hands on sight. They witnessed those hands toiling in the shop. They watched his hands gesture as he taught gospel doctrine. They saw those hands pass the ketchup, tickle their kids, and break bread. Those hands had held them as they sobbed.

They knew those hands.

When you're close enough to know someone's calloused hands, you're close enough to know his or her soul.

・・・

IF YOU CROWDED ALL THE HANDS in the world into one giant police lineup—billions of thumbs, pointers, middles, rings, and pinkies in a row—I'd spot my father's hands in a second. They're the electrician's hands, nicked by a lifetime of snipping wires and installing panels; the softball pitcher's hands, with a right index finger curved inward from throwing countless sinkers; the broken sinner's hands that trembled violently when he repented of a year-long sin that nearly broke our family; the justified saint's hands he loves to lift when he worships King Jesus. On Sundays I see that crooked index finger pointing up to heaven as we sing.

I know my dad's hands.

I know them because he has reached out to me for more than forty-six years. They held me at my birth in '73 at St. Vincent's. They worked summers beside me in hot New England attics as we wired ceiling lights. They dominated the Greater Boston Men's Softball League: he on the mound, me at shortstop. Those same hands clung to my neck as I dragged him into the emergency room the day he almost died of food poisoning.

I know my dad. I know his hands. And I know his soul.

...

SADLY, THIS KIND OF WILLINGNESS TO know and be known is rare in the American church. We love to do gospel ministry from across the room, across town, or across social media. We have mastered the art of keeping ourselves at arm's length.

But Jesus calls us to know our church family the way I know my dad's hands.

Imagine what Paul's speech might sound like if it were given today:

> You yourselves don't really know at all how I lived among you, since I didn't really live among you. I lived near you. You did see me across the sanctuary on Sundays, and at some important church meetings here and there, and I think once in the cereal aisle at the supermarket. You do know (don't you?) that from the first day I set foot in my newly constructed home, several zip codes removed from the church, at a safe emotional distance, when Facebook trials came upon me, how I did not shrink from recommending to you several things I found uplifting from various devotionals, teaching you in public and, uh, well, only in public, having never actually stepped into your home, as I have no idea where you live.

This is the tenor of American church ministry.

It's easy to understand how we got here. Relational intimacy comes with a warning label attached that would make a pharmacist shudder.

Getting close to others is a good way to get hurt. When some admissions counselor at a faraway college rejects your application, you get over it fast. When a member of your church whom you've loved and served and preached your heart out to and visited in the hospital suddenly flips you a midnight email explaining why he is leaving the church, you can't sleep for two days. The nearer you get to someone, the deeper he or she can cut you.

Relational intimacy also takes time. As a ministry grows, calendars fill up, inboxes clutter, and more and more (and more) tasks need accomplishing. Time with people can be pushed aside. Although no one is saying faithful gospel ministry requires we be on a first-name, in-home basis with every member of the church, it does require being deeply invested in the lives of somebody—lots of somebodies. That takes time. How much depends on our context. Paul gave the Ephesian saints 1,000-plus days of his life, and it was enough to develop a lifelong bond that left them weeping on the beach at his departure. Depending on where we live, it might require 3 months or 30 years, but it will take time.

Relational intimacy doesn't come fast. Or cheap. This begs the question: if relational intimacy is so emotionally dangerous and time-consuming, where do we find the motivation to actually give ourselves to it?

Answer: Jesus.

. . .

THE DOCTRINE OF JESUS'S INCARNATION IS the theological foundation upon which we build relational intimacy. In the Incarnation, Jesus "became flesh and dwelt among us." He moved toward us—into the neighborhood, onto the block, into the apartment upstairs—in love and with abandon. Day and night, year in and year out, He walked and talked and ate and slept with His disciples. They saw Him exhausted, frustrated, elated, troubled, delighted. They smelled His morning breath and sweaty sandal feet. They knew His voice. His stride. His hands.

Do you remember Jesus's last meal? The "disciple whom Jesus loved" was so near to Him he was reclining on Jesus's chest at the table. Literally. This was no anomaly. This wasn't Jesus suddenly chumming up to the nearest warm body because He knew His time had come. This was Jesus's way. It's no wonder that, as a grizzled old apostle, John begins his first letter with these tender, intimate words: "That which was from the beginning, which we have heard, which we have seen with our eyes, which we looked upon and have touched with our hands ..." The Savior drew near to sinners, chest to chest, hand to hand.

Of course, Jesus's hands were unlike any other hands in history. His were the righteous hands violently pierced, nails driven through so He might win a sinful people to Himself. His were the glorified hands that doubting Thomas knew on sight. The ones with the holes. You and I and all the saints will one day see those same hands, and we'll recognize them immediately, because no one has ever served more loaves and fishes, touched more cripples, chased away more demons, hugged more mourners, than the hands of our Savior. What His hands accomplished provides the foundation for the gospel we hand to our people.

Would anyone in our church know our hands? They can.

– BLUEPRINTS –

1. Know names.

I love the end of Paul's letter to the Christians in Rome. After fully wielding his apostolic authority and dropping mind-blowing theological argument after argument, he shifts effortlessly into relational intimacy. Not only can he rattle off name after name of his gospel coworkers—he is able to comment specifically as each one comes to mind. This big-shot apostle was on a first-name basis with Phoebe, Priscilla and Aquila, Mary, Andronicus and Junia, and the others that he greeted with a holy kiss.

To some degree, you should be, too.

When Seven Mile Road was first planted, we had two children in the church, total. Both were mine. Our "nursery" was my wife standing in a dusty hallway, half-listening to the preaching and half making sure our boys didn't wander outside into the traffic. Twelve years later, our church has more than sixty children. Every Sunday, before sending them to their classes, we pray for them up front as part of our liturgy. As they careen down to the front, I greet each by name. Getting there has taken some work (we have three girls named *Ada*), and some mornings I miss a name or two. But I am trying to model for our people relational intimacy. I want our children and parents to grow up knowing "My pastor knew me, and I knew him."

2. Write notes.

Handwritten notes are another way to forge relational intimacy. You can't write a personal note if you are unaware of something personal to write. So, disciplined note-writing forces you to move toward people. A note communicates, "I know you personally. You matter."

A third grader in our church recently made the all-star team in his little league. (At his age, I believe, all this means was he knew to run to first instead of to third.) When I found out, I wrote him a note with ALL-STAR! in big letters, complete with illustrations of a glove, bat, and ball. He raved about it for weeks. He knew I knew him, and he may now receive gospel encouragement and correction in a deeper way from me as he grows up.

3. Be in homes.

Be around. Be in your flock's homes, at their weddings, by their pools. Share meals, confess sin, and greet them with a holy kiss. Help them move and paint. Take them to the airport. Know their favorite band, their go-to outfit, their deepest wound, their highest joy.

Perhaps nothing has been more helpful in fulfilling the essentials of my pastoral ministry than being in our people's homes. This is intense. Walk into a young couple's home and find unwashed dishes piled up all over the kitchen and the husband sitting on the couch drinking a beer and playing *Madden NFL*? Sit on a secondhand couch with an unemployed dad and pregnant mom with three children who can't offer you anything but water or milk? Time to encourage and give. Being in homes is the anti-Facebook. We belong there.

The reverse is true as well. The people you are discipling should know what your home looks and smells like. For fifteen years the door of our home has been open. More than simple Christian hospitality, this is an invitation to the people Jesus has sent us to: "Come and see our home. Our table. Our couch. Our dirty dishes. Our family. Our life. Our hands."

18 | TEAM

Church can be unified.
On working together for gospel advancement.

... to those who were with me. —Acts 20:34

IF YOU SPENT SOME TIME AROUND Seven Mile Road, you would notice that almost all the gospel ministry gets done in teams. Seven Milers differ from each other in personality, family background, level of foodiness, musical tastes, and preferred time of day, yet we all work together for the glory of God and for the good of the people we've been given and are sent to. We've got Americans, Brazilians, Puerto Ricans, Haitians, townies, transplants, night owls, early risers, TB12ers, Beachmont Roast Beefers, mountain climbers, beach bums, on-timers, and fashionably-laters, all working side-by-side for gospel advancement.

Our church is not led or governed by a rock star. It is led by a pastoral team. Our thriving student ministry is run by a team. Our leadership development tracks are led by teams of two leaders. Compensation is set for our pastors by a team of our members. Our curriculum is chosen by a team. Our songs are selected by a team. Even our lawn is mowed by a team.

In fact, the idea of Seven Mile Road becoming a family of churches emerged from the simplest of premises: we can accomplish more gospel work together than we ever could apart. Jesus never intended for us to function as lone wolves, but as partners, laboring side by side for institutional health and gospel advancement. Whether it's ministry initiatives, gospel communities, community engagement, leadership development, or sermon preparation, all our gospel work now is the direct result of a team effort. We are in this disciple-making, church-building, gospel-advancing work *together*.

But this is not how things began.

. . .

WE PLANTED THE ORIGINAL SEVEN MILE Road with a core "team" of eleven souls: my wife, my father and mother, one couple from our sending church, my childhood best friend, and four teenagers. Calling us a motley crew would slander the word *motley*. While I worked tirelessly in those early years, I did a terrible job of inviting and mobilizing others to share the work with me.

Here was a typical Sunday in my life circa 2003:

5:00 a.m.: Wake up, finish typing my sermon, attempt to print it out on the worst DeskJet printer HP ever marketed.

7:00 a.m.: Take a shower, put some gel in my hair (old days), throw on jeans and a black shirt, and drive to the Emerson School Hall.

7:15 a.m.: Unlock the doors, turn on the lights, set up the chairs, drag out the speakers, plug in the sound system, put up the signs, clean the bathroom, put the bulletins on the chairs, and hook up the laptop to the projector. (If I could have tuned the guitar, I would have.)

9:30 a.m.: Go over the chords and lyrics with our Massachusetts-born, Hendrix-esque, not-yet-saved guitarist.

10:00 a.m.: Open the service in prayer, lead the singing, do the kids' sermon, take the offering, read the Scripture, preach the sermon, and pray the benediction.

Noon: Reverse engineer everything, then go home and crash.

And it wasn't just Sundays when I was doing most of the work. I was populating attendance spreadsheets, updating the website, knocking on doors in the neighborhood, raising money, running VBS, choosing songs, and delivering fifty-one sermons a year.

Here's how I say it now: for the first few years, Seven Mile Road was a drum solo.

Drum solos are cool—for two or three minutes. But then you find yourself longing for the other instruments to rejoin, because the boom-pop-buhdoomdoom-pop is only one element of a strong band. Alone, that act gets tired, fast. So does the drummer. You can solo only so long before your arms throb and your foot starts to cramp.

Drum solos pass for gospel ministry in lots of American churches: one guy or one girl, grinding alone, gifted deeply but narrowly, with no complementary players around him or her. Everything falls on the soloist, and the church and the minister and the mission suffer because of it.

That was me, unknowingly, for years, but then something beautiful happened. We matured to being led by a plurality of shepherding elders: Kevin Luce (now a missionary in Africa), Ajay Thomas (now lead pastor of Seven Mile Road in Philadelphia), and me. Each different from the other. We began working together, and boom!

The church began to get healthier.

I began to get healthier.

More and better gospel work began to get done.

I am not saying teamwork was the only thing that moved us toward health, but I will tell you this: the first thing I say when people ask what strategic change helped our church become viable is "We went from a drum solo to a band. And we are never going back."

• • •

TEAMWORK SHOWS UP AT THE BEGINNING of the biblical story. In absolute sovereignty, by infinite wisdom, and from an overflow of trinitarian love, God—Father, Son, and Spirit—created the world. The earth—beautiful, raw, wild—was just sitting there, ready to be worked in and worked on for good.

In Genesis 1 we see that at the height of His creative flourish, the pinnacle of His creation, the Lord creates man—male and female—and issues a mandate: "See this earth? Fill it and subdue it. Bear my image across it through procreation and cultivation."

Then in Genesis 2, we get a zoom-lens look at the creation story, and we see that God didn't create man and woman simultaneously: He created them in order. He created man first, alone, and set him to work. And then, for the first time in the story, we read something was not right. The man was alone, drum-solo alone, and that was not good. He needed a helper, a partner, a teammate. The creation mandate, the cultural work God assigned humanity from the beginning, was way too big to be done except in community.

What was true with the creation mandate is just as true with the redemption mandate—the gospel mandate, the Great Commission. At the beginning of the new creation, forged in His blood on the cross, Jesus stood with His disciples and looked out at the earth with them and said, "Go into all the world and make disciples, baptizing them and teaching them to obey everything that I have commanded you." You thought Adam and Eve were given a big job? Look at the work Jesus has given His church: *advance the gospel across the earth!*

And what was the context of Jesus's command? Was He huddled with one solitary super successor? Did the mantle of His ministry fall on a single apostle? Had Jesus pulled Peter aside in a private conference and said, "Listen, this is on you; you gotta run things now"? Nope. He was speaking to His team, a community, commissioning them, *plural*, to the *together-work*. And so, all through the rest of the New Testament, we see ministry plurality. Teams. Working together.

At Seven Mile Road, we spent two years preaching through the book of Acts. We began to realize it was the anomaly, the exception, the outlier, to read a story in the early church where only one person was at work. We saw Philip evangelizing the Ethiopian eunuch and thought, "This is weird. He is all alone on the road here. Where's his backup? Where's everyone else? This almost never happens." We had grown so accustomed to seeing partners, trios, teams, and entire churches working together that solo Philip was dissonant. *Team* is the norm in the book of Acts, and it's exactly how Paul did his work in Ephesus.

・・・

THIS JUMPS OUT AT US TWICE in the text of Acts 20.

Luke (the author of Acts) sets up Paul's speech like this: "Now from Miletus he sent to Ephesus and called the elders of the church to come to him."

Greek has something called a "plural accusative form." I Googled it and learned it signifies that the direct object in a sentence is plural. That's the form used here for *elders*. In other words, this church community in Ephesus was led not by one man but by a team of called, gifted, and qualified men. In fact, everywhere you see *elders* in the New Testament, the form is plural.

No drum solos. It's plurality, always.

A potential objection arises here. "Sure, that's how the church was governed, but is that really how it was founded? Didn't they need super-apostle Paul to roll into Ephesus to start the work? Wasn't Paul a one-man Holy Spirit hurricane who preached sermons and converted cities and battled heretics and raised money and wrote epistles that ended up in the Bible? Didn't he establish these churches solo and then hand them off to secondary leaders to do the daily dirty work? Paul didn't need the whole team thing. Right?"

Hardly. Paul explicitly mentions his team in verse 20: "You yourselves know that these hands ministered to my needs and to those who were with me."

The phrase "those who were with me" has become beautiful to me. Paul was a part of a ministry team. He didn't roll into Ephesus in the back of a limo with some handlers and a Dunkin' Donuts run guy. He didn't lounge around greenrooms sipping green tea before giving TED talks to adoring crowds. He didn't have a corner office behind two secretaries and a security guard. He labored side by side with others. Silvanus, Timothy, Luke, and others were as vital to the Ephesus mission as he was. The collections of names of co-laborers that appear at the end of Paul's letters are longer than a feminist's grievance list. Team ministry was the norm for Paul. And if it was for him, it must be for us.

· · ·

IT'S IMPORTANT TO DEFINE WHAT WE mean by *team*. If we mean "committee," I understand anyone's knee-jerk trepidation. I've served on some church committees, and I'd rather pencil-dive off the John Hancock tower. So, it becomes important that we embrace not only the biblical mandate for team ministry but also the biblical ethos of it.

I attended a human rights commission meeting at our town's city hall. We were hoping to serve at their annual welcome meal for immigrants who are new to the city, and I wanted to learn more about their work. I would have had a more exciting night playing Scrabble with my Russian-speaking friends. The commission was technically a "team," but there was no philosophical unity (zero members shared an understanding of what "human rights" entail or where those rights come from). There was no relational unity (the members didn't seem to know or even like each other). And there was no missional unity (there was thirty minutes of wrangling about whether a specific event should be added to their calendar). The meeting was just a tense, aimless three-hour ordeal of power plays, passive aggression, and competing agendas.

That's not the ethos of the biblical mandate for team ministry. Tucked into Paul's letter to the Philippians is the essence of gospel-centered teamwork. Writing from prison, Paul let his Philippian friends know that he was going to send Epaphroditus to see them. Epaphroditus was a partner of Paul's. They had served on a disciple-making church-planting team together. Listen to how Paul describes his teammate:

> I have thought it necessary to send to you Epaphroditus my brother and fellow worker and fellow soldier. (Phil. 2:25)

No three nouns communicate more clearly the logos, ethos, and pathos of team ministry.

1. MY BROTHER

First, Paul calls Epaphroditus "my brother." Without hesitation, the first Christians co-opted family language to talk about being a part of Jesus's church. If, through the gospel, God has become our Father, and Christ our elder brother, then we are family.

Brothers and sisters. The blood of Christ unites us as if the same DNA were in our blood.

This doctrine has implications not just for racial, ethnic, gender, and socio-economic reconciliation, but also for team ministry. When you hear "brother," you are supposed to hear "love." Paul begins his description of his gospel teammate with the most intimate word available to him: *brother*.

Don't ever rush over the word *brother* in Scripture. Hear it for the powerful analogy that it is. Paul says, "When I talk *gospel team*, I don't mean *committee members*, or *cubicle mates*, or *two-year contracts*. I mean *family*. He's my brother."

I grew up with one brother, and we were close. Fifteen-months-apart close. We shared the same last name, same house, same little league teams, same friends, same youth group, same high school, and same backseat in a 1982 yellow Subaru. James played Division I basketball in college, and when his Golden Eagles beat Arkansas, I was the first one on the court celebrating. (No, seriously—rewind SportsCenter from November 23, 1997. That tall, skinny kid with the mullet at center court. That's number 33's brother.) And Paul says: that is how I feel about my gospel teammates.

2. FELLOW WORKER

Second, Paul calls Epaphroditus "fellow worker." Co-laborer. Associate. Helper. Being a gospel team involves not only warmth but also *work*. The Greek word for this is *synergos*, from which we get our English word "synergy." Synergy ("together working") is the interaction of two or more "agents to produce a combined effect greater than the sum of their separate effects."[45] In mathematical terms, that's when 2 + 2 > 4. Although Paul didn't know that this word would take on that meaning in English, it signifies exactly what he was getting at. No matter how talented, energetic, or experienced any of us is, there is a narrowness if we're alone. But if you add people, you multiply talent and energy and experience. You subtract blind spots. You neutralize weaknesses. You amplify strengths.

Bostonian hoops junkies know this to be true from experience. Celtic greats like Kevin Garnett, Paul Pierce, and Ray Allen won zero championships before teaming up with the Celts. Their non-Celtic accolades were impressive, but none had won a title. But then, through the machinations of general managing savant Danny Ainge, the three became teammates and together ran roughshod over the league from their first preseason game to banner seventeen.

Paul loved this truth, and that's why he uses *fellow worker* so often. Twelve times he employs it in his letters, almost always attaching it to a named teammate like Priscilla, Aquila, Urbanus, Timothy, Titus, Epaphroditus, Euodia, Syntyche, Justus, Philemon, Mark, Aristarchus, or Demas. As Jack Johnson sang, "It's always better when we're together."

3. FELLOW SOLDIER

Third, Paul calls Epaphroditus his "fellow soldier." In Paul's mind, a gospel teammate is someone to love or labor with, and someone to go to war alongside. Team is easy when it's all cinnamon buns and smooth jazz and blue skies, but what about when it's wet socks and foxholes and thunderstorms? Paul and Epaphroditus had been through some things.

Ten minutes before the start of every Friday night service at the youth group I grew up in, a handful of leaders would circle up and pray together. One night I was invited to join in. I'd never participated in this traditional prayer, and so I was half-praying, half-sweating, and half-looking around to see how it worked. Pastor Wayne (nicknamed P-Dub) spoke that night, and he asked that someone pray for him. One of our youth leaders (a doppelganger of a twenty-two-year-old Krusty the Clown) launched into a prayer I will never forget: "Satan, you listen to me. P-Dub is preachin' tonight. He's our pastuh. You mess wit' 'im, you messin' wit' alllllll of us." While I don't defend the orthodoxy of that prayer, I love the spirit of it. We are fellow soldiers, at war against our flesh, this world, and Satan. We love and labor and live and die together.

Put that all together, and you get the ethos of *team* in the gospel sense. Love. Suffering. Encouragement. Accountability. Complementarity. Loyalty. Synergy.

This is what Jesus calls us to.

But none of it is easy.

• • •

TEAM MINISTRY SOUNDS NICE IN THEORY, but when it comes to stepping into it, pastors hesitate more than a Republican at the Massachusetts border. We know the cost will be steep. Our souls, our futures, our comforts, and our preferences are placed in jeopardy the minute we tie ourselves to the opinions, performance, reliability, and goodwill of others. Saying yes to team ministry opens the door to the sharpest of sanctifications.

At least three reasons cause us to vacillate on team ministry:

1. WE ARE PERFECTIONISTS.

Many of us naturally insist that everything be done our way. The old adage "If you want a job done well, do it yourself" is common, but it's not brilliant.

A few years ago I was reading *Fast Company,* and the mag profiled a world-famous interior designer, the kind of creative personality who would put up the best Pinterest board in history. The interviewer asked him something like this: "Tell us what it looks like for you to do your work." The designer's answer was a drum solo—basically, "I meet with the client, and I listen, and I ask questions. And then, I go into my office, and I close the door and I work, alone! No interruptions, no phone calls, no conversations, no outside opinions, no team meetings, nothing. Sometimes, I am in there for days without coming out. Sometimes weeks. And then, I meet with the client and I tell them, 'This is what you need to do. Present, explain, pitch, defend, voila.' If they don't agree, I walk away. If they do, I let my staff implement my design."

We all have that in us. My wife is this way with the dishes. Most preachers are this way with their sermons. I am this way with budget reports, the website, our children's space, and the setup of the chairs in our sanctuary. Every time I go to my son's middle-school basketball games, I want to grab the clipboard and run the offense.

Healthy gospel ministry requires that we humble ourselves and reject this false narrative. A perfect sermon is not the point. A perfect budget report is not the point. Perfectly aligned rows are not the point. The glory of Jesus through making disciples is the point, and that will happen better if we allow the team to share the work.

2. WE ARE DIVAS.

Team ministry makes it about "us," but I want it to be about me. Sure, there is no *I* in *team*, but there is a *me* in there. All eyes and all accolades on me is how I like it. I'm a lanky six-foot-three balding diva.

My senior year in high school I worked at a television station called KOTV. They wouldn't let me on the air thanks to my accent, so I worked behind the scenes in video production. I hated that semester. If you are looking for the most concentrated gathering of giant egos in a city, head to the television studio. You will find that the very nature of the business is where the individual is a brand unto himself. TV breeds cutthroat competition, perpetual maneuvering, and endless backbiting. It was every anchorman and anchorwoman for himself or herself. This is not how it should be in Jesus's church. Gospel-centered team ministry means being as excited about others' successes as our own. For Paul, this looked like writing epistles with a thousand other people's names in them.

3. WE TAKE THE PATH OF LEAST RESISTANCE.

Team ministry is hard, and the objections to it are endless: "That's so much extra work." "I hate dealing with conflict." "Training people takes so much time." "She's always late." "It'll go faster and smoother if I just do it myself." "They are going to slow me down." You are right. Team ministry is costly. There are days when I don't want to weather Justin's sarcasm, or Matt's feet on the table, or Clint's culinary opinions, or Dan's Cubs paraphernalia, or Bryan's hockey references, or Heather's whirlwind of debris. And more days exist when these men and women don't want to deal with *my* idiosyncrasies. But Jesus calls us to it, for His glory and our joy and fruitfulness.

• • •

OUR EXECUTIVE ELDER BOARD (the team of pastors who are leading and serving Seven Mile Road) recently nailed down a simple mission statement for why we exist as a team. We were hoping this one little sentence would serve as a helpful guide for everything about the way we work together:

> Become a holy, prolific, and uncommonly unified pastoral team for the good of our people and the ungospeled Bostonians we are sent to.

Every phrase in there is pregnant with meaning, but the words *uncommonly unified* blink like landing lights on a runway.

Here is how I explained *uncommonly unified* to the team:

> Men, we are pursuing a hard thing together. We are one church with multiple, contextualized congregations and missions who love each other, share everything, yet are free to do what's needed at the local level to see gospel work done among distinct Bostonian people groups. Any old level of unity won't cut it. We need to be 'uncommonly for each other.' We have early birds, night owls, multitaskers, lone wolves, and more on this team. We need to be aware of this reality and give and take as needed, with an emphasis on 'give,' meaning both accommodating to the needs of the team and movement when our natural tendency is not to, as well as bearing with and thanking God for a brother who rolls differently. And we need to fight holy. Healthy families sometimes see things differently from one another. They are not afraid to challenge, to press, to dissent, to ask for explanations, to agree to disagree, etc. The key is that they do all of this with both affectionate love and fierce loyalty remaining intact. We need to get and live there.

Church can be a place where love, loyalty, and God's people unite.

– BLUEPRINTS –

1. Always ask, "Who is leading with me?"

Whatever the ministry or mission initiative, whether it's continuous or stand-alone, don't begin until you've prayerfully landed on who is going to be involved and how. And don't begin until you have been clear with everyone about vision and execution. It's not always going to be as dramatic as the coming together of the Fellowship in Rivendell, but it's crucial to know "I'm not in this alone, and here is who's with me."

2. Grow in leading a team.

There are hundreds of helpful books and videos to aid in this effort. Pick your favorites, and commit to implementing their counsel.[46]

A well-led team agrees 100 percent on the answers to the following:

- Why does this team exist? In other words, "This is what success looks like." The answer should be big and bold and compelling (completely idealistic is good!), as it will energize and inform everything the team does. *Checkpoint: The members of the team know, agree on, and are passionate about the reason the team exists.*
- What does this team do? In other words, "Here is how we accomplish that mission." Be simple and concrete. *Checkpoint: Each activity the team undertakes can be tied directly back to the team's purpose.*
- What is most important right now? In other words, "If we do just one thing really well during the next stretch, what should it be?" This drives action and accountability. *Checkpoint: Team members have a clear, current goal around which they are rallying, and they feel a collective sense of ownership of that goal.*
- Who is doing what? In other words, "Everyone is mobilized to do his or her part." Be clear who is responsible for what. Be clear that they are empowered. *Checkpoint:*

Team members understand their own and one another's roles and responsibilities, and they are comfortable asking questions about each other's work.

3. Serve the others on the team like crazy.

If you are the leader of a ministry team, your team members should know you are striving for the success of the team and not just your self-actualization or the accomplishment of a task. Pray for the people on the team. Ask them before meetings how they are doing. Send encouraging texts. Show an interest in their thoughts and perspectives. Love them.

19 | HUSTLE

Church can be hardworking.
On breaking a sweat.

By working hard ... —Acts 20:35

WERE YOU TO COMMISSION A PORTRAIT of the average Seven Miler, you'd receive a no-nonsense New Englander with a sweaty brow, bent back, and calloused hands. In a mostly apathetic or antagonistic environment like ours, you cannot build a church from scratch without a critical mass of men and women who are both optimistic and willing to work.

Church planting requires hope and hustle.

Although not a prerequisite for ministry at Seven Mile Road, almost all our pastors and church planters are or have been "tentmakers." Their side jobs have included teaching high school, balancing books, plowing snow, swinging hammers, guarding fishing docks, teaching Greek, chaplaining Army cadets, and myriad other tasks to make ends meet. Along the way, they made disciples and helped plant a church. Those who didn't tent-make did raise money, write prospectuses, chase leads, and master their elevator speeches. Meanwhile, these men have relentlessly loved and served their wives, sons, daughters, fathers, mothers, and neighbors.

Then there are the real super-hustle-heroes: our wives. Rome wasn't built in a day, but if the wives of our Seven Mile Road pastors were on the job, it might have been. These unashamedly feminine women have tirelessly supported their husbands, not only "hustling at home," as Titus 2 (my translation) so beautifully requires, but also hustling at church. Our wives welcome newcomers, disciple younger women, teach children, visit the sick, engineer podcasts, plan events, and do the kabillion invisible things godly women have done throughout the ages. My wife and my sisters in Christ hustle in the mold of those venerable Ephesian widows who (to paraphrase Paul) brought up children, showed hospitality, washed the feet of the saints, cared for the afflicted, and devoted themselves to every good work.[47] Every Christmas, when our broader Seven Mile Road pastoral team and their wives gather for a meal, I inevitably choke up with gratitude as I thank them for their partnership in the gospel.

One icy January day, when our pastoral team was wordsmithing how to tell prospective church planters what it means to partner with Seven Mile Road, we wrote the following triad on the whiteboard: "Really hard work. For a really long time. In a really hard place." Although we eventually passed on this grim summary for the sunnier "A Family of Churches Built to Love and Lead New Englanders to the Real Jesus," the three-part pitch packed power. To pastor or plant a healthy and holy church in a post-Christian context, you have to come ready to work.

Really hard.

For a really long time.

. . .

ONE OF THE DIDACTIC TOOLS SEVEN Milers use is what we call *gospel continuums*. As sons of Adam and daughters of Eve, we all gravitate toward sin the way a New England socialist gravitates toward other people's money. It's in our nature. But we don't all sin in the same direction. The prodigal son and his big brother were both lost, but in opposite woods. Simon the Pharisee and the woman at the well both needed rescuing from their sin, but their pasts looked nothing alike. Jesus had a zealot and a tax collector on his team, each of whom had believed a different set of lies about how to live in this world. Ditches flank each side of the straight and narrow path Jesus called us to walk. The devil doesn't care which ditch our people stumble into, as long as they stumble. We need to warn them of both.

This doesn't mean we emphasize all ditches equally. Different people groups, and different individuals within those people groups, have different sin tendencies. A good pastor will know this and, while not neglecting to declare the full counsel of God on every matter, will incessantly hammer on the specific sin tendencies of the people he is dealing with. Jesus's apostle Paul quoted a local Cretan poet to Titus, advising him that his fellow islanders were "always liars, evil beasts, lazy gluttons" (Titus 1:12). He was helping the young pastor know what to emphasize in his discipleship. A twelve-week series on "practicing Sabbath" would have been barking up the wrong tree. Yes, Titus needed to disciple his people in the importance of Sabbath rest—but the Cretans he was sent to were more likely to slide off their couch, joystick in hand, into a ditch of indolence. Titus needed to go hard on sloth, not Sabbath.

Because virtually every obedience is confronted with twin temptations, leveraging a gospel continuum clarifies two things:

1. Polar opposite temptations of unbelief and disobedience besiege every soul.
2. The pole most attractive to our people is …

Here is how we have used a gospel continuum to disciple our people around work:

A GOSPEL CONTINUUM ON WORK

Slacker ———————————————————— Workaholic

THE SLACKER DITCH

When it comes to work, one temptation we can fall into is the slacker ditch. It teems with the remains of Cretans, innumerable fifteen-year-old males, summer school students, and, sadly, American pastors. Proverbs collectively calls slackers "the sluggard." Some slackers are lazy, like the prototypical couch potato who spends hours watching Netflix while downing Nutter

Butters and chocolate milk his mom brought home. Others have PhDs in procrastination; they keep themselves busy but seldom accomplish anything significant. We call this "fake working," flitting about with meaningless tasks to avoid the harder tasks.

Slackers don't hustle.

THE WORKAHOLIC

The other ditch swallows up workaholics. Whether driven by greed (more work gets me more money), or pride (more work means more status), or fear (everything rides on my performance), workaholics hurtle toward burnout. While attending a panel on the workplace at J.R. Vassar's Apostles Downtown church in Manhattan, I heard speaker after speaker articulate God's grace in bringing them to repentance over their refusal to rest on the Lord's Day. This didn't surprise me at all, given that Vassar's congregation was filled with ambitious twenty-year-olds who had come to Wall Street or Madison Avenue to make their mark in the world.

Workaholics hustle, but idolatrously.

SWEET SPOT: GOSPEL HUSTLE

The holy and healthy spot on this continuum is what we call "gospel hustle" or "grace-animated effort." We hammer the truth that our identities are grounded in who we are in Christ, not in what we do or in how much we accomplish. This gospel truth propels us into our homes, churches, and cities with vision and vigor to do great things for the common good and the glory of God.

Jesus is our exemplar here. At the start of His ministry, He emerged from the waters of baptism to the sweet sound of His Father's affirming voice: "This is my beloved Son, with whom I am well pleased" (Matt. 3:17). From this starting line of acceptance, Jesus hustled. He traveled, preached, healed, exorcised, confronted, debated, explained, and ultimately died exhausted on the cross, His one mortal life fully spent. I've always loved that Jesus was once so tired from working that He slept right through a mini typhoon. Jesus nailed the gospel work continuum, hustling perfectly, by the Spirit, in submission to and in tandem with the Father, and in love for others.

As pastors, we are called to do the same.

This is why we coined our pastoral training program the Ox Track and not the Diva Track or Hammock Track or One-Day-Work-Week Track. While Scripture's reference to an ox is made primarily in defense of compensating ministers generously, it's no accident that the ox was the Spirit's metaphorical animal of choice. An ox is a beast of burden with a daily routine that includes putting its head down and dragging a heavy load through a rocky field all day long. And then getting up the next day and doing it again. That is our fundamental self-understanding of pastoral ministry: head down, muscles straining, legs pumping. After heavy lifting and hard work, look back one day to see a great harvest.

• • •

JESUS'S APOSTLE PAUL WOULD CONCUR WITH this sentiment. In the last sentence of his speech, Paul presents yet another mark of the faithfulness of his gospel ministry by saying, "I hustled." Here is how he said it:

"In all things I have shown you that by working hard ..." (Acts 20:35).

For three years, Paul did not cease, night or day, to work hard for gospel advancement among the people he was sent to. For at least one of those years he held down two jobs: tentmaker by day, apostle by night. This fact does not normalize bivocational ministry, but it does normalize hustle. When outside funding enabled him to "go full time," Paul threw himself into teaching, preaching, visiting, exhorting, helping, loving, and hustling tirelessly.

Unfortunately, American pastors of recent generations lack a reputation for such diligence.

Some of this stems from a common misunderstanding of the rhythms of pastoral ministry. What pastor hasn't heard the quip, "You work one day a week, right? That must be awesome!" Many people assume that a pastor's job description includes little more than preparing sermons, getting coffee with people, coordinating water bottle deliveries, replacing the toner on the copy machine, and reading theology books. (Bonus if you are a church planter: You get to hang out at Starbucks all day.) But much of this confusion is a direct result of pastors' sinful lack of hustle or ambition. Yes, some pastors burn out—but many more glide through their ministries, heart rate unraised.

In the early years of planting Seven Mile Road, I was connected to the Malden Clergy Association. Attending the group's meetings was like visiting Plymouth Plantation, where everyone dresses in odd clothing, employs long-extinct vocabulary, and engages in practices that the modern world left behind centuries ago. At one luncheon, I sat across from a youth pastor at a congregational church in our city.[48] I was immediately miffed when I realized the church was living on the rancid fumes of endowment interest. I choked when I heard the congregation employed him full time to pastor its six to eight total teenagers. When he began whining and complaining he was required to lead "both middle and high school youth groups," I wanted to vault the folding table and throttle him. Silently I screamed, "You are being paid full time, with Jesus's money, to love six to eight teenagers, and you are complaining about the workload?!" (At the time, I was working three jobs to provide for my wife and newborn son while attempting to gain some traction with our church plant, so I confess my heart's response was poor.)

I really should have befriended this young man, loved him, and said, "Let's talk about the glory and the goodness of working really hard."

...

BY GOD'S PROVIDENCE, I HAVE WORKED bivocationally throughout the planting of Seven Mile Road, helping to manage finances for a local school district. My team there is composed mostly of middle-aged Bostonian women with hearts as thick as their accents. Every time the Powerball lottery crests $500 million, a buzz surrounds our water cooler, and I am bullied into pooling $5 into a bulk purchase of tickets. For days everyone waxes wistfully about what they'd do if the office won. Most agree on one point: "If we hit it big, I am not even coming into work the next day!"

That is their big dream—to not have to work ever again. Work is viewed as a necessary evil, required to pay the bills. If there were any way not to work, they'd quit immediately. Real joy would come in doing as little work as possible.

We Americans (pastors included) love this siren song. We made *The 4-Hour Workweek* a *New York Times* Best Seller and turned TripAdvisor into a billion-dollar enterprise. We see work as a means to other ends, never as a happy end in itself. But the clear teaching of Scripture is that our Father is a worker. "Creator and Sustainer" is how the creeds convey this doctrine, meaning God did the work of making all things, and He continuously does the work of keeping all things going. Jesus noted this succinctly in His wrangling with the Pharisees: "My Father is working until now, and I am working" (John 5:17). (This verse is why those father-and-son business names on old, beat-up trucks have always delighted me.) This working of Father and Son (and Spirit) is never done in a foot-dragging malaise. It's done with energetic joy.

Not only is our Father a worker—He created workers, preparing "good works" for us to do, first in the garden, then in the church (Eph. 2:10). Work both precedes the fall and follows the resurrection.

I've always resonated with imagined accounts of creation (like the one in C.S. Lewis's *The Magician's Nephew*) that depict God singing creation into existence. Work, at its uncursed core, is not an aimless, random, boring drudgery or an unfortunate necessity, but a creative, purposeful, productive, meaningful exertion, the kind you sing (or whistle) while doing.

We pastors were made to join God in that song.

– BLUEPRINTS –

1. Develop leaders who have already proven—pre-paycheck, pre-position, pre-title—that they'll hustle.

Every Thanksgiving, all the Seven Mile Road guys pull together for a three-hour game of pickup at the local Y. Burning off a few thousand calories before noon is perfect justification for our reckless eating later in the day. One icy November 27, a young man new in our pastoral track showed up. And one thing was obvious from the tip: basketball was not his sport. He was built more like a fire hydrant than a shooting guard. Despite this, he threw himself into the games with abandon. He ran, jumped, screened, and dove for any loose balls, all with a smile. One hour into the game, I thought, "I could trust this guy to pastor with me."

Over the years, charisma and competency have lured me when I have thought about whom to invite into our leadership development tracks. Although these qualities are important, they pale in comparison to a proven track record of humble, holy service to the church. We want to train leaders who have hustled for the good of others—with no cameras on them and no carrot before them.

2. Set the expectation that the people (not the professionals) own the work of the ministry.

We've tried to build a culture where it's clear that if everyone doesn't serve, the mission doesn't function. Although paid staff tend to drive the mission of the church, the people of God must own it.

For example, Seven Mile Road's ratio of children to adults is beautifully ludicrous. From our last count, we have 1.2 adults per child. (Give us nine months, and we'll likely be outnumbered.) This calculus presents numerous challenges to our church, one being how to care for those kids during the preaching on Sundays. We've been honest with everyone, saying, "You need to hustle at this. We need all hands on deck in loving our sons and daughters if this church is going to work." Each week, forty-eight Seven Milers serve our children—nearly half of the adults in Seven Mile Road. That's hustle!

3. Systematically avoid burnout.

"Working hard" is not code for "burning out." We've been careful to build non-negotiable rhythms of rest for our staff and people. These may differ in your context, but ours include the following:

- Make July as chill as possible. We have zero expectations of ministry initiatives advancing, gospel communities

meeting, or any organization doing heavy lifting in July. It's New England. It's summer. Enjoy it.
- Nobody serves formally every week. Our all-volunteer band rotates members. Children's volunteers serve once every six weeks. Our setup team rotates monthly. Same with our welcome team. This gives everyone plenty of reps to enjoy the means of grace in worship on a regular basis.
- Volunteer appreciation: Twice a year we create space to love and thank all the Seven Milers who make the church life go. In December, it's a fun Friday night by a fireplace somewhere. In June, it's a big picnic at the park. Both serve as simple, invigorating Sabbath time.

20 | SPEED BUMPS

Church can be compassionate.
On not running people over.

We must help the weak. —Acts 20:35

ONE OF THE VERY LAST THINGS we do in each of our year-long leadership development tracks is work through CliftonStrengths,[49] a personality profiling exercise that helps identify some of the natural strengths our future leaders possess.

The timing is important. We don't lead with a personality test; we finish with it. Having a full year of gospel conversations under our belts before exploring our unique wiring helps us keep the exercise in proper perspective. The results are not a prison, defining and limiting us, but a window into how the Spirit intends to use and grow us.

"StrengthsFinder Night" is always lighthearted, and sometimes it's hilarious.

Each person submits his top five strengths to the track leader, who then anonymously prints and posts them on the wall. Everyone tries to guess who's who. Sometimes it's super obvious (the guy who never puts a book down is a Learner). Other times, not at all. But we have a good time affirming (and needling) each other about our God-given idiosyncrasies.

No one has ever had a hard time tying me to my results. I wear my top five like a neck tattoo: Learner-Maximizer-Analytical-Discipline-Focus. Not exactly the life of the party. If my StrengthsFinder was a sign on a chain-link fence it would read "Beware: Alpha Dog."

Here's a sampling of what the "Maximizer" strength entails:

> Excellence, not average, is your measure. Taking something from below average to slightly above average takes a great deal of effort and in your opinion is not very rewarding. Transforming something strong into something superb takes just as much effort but is much more thrilling.

> Strengths, whether yours or someone else's, fascinate you. Like a diver after pearls, you search them out, watching for the telltale signs of a strength.[50]

In other words, show me a person or project that has the potential to be spectacular, and Red Bull starts running through my veins. Is someone selling a historic but dilapidated church building with strong bones and Bostonian character? Buy it and name me project manager. (We did this in 2011.) Do you have a few athletic and teachable middle schoolers who love to ball and need a coach? Give me the whistle, and we'll go undefeated. (This happened several times.) Are you gathering two hundred high-powered future leaders who are interested in gospel-centered church planting in New England? Assign me the TED talk (or better yet, a one-hour sermon) and I'll nail it.

Show me strengths that can be nurtured, steered, and maximized, and I'm in.

This can be helpful as far as it goes, but Maximizer has a dark side.

If I don't sense, immediately and intuitively, a high probability of blazing success in a relationship or venture, I hit the eject button before we are wheels up. If I can't get an A+, I don't bother. My radar is always searching for high-potential ROI. I want to go fast and furious, big and Broadway, or I don't want to go at all.

I don't do average, pedestrian, or mediocre.

And I definitely don't do weak.

• • •

I HATE SPEED BUMPS. THE PARKING lot at my son's high school is filled with them. His freshman year I was assigned morning drop-off. As a Maximizer I made it my ambition to map a route that avoided as many speed bumps as possible. Whether that meant swerving erratically through empty parking spaces, entering via the exit (or vice versa), or driving with two tires up on a slight curb, I was not letting those speed bumps slow me down. If avoidance was altogether impossible, acceleration was my backup strategy: hit the gas and hammer right over the bump.

Avoid if possible; run over if necessary.

Just don't ever slow down.

Sadly, with those I deem "weak," this is my MO. My tendency is to swerve violently away from anything or anyone who's going to slow me down. I don't view someone who is hurting or fragile or dysfunctional or incapable as a God-given opportunity for displaying gospel love, or an invitation to serve like Jesus. Instead, I see them as speed bumps, as obstacles to be zoomed past or accelerated over.

...

IT IS DIRECTLY INTO THIS UGLY (but not unusual) tendency that Paul issues a beautiful yet jarring admonition: "We must help the weak …" (Acts 20:35).

Feel the weight of that word *must*. This is a command. A have-to. An imperative. And it's not given only to the naturally tender or nurturing among us. It's not reserved for those drawn to the helping professions. It's given to every shepherd, to every disciple-maker, to every Christian.

We dare not job-description our way out of this. "Well, I am the Pastor for Teaching and Vision. My duties are planning and delivering the weekend sermons, maintaining the culture, and training future leaders. I don't have time for the weak."

We dare not excuse ourselves based on our Enneagram, Myers-Briggs, or CliftonStrengths results. "Hey, I'm a Maximizer. The church benefits the most when I am free to run with the strong. I'll leave helping the weak to my associates."

We dare not rationalize this requirement away. "It's very important that we foster a spirit of excellence in all that we do here at our church. So, we need to platform and invest in our high-potential members. We just don't have the time to give to the weak."

We dare not sidestep, delegate, or fake our way around this.

If we are going to be faithful gospel ministers, we must help the weak.

I can quickly catalog a dozen verbs I'd prefer the Spirit to have inspired right there: Sidestep. Delegate. Despise. Mock. Pity. Dismiss. Patronize. Avoid. Hand off. Gripe about. Judge. Chase away. Ignore. Crush.

I'm too embarrassed to type the rest.

But help?

Yes, help.

We are called to move toward the weak in our churches with gospel love. To slow down and help them. To empathize with them. To serve them. To mobilize our strengths not for our own good or comfort or promotion or actualization, but for theirs.

· · ·

THINK ABOUT PAUL'S TIME SERVING THE Ephesian church. For three years, by God's grace, Paul was in a place of strength. He was strong physically, in good enough health to do the grueling physical work of tentmaking. He was strong emotionally, surrounded by beloved coworkers and experiencing fruit from his discipleship efforts. He was strong theologically, decades deep in living out sound doctrine. And Paul happily employed all of that strength, not for his own good, nor exclusively for the good of the strong sheep, but for the weak.

He was not frustrated by them. He did not domineer them. He did not expect some sort of equitable reciprocation. He did not ignore or sidestep or patronize or demean them. He helped them.

You could say it like this: Paul viewed the weak not as the blight of gospel ministry but as the fruit.

We need those eyes. And Jesus will give them to us.

...

FOR THE FIRST SEVERAL YEARS OF our church plant, almost all the fruit was borne in the hungry soil of my own soul. If you were looking for growth in the normal metrics of conversions, baptisms, and Sunday attendance, you'd have said the branches hung fruitless. But my soul? My soul was sprouting like Eden.

One of the graces the Lord was growing in me was unexpected affection for the weak. He did this by putting speed bump after speed bump in my path.

The earliest speed bumps had names: Jen, Vin, and Gerry, each of them overqualified to be called "weak."

JEN

As a six-foot-tall Medford girl with a room-owning smile, Jen could roll out of bed into gray sweats, a wrinkled tee, and a Sox hat pulled down just above her eyes and still turn heads. She got pregnant as a high school junior. She married right after graduation, had another baby at 20, and at 21 gave birth to twins.

Everything spiraled downhill from there.

When I met her, she was in poverty and addicted to painkillers, prescribed because her alcoholic husband had beaten her badly in front of their four children. Single, poor, and overwhelmed, Jen dropped the kids off at the Department of Children and Families and checked herself into McLean Hospital for psychiatric treatment.

I remember getting the call and praying as I drove forty-five minutes down 128 toward Waltham. More precisely, the holy part of me was prayerful, asking the Spirit for wisdom and grace. The unholy part complained: "A ninety-minute round-trip drive to deal with this? I love Jen and everything, but she's years away from being a functioning member of this church plant. We've got work to do. I don't really have time for this speed bump, Lord."

When I arrived at McLean, I parked and walked briskly into the cold, gray psych ward. Jen was sitting in the corner, facing a window. Her shoes were laceless, her stare blank. Thick dark lines circled her sky-blue eyes like moats around an abandoned castle. Her natural beauty lay buried under years of abuse and neglect and addiction. Our conversation was fitful. Pauses outweighed words. I stammered a bit, affirmed my love for her, and affirmed Jesus's love for her. I left uncertain, feeling like little had been accomplished.

But Jesus was teaching me to help the Jens.

VIN

Vin, 42, was ex-military, retired on disability. His hair was shaggy, his clothes ragged. He always missed a few streaks of his graying beard when he shaved. Within three years of being discharged from the Army, he had met a girl, gotten her pregnant, married her, divorced her, then gotten her pregnant again. His second daughter was born a deaf, mute quadriplegic. Mom wasn't interested, and so the two girls soon fell into Mark's custody. Unemployed and disabled, he was barely functioning.

One afternoon Vin asked Grace and me to watch his daughter while he went to court. We happily agreed. I remember sitting on the ground with her, a young pastor trying to process the sovereignty of God in disability, talking quietly to this little girl, her limp arms and legs sprawled across our living room floor. As I built a DUPLO castle, she stared off, oblivious. Then, without warning, she vomited all twenty ounces of the red Gatorade she'd consumed. It got all over her, and me, and our light-blue rug.

As Grace and I cleaned her up, I thought: "All morning, I've been sitting and playing with a quadriplegic five-year-old and cleaning up her puke? I love Vin and everything, but he's never going to be a functioning member of this church plant. I have a sermon to write. I don't really have time for this, Lord."

It took Grace and me twenty minutes to clean up her vomit. Her dad picked her up late, downcast, fidgety. My sermon remained unwritten.

But Jesus was teaching me to help the Vins.

GERRY

Gerry, a quiet, overweight teen, plummeted into a pornography addiction. One night while binging, he caught an unitended glimpe of a very young girl in one of the images. Realizing he had crossed a dangerous threshold, he panicked. Then he shut down. Completely. His mom had no choice but to check him into a psych ward.

The call from the hospital forced me back into a familiar forty-five minutes down 128 toward Waltham. Back to McLean. Again.

"Jesus, are you serious? I mean, again? I love Gerry and everything but … he's never going to be a functioning member of this church plant. I've got work to do. I don't really have time for this speed bump, Lord."

But Jesus was teaching me to help the Gerrys.

I now look back at those early years not with frustration but with gratitude for my Savior, who taught me to love the weak. Jesus was equipping me to be a good shepherd, slowing me down, fixing my gaze on the eyes and stories and names of broken people. Every single person, not just the super strong, Jesus brought to Seven Mile Road was His way of ensuring that our church would be a safe place for the weak.

There's a reason engineers place speed bumps in roads: they ensure the pedestrians stay safe. They slow some of us down so no one gets hurt. They are a bright yellow means of grace, without which a parking lot would be deadly.

The same holds true for Jesus's church. Jesus intends for His church to be a place of gospel safety. People are supposed to get healed, not hurt. To be lifted up, not sized up. To be loved on, not left behind. Jesus fills His church with weak and broken people—and then teaches us to help them.

It is among the weak, and only there, that we learn the true nature of gospel ministry. We are not running Fortune 500 companies that recruit and hire the best. We are not coaching Division I teams where everyone must be six foot ten or lightning fast to make the team. We are not directing Hollywood epics where only beautiful and articulate dons and divas need apply. We are ministering the grace of Jesus to all comers: highly functional, regularly functional, or barely functional.

If we lose sight of this, it's not only the weak who will be in danger in our churches. We all will be in danger of losing the gospel itself.

...

JESUS NEVER SAID A BLAND WORD. Every sermon, parable, promise, comfort, and woe were beautifully, forcefully, and eternally true. His listeners were rocked by them. No one ever dozed off when Jesus was at the mic.

His words are supposed to jolt us every time.

But different truths jolt us differently. Because I'm a Maximizer, Matthew 11:28 has always stopped me in my tracks.

In this text, Jesus looks at the crowds and offers the following invitation:

"Come to me, all who labor and are heavy laden, and I will give you rest."

The words "labor and are heavy laden" are meant to amplify each other and must be taken together. Jesus is not talking here about run-of-the-mill, everyday tired that we all experience at the end of a rugged shift or a weekend with the in-laws. He is talking about someone who is wearied, spent, faint, exhausted, and burdened down to the point of being helpless. Someone with little to nothing left. The heavy laden have tried and come up short. They couldn't beat the system or keep it together or get it right. They and the real world went antlers to antlers, and the real world won. Their weakness has been exposed.

In Bostonian, we would translate "labor and heavy laden" like this: "wicked weak."

But what is jolting here is not the fact that the world (and our churches) are filled with weak failures. It's that Jesus wants them. He is not trying to fly past them or mow them down. He's moving toward them, beckoning them, recruiting them, inviting them. Jesus is looking to minister to, among, and with the weak.

Here's how Jesus's words in Matthew 11:28 would read if I had written them:

> Come to me, all who are:
>
> highly functional,
> gainfully employed,
> multitalented,
> college educated,
> biblically literate,
> good looking,
> kind of sarcastic,
> low maintenance,
> and gospel fluent,
>
> and I will leverage your strengths toward the building of a highly successful church.

Those are the people I hope walk through the doors of Seven Mile Road or into my basement on gospel community night. I can get some serious work done with a team like that! Nothing's going to slow us down!

But that's not who Jesus calls to Himself, or sends us to.

Read the Gospels. You can't get two pages without seeing Jesus slow down to help, care for, love, assist, heal, and identify with the weakest folks in Israel. He scoops up little children. He touches lepers. He teams up with fishermen. He lets ex-prostitutes wash His feet. He preaches to peasants, people who wrestle with demons, adulterers caught in the act, and divorcées who have been married five times and are living with a new partner.

This is the heart of the gospel we love and proclaim. We're all weak, helplessly and pathetically weak. We've made our attempts at keeping it together and have fallen short. Yet Jesus loves us and died for us and covenants with us anyway.

No other religion, not even the watered-down ones, is like this. Every other religion calls to the dons and the divas, the strong, the capable, the disciplined, the driven:

"Come to me, all who can meditate for hours on end with your legs bent like a pretzel."

"Come to me, all who can hold to a rigorous moral code."

"Come to me, all who can devour thick books and interact with opaque philosophical ruminations."

"Come to me, all who can keep a seven-times-a-day prayer schedule."

"Come to me, all who have never smoked crack or gotten pregnant or racked up credit card debt."

"Come to me, all who are witty and intelligent and in shape and can quote *Seinfeld* and Springsteen."

"Come to me, all who are successful and strong."

Hear me clearly. These are not the invitations of Jesus and His gospel of grace.

Jesus says:

"Come to me, all who are weak and pathetic and incompetent and sin-addled and unattractive and messed up and unsure and scared and addicted and smelly and illiterate and tone deaf and easily depressed, and I will give you rest. You are safe with Me. I will be strong for you."

This is why Paul echoes Jesus's command to us to help the weak.

. . .

IN HIS LOVE FOR US, JESUS keeps bringing the weak to Seven Mile Road.

You would love our friend Greg. He's a fifty-nine-year-old from Winthrop with Down Syndrome. He gets to church ninety minutes early every Sunday and hands me a crinkled sheet of paper with a scribbled Bible verse. He never gets the references correct. "Joob 134:5697" is my favorite. When I am preaching, Greg will interrupt with a sudden laugh, or answer a rhetorical question from three paragraphs ago. One time, while I was preaching about beautiful Abigail, he blurted out, "I like girls."

Old Maximizer Kruse would be bothered by Greg. Frustrated. Tempted to avoid him or run him over or chase him off. But Jesus is teaching me to love him. Our church needs to see me love him.

On Easter Sunday, I was given that chance.

Greg was scheduled to go to his brother's house for an earlier-than-usual lunch, which meant cutting out of church before it was over. I wasn't three minutes into my Resurrection Sunday empty-tomb sermon (biggest audience of the year—a Maximizer's delight!) when Greg suddenly stood up, buttoned his leather Boston Bruins jacket, and shuffled straight to the front of the church. All I could see was a giant black-and-yellow speed bump coming at me. "How fast can I fly over this thing?" I thought. But I was reminded of Paul's words: We must help the weak. Slow down for them. Love them.

So I stopped preaching, stepped to the right of the pulpit, and threw my arm around Greg. "You going to your brother's?" He nodded and said some things I couldn't understand. I told him that we loved him. He released his grip and shuffled out. Church went on.

Jesus was teaching us to love the Gregs.

. . .

LET'S HELP THE WEAK. LET'S MOP up their puke. Let's dig in as they battle with addictions. Let's preach a little shorter if it helps them understand gospel love a little better. Let's sit in awkward silence with them and trust God with their minds and souls. Let's say the same things over and over again, even when we think they should get it by now.

Let's give a lot of money when others just can't, even if that's because they foolishly squandered theirs away. Let's set up chairs because Jesus has made our legs and backs strong enough.

Let's see the weak not as speed bumps but as means of grace, ensuring that our church will be safe places of healing and hope.

Better yet, let's see them as mirrors, reflecting our own weaknesses Jesus has so patiently borne.

By God's grace, we are no longer the blind leading the blind. But we will always be the weak leading the weak. So, even when we are graced with seasons of strength, let's slow down, lean in, and love the weak.

– BLUEPRINTS –

1. Be among the most broken people.

When the house phone rings at 4:45 a.m., you know a bad conversation is coming.

My dad was calling. Before dawn, my mom had mistaken the top of their stairs for the entrance to her room, tumbling down the flight. She had fractured her arm, broken her nose, concussed her brain, and bruised just about every other muscle in her sixty-nine-year-old body. Soon after I arrived, I watched first responders secure her to a stretcher and then race the seven miles to MGH in Boston, my dad and me disregarding all traffic laws in their wake.

Three days later, the doctors assigned her to a rehabilitation center/nursing home in Stoneham. For the next two weeks, I visited daily—not only to console my mom but also to sit with the other residents, their bodies or minds unable to keep pace with the demands of everyday life. Almost to a person, they beamed because a stranger was willing simply to look them in the eyes and ask their names. Those weeks were a gift to me, allowing me to obey the fourth commandment by slowing down and loving on these folks society had forgotten.

Wherever those folks are in your context—nursing homes, substance rehabs, housing projects, hospitals, prisons—be present with them.

2. Let the babies coo.

A culture's posture toward its babies—the costliest, least efficient members of society—speaks volumes. The rabid support for abortion-on-demand in America is obvious evidence of the dark state of our nation's soul. But in the church, we must remember that Christ took into his arms infants and little ones. His disciples saw them as helpless, loud, stinky, distracting, and unproductive. Christ saw them as image-bearers to be embraced.

Whenever I see a new family in our service with a baby, I make a point to assure them (moms especially) how glad I am they are there, and that they should have no worries about their little one making some noise in the service. Let the reader understand: we have a cry room for sustained, concentration-rattling crying. But I am talking about the chatter that comes with a fussy baby or a toddler who hasn't mastered the art of whispering. This speaks volumes about the church's love for the youngest image-bearers.

3. Be familiar with all the texts that remind us of God's calculus for who finds their way into His kingdom.

God does not idly repeat Himself. Scripture is littered with these verses for a reason: Deuteronomy 7:7; 1 Samuel 16:7; Matthew 8:3; Matthew 25:40; Mark 4:31; Luke 6:20; Luke 14:13; 1 Corinthians 1:26. We need constant reminders that grace to the undeserving and underperforming is the heart of the gospel.

21 | SUPERGLUE

Church can be generous.
On giving (literally) everything away.

It is more blessed to give than to receive. —Acts 20:35

IN 2007, A BRIGHT-EYED, SUPER SKINNY, really young couple landed at Seven Mile Road. They were recovering from spending four years in the frozen tundra of a campus called Houghton College in upstate New York. They threw themselves immediately into the fray of our community and mission. They began to love and learn and repent and serve. They would suffer an hour-long commute from South Hamilton to West Medford every Tuesday night just to be discipled. They watched children and painted walls and gave people rides to the airport and loved their upstairs neighbors. They did it all with joy: no complaints. The husband's desire was to shepherd people, so he ran through our Ox Track. Twice. Just to be sure he was ready. They were some of the best disciple-makers we've had.

Then they left.

My math may be fuzzy, but I believe that was the 3,245,673rd time that has happened to us.

One of our newer members, who had observed the constant churn of people, asked, "So, do you ever get scared that one day there's not going to be anyone left?"

Only every Sunday.

SUMMARY OF SEVEN MILE ROAD TO DATE:

First four years: Start, grind, experiment, fail, grind, read, learn, pray, preach, disciple, love, falter, stumble, muddle, grind, reel, learn, repent, muddle, grind, repeat.

Next four years: Fwoosh. Broad and sudden and deep gospel wakefulness, new people everywhere, rapid growth, chairs in the

	hallway, momentum, budget surplus, cash on hand, sustainability, hands full.
Next four years:	Give it all away.

Among my hundreds of Evernote entries, there is one particular note I have to fight to love. It's entitled "Shaped and Sent by Seven Mile Road," and it lists the names of more than two hundred adults who have left our young church. (Our average Sunday attendance is ninety adults.) It's probably the most frequently updated note I have because we are constantly giving our people away.

Let me use numbers to make the point.

From 2011 to 2015, we have …

- Sent sixty of our members (plus their kids, eighty-five total persons) out the front door for two church plants, each less than three miles away;
- Sent another one hundred members to Alabama, California, Colorado, Connecticut, Florida, Hawaii, Illinois, Kansas, Kentucky, Maine, Minnesota, Nebraska, New Hampshire, New York, North Carolina, Ohio, Oklahoma, Pennsylvania, Rhode Island, Texas, Virginia, Wisconsin, and Washington. We sent a family to Ghana. We sent two of our best families overseas to do gospel work in Tanzania and the Comoros Islands. We gave away dads, moms, singers, nursery workers, pastors, deacons, teachers, drummers, electricians, doctors, and professors. (I don't even want to think about how much recurring giving they took with them, but a lot of zeros were involved.) Every ounce of sustainability we had built either moved a few miles down the road or boarded a plane at Terminal C.

And it's the best thing that could have happened.

• • •

THERE ARE TWO DIFFERENT TYPES OF people when it comes to managing what ends up in our hands: spenders and savers.

SPENDER: Just got paid. Friday night. Party's hopping. Money's gone by Saturday.
SAVER: Just got paid. Friday night. Party's hopping. Tell me how it goes. I'm headed to the bank.

SPENDER: Two hours in the Meadow Glen Mall, and you come out with arms full of bags.
SAVER: Two hours in the Meadow Glen Mall, and you come out with nothing but an attitude because the clerk at Chess King wouldn't give you a discount on a pair of two-tone jeans you wanted.

SPENDER: Twenty minutes on Amazon, and you're cramped up from clicking "Add to cart."
SAVER: Twenty minutes on Amazon, and your cart is empty.

SPENDER: UPS driver is invited to your wedding.
SAVER: UPS driver has never visited your house.

SPENDER: You go to the movies, and you buy a bucket of popcorn, Cracker Jacks, Goobers, a beer, a foot-long hot dog, and a movie poster.
SAVER: You go to the movies only when someone gives you a gift card for Christmas, and you stuff a water bottle in your cargo pants and candy in your hoodie.

SPENDER: Credit card statement: only nineteen pages long this month. (But look, my cashback reward bonus is growing, rapidly! Every time I buy something they give me money! This is great!)

SAVER: Credit card statement: Inactive account ...

These are the default categories of our human hands when it comes to our stuff. Neither is necessarily sinful. We can spend to the glory of God, and we can save to the glory of God. Jesus has given me responsibility for a family of six. We spend some serious money. Our Discover card statement is nineteen pages every month. We need to eat and dress and heat the house and educate our children and take vacations and enjoy God's world. We also save money—I'm the guy with the water bottle in his cargo pants at the movies. We have some simple financial goals and are working toward some really good future ends for our family. But if we are not careful, these two options very quickly become the only two things that we ever do with what we've been given.

What's ironic is that, although they appear to be opposite tendencies, spending and saving are just two sides of the same coin. In both cases, we are grasping everything for ourselves, whether it be for now or later. Consuming and hoarding are both born of self-interest—they just have competing time horizons. Think of a girl on Halloween night. Whether she eats every Kit Kat, Almond Joy, and Snickers bar immediately or stashes it all away, she is still keeping it all for herself.

At Seven Mile Road we call this tendency *superglue*. What hits our hands tends to stay in our hands. Whether it's money, people, assets, resources, candy, jeans, or Cracker Jacks, it all runs down a one-way, dead-end street.

There is, however, a third thing we can do with what we've received. It is not the default action of any human heart or hands. It's the anti-superglue. It's a counterintuitive, unusual, selfless, gospel-driven way to deal with things we find in our possession: to give it away.

Has anyone ever gone to the Meadow Glen Mall for two hours, waited for someone to approach the checkout, then swooped in and said, "Hey, I got this. How much? Here's my card. Swipe it. My gift to you." Has anyone ever left their Amazon cart empty, then clicked on their church's online giving app and filled that up instead? Has anyone ever waited for the UPS truck to drive down their block, waved it down, and handed the driver a brown box with some brownies and a $100 bill in it? Has anyone ever gone to the movies and snuck in M&M's for their entire row?

That's not us. We are all natural consumers and hoarders. We believe the best and wisest course of action is to get and then hang on to what we've got.

Our maxim: it is more blessed to receive than to give.

. . .

BELIEVE IT OR NOT, I AM Puerto Rican. *Si, mi hijo.* My fair-skinned mom married the whitest white guy in the history of Queens. But most of my cousins are 100 percent Latino. The dominant last name in our family used to be Quintero. When I was a kid, every Christmas all the Quinteros would get together for "A Quintero Christmas"—sixty Puerto Ricans crammed in a two-bedroom apartment in Manhattan or Brooklyn. Because there were so many kids, each child would receive one present. Each present would be given away one at a time, and we'd all have to watch the opening and the thanking before moving on to the next. The process took hours. Scotty! Ricky! Alizia! Benji! My brother James and I would wait, and wait, and wait, until finally our names would get called. Some years we would receive an amazing gift like Voltron, or a mini pinball machine, or a Jets jersey. Some years it was a sweater. But either way, if you had asked us, we would have said the best part of the night was the moment our name was called.

That is how our hearts are wired. We love to receive.

Have you ever noticed how people suddenly beam when they receive even the most inconsequential trinket? We took our family to Florida for vacation once and attended a Miami Marlins game (along with maybe nine hundred other people). No one made a sound when the Marlins got a hit or turned a double play, but when the cheerleaders emerged onto the promenade to shoot free T-shirts at the crowd, you would have thought Jesus had returned. Everybody began jumping and shouting and jockeying for a position to catch a cheap black shirt co-branded by the local erectile dysfunction clinic.

If you want to see Seven Mile Road people happy, have free Kane's Donuts in the foyer on a Sunday.

I get excited when the guy at Trader Joe's offers me a paper bag.

We are convinced: receiving is the best.

What's true about us as individuals becomes true about us as churches. We, too, believe it is far better to receive people, money, assets, influence—and to hold on to all of it for dear life—than to give them away. No one consumes and hoards like churches. I have the financial statements and attendance charts to prove it.

This is why the final flourish of Paul's speech has become so important to me. He reminds me, gently, that while spending can be good, and saving, too, the happiest, holiest, best thing we can do is give.

• • •

AT THIS POINT IN HIS SPEECH, Jesus's apostle Paul has spoken about the generosity with which he lived as a church planter and pastor in the city of Ephesus. He worked tirelessly with his hands, providing an income for himself and his teammates, so the church would not have to worry about his compensation in the early years. He coveted no one's money or material things; he was content with the basics. He worked hard and gave away much of what he received. Now he gives the doctrinal ground for that generosity.

He says it like this: "We must ... remember the words of the Lord Jesus, how he himself said, 'It is more blessed to give than to receive.'"

Let the weight, wonder, and weirdness of those words hit you: "It is more blessed to give than to receive."

While those words do not appear in this exact form in any of the Gospels, they were part of some broader tradition of Jesus's teaching that was being passed down from disciple to disciple. They are not a typo. Nor are they a pithy proverb that belongs on a coffee mug or fortune cookie or yoga mat. They reflect a truth that is rooted in the infinitely holy character of the Trinity itself.

• • •

WERE YOU TO READ THE ENTIRE Bible front to back in a month, you'd see that the concentrated truth—undiluted by piecemealing the story over several months or years of reading—is that the God behind the story is generous. He gives and He gives and He gives.

Book 1, Chapter 1, He is giving. He gives mankind a garden home, a breathtaking, beautiful, bountiful, rich land filled with visual and aromatic and culinary and sexual delights.

Book 1, Chapter 2, He is giving. In one of the most romantic texts of Scripture, setting the stage for the gospel story to come, He fills in the details of giving the man a wife. He knocks him out, fashions her from his side, a perfect fit for him, and then nudges him awake and presents her to him, a better gift than any ever given at Quintero Christmas. "Here you go, Adam. For you. And Eve, for you. Each of you, for the other." Biblical marriage was—and remains—a beautiful gift from God.

Book 1, Chapter 3, He is giving. He makes warm, durable clothes for Adam and Eve when their best idea for clothing was to wrap their naked bodies in leaves. And He makes Eve the gospel promise that one of her descendants would reverse the curse she and Adam had brought down on creation.

Book 1, Chapter 4, He is giving. He gives Eve three sons, one in partial fulfillment of His gospel promises to her.

The story just rolls like this. God constantly opens His hand and gives. He gives Sarah a son, Isaac a wife, Moses a staff, the people a way through the Red Sea and manna in the desert, Joshua the land, Samson strength, Jonathan a friend, David a kingdom, Solomon wisdom, the widow of Zarephath her son back, and Naaman his skin back. We could cite hundreds of examples of God's generosity in the old covenant, but ultimately, all of this giving points toward the wildest, most openhanded gift of all: "For God so loved the world, that he gave his only Son, that whoever believes in him should not perish but have eternal life" (John 3:16). The Father, openhanded with His most treasured possession, gave His Son.

Paul asks a rhetorical question in Romans 8:32: "He who did not spare his own Son but gave him up for us all, how will he not also with him graciously give us all things?"

The staggering answer is "He would never not."

If God, who always acts in accord with what is good, true, beautiful, and right, never holds and hoards—but instead *gives*—we who have been adopted by Him must do the same.

Paul lived as though this was true, and we get to as well. We get to plant churches, even if it means giving away some of our best leaders and workers. We get to invest money in God's people, even if it means enduring a deficit for a year or foregoing some bells and whistles. We get to give away our sermons and songs and skills and time and energy, even if it means losing recognition and fame.

This math of the gospel, the upside-down way of thinking and living in God's kingdom, doesn't compute with the world.

QuickBooks is never going to comprehend it.

Excel has no formula for it.

Actuaries would never sign off on it.

Instead of accumulation by addition, it's multiplication by subtraction.

• • •

ONE OF CHRIST'S MIRACLES RECORDED IN all four Gospels is His feeding of the thousands. More gospel truths poke out from this story than cigarette butts poke out from

Revere Beach. One truth is that God gives generously to His people and to His servants.

To set the scene: John the Baptist has been murdered for standing up for biblical sexuality. Jesus retreats to a desolate place to mourn the death of His cousin, the greatest prophet there ever was. The crowds hunt Him down, and He spends the day loving, healing, and teaching—giving of Himself all day long. As the sunlight wanes, His disciples say, "Jesus, awesome job. It's getting late, and you must be exhausted and hungry. Let's send everyone home. They need to sleep and eat, too." But Jesus responds, "You give them something to eat." The disciples look down; they have barely enough food for themselves: five loaves and a few fish. They think, "We can't give this way, and what good would it do anyway? Giving this little can't feed all these people." But Jesus takes the food, prays, and begins to give to the disciples. They begin to serve the crowds, open-handed, not hoarding what they have on hand, but giving it away. Everyone eats.

This is beautiful, but don't miss the rest of the story. At the end of the meal, there are twelve baskets filled with food. This is no coincidence: twelve baskets for twelve disciples. It's a metaphor for doing gospel ministry. We are called to give, and give, and give, even when it seems like bad math. The disciples initially thought, "We can't give. We have to hold on to what we've got, or we will go without," but when they finished giving, they had more than when they started. This is not prosperity gospel garbage, where we give so we get. This is true gospel glory, where—without fear, without hesitation, without worry—we give because we know that's best: God owns everything, and He will take care of us in the end.

"MULTIPLICATION IS NEVER SEXY FOR THE multiplier." One of my brothers in Christ quietly said those helpful words to me once as I confessed some struggles to have joy in my pastoral life. We had recently gone all-in on giving away our original Seven Mile Road in the form of aggressive church planting. I had just gotten back from visiting with a church we had planted, which was younger than half the age of "mine," but already it had more people, more money, more space, more volunteers, more programs, more stuff, more everything.

I know our success does not consist of possessions and programs—but my Type-A, quantitative, neatnik, glory-seeking side so wants it to. I want to be able to get a camera, take some pictures, and show the world: "Look. See? There it is. I'm doing this well. I'm no joke." I want to be able to post a 102-page PDF with colorful charts and bars and lines racing to the top-right corner of every page. I want *Fast Company* to publish a piece on thoughtfully managed, highly successful church startups and lead with mine.

I want my joy to be in what I've accumulated under the tent with my name on it, but every time Christ calls me to give another leader, member, or dollar away, it's a new nail in the coffin of that myopic dream.

Praise God for the hammer of the Spirit.

Praise God for every one of those nails.

Praise God for walking me to the sink, repeatedly, to wash the superglue off my hands, that I might open them and give.

Praise God for calling me to invest tons of time, energy, love, instruction, correction, care, and encouragement into young men who will leave "my" (there it is again) church, take lots of "my" people and money, and go grow churches of their own, none of which will add to the bottom line, attendance figures, giving counts, or volunteer list of "my" church.

Praise God for helping me see this as not just OK, but beautiful. Jesus didn't say it was more blessed to hang on to, hoard, conserve, or lock down. He said it was more blessed to give.

· · ·

THIS POSTURE OF BOLD GENEROSITY IS crucial not only for our own usefulness and joy as shepherds but also for that of our sheep.

We like to say that Seven Mile Road is "a church built for Bostonians." It's our way of capturing the missiology that anchors us. The "church" part points backward, to the life, death, and resurrection of Jesus and His establishment of the Church. The "Bostonians" part points outward, toward those He has sent us to.

People often press us on what we mean by *Bostonians*, so we've come up with three profiles:

BORN AND RAISED. These are the townies who grew up just north of Boston and couldn't imagine living anywhere else. They know all the words to "Sweet Caroline," correctly pronounce *Peabody*, *Worcester*, and *Quincy*, have six pairs of Adidas in their closet, and know where the best cannoli are in the North End. They spend zero time on Zillow looking at housing prices in places like Carolina, Indiana, or Texas. In the age to come they are still going to drive crazy, play Keno, and call stuff "wicked." They are my people.

PASSING THROUGH. We don't spite these people. They are headed somewhere in life, and our city is where they are going to be educated or become qualified to get there. They come with a million cultural oddities, and they're serious about enjoying, respecting, and experimenting with Bostonian culture. Many of them love the gospel and throw themselves fully into the life of the church for however long they are here. In membership interviews many of them tell me, "So we're here for three years and then we're moving back to central Pennsylvania." We get it.

HERE TO STAY. These folks land with us and are so affected by the need for good, gospel-centered churches and so enamored with our vision that they re-envision their lives as missionaries sent by God to live and die among the people of Boston.

The clearest barometer I have for how generous Seven Mile Road is being is how our "born and raised" and "here to stay" folks relate to those "passing through." Are we willing to give ourselves fully to those who might not be around for the long haul? Or are we closing off our lives and hearts?

I don't have sisters, but Jesus has given me dozens at Seven Mile Road, and Patti Rosell is one of them. She's every pastor's dream: an honest, generous, selfless, no-nonsense, optimistic, energetic team player who loves the gospel, embraces her femininity, and does whatever it takes to see the church thrive. For years, she has led our Kalos Track[51] by my side, bringing to every conversation her ferocious appetite for gospel truth, accumulated wisdom from decades of marriage and motherhood, and keen sense for what our women need to hear. She's also watched as almost every person in my Evernote has come and gone. But rather than allowing the openhandedness of our church to discourage her, or drive her to the margins of the church, she has embraced it. A few Sundays ago, while guarding the stairs to make sure none of our fifty little ones tumbled down, I mentioned that a couple we had cared for years ago during a terribly difficult crisis of trust was somehow still married and thriving in Christ. Her eyes suddenly filled with tears, but not the tears of sadness or frustration that they weren't with us anymore. They were tears of gratitude that the Lord would allow us to be a means of grace in someone's life, even if He called us to give them away.

We can lead our people to that gospel place.

· · ·

THIS HAS BEEN ESPECIALLY CRUCIAL for us as we have sought to become a family of churches. Here are the non-negotiables for being a Seven Mile Road church, with the first and last bookending everything.

LOVE: We are fully committed personally to one another. Take-a-bullet committed.

THEOLOGY: We have a unified statement of faith and shared theological distinctives.

BYLAWS: We have unified bylaws.

MONEY: We share a budget process and fund certain unified realities (back office, church planting, etc.).

MULTIPLICATION: We plant as a family, not as individual churches, and we require unanimity on approved Seven Mile Road planters/church plants.

HUSTLE: We invest the time, money, energy, travel, etc., to meet together frequently enough to function as a unified team.

GENEROSITY: We openhandedly share everything Jesus places in our hands, from finances to people to content.

To my amazement and delight, our people are bought in. They believe Jesus wants us to be more than stand-alone churches. And every time a new cost calls their bluff, they've responded with open hands. Our small, original church has kicked in hundreds of thousands of dollars to see other churches planted, and these newer churches make many sacrifices of their own, and no one regrets it for a second.

Jesus wasn't lying. It is more blessed to give than to receive.

Let's lead our people there.

– BLUEPRINTS –

1. Measure beyond accumulation.

I am a numbers guy. Numbers tell me stories. Give me a spreadsheet, and I can write you a novel. It's the product of my brain's wiring, a Boston University MBA where I transformed haphazard buckets of numbers in profit-generating recommendations, and countless hours reading baseball cards.

Numbers are good, but we have to be careful with them. Attendance, giving, membership, etc.: these cannot be the only metrics we use to measure success. Take time with your team, and make a list of "softer" metrics that are about investment, not accumulation.

2. Make sure your church is paying her pastors well.

One place churches can model gospel-driven generosity is in setting generous compensation levels for their pastors and staff.

In *Marriage to a Difficult Man: The Uncommon Union of Jonathan and Sarah Edwards*, Elisabeth Dodds wrote about the contention around ministers' pay in the colonies, penning this fascinating paragraph:

> The Boston News Letter [*sic*] of November 18, 1728, printed a sample budget for 'persons in families of middling figure who bear the character of being

genteel.' It allowed for beer, for soap for baths once in four weeks, for three candles [at] night, for a maid at £10 a year, and three pairs of shoes each year. The sample budget made no provision for the entertaining Sarah did incessantly, for charitable gifts, for letter writing, or for schooling. All these were necessities of life for the Edwardses.

In other words, the benchmark for paying pastors failed to consider their generosity in hosting and above-average giving of their time, treasure, and talent.

Almost three hundred years later, this conversation is unchanged. How does a church compensate her pastors generously, given the call on their lives? What factors need to be considered? Are there pay premiums for things such as hospitality, study resources, and children's education? Whatever the specific answers to those questions are, generosity should drive the conversation.

At Seven Mile Road we have an Independent Compensation Committee that works from the following convictions:

1. DOUBLE HONOR

Scripture is explicit that we "let the elders who rule well be considered worthy of double honor, especially those who labor in preaching and teaching" (1 Tim. 5:17). We should gladly provide for our pastors who bear the intense weight of ministry in a way that honors their work and office.

2. LIVING LOCAL

We desire our pastors to live among the people they are called to serve. Our compensation levels should allow this to happen by considering the amplified costs of living in New England, compared to other regions of the country.

3. LONG GAME

Long-term leaders provide the church with stability, familiarity, efficiency, and effectiveness. At Seven Mile Road, our goal is to compensate our executive staff in ways that allow growing families to serve the church fruitfully for a long time.

4. JOB DESCRIPTION AND PERFORMANCE

We desire skilled, prolific pastors to serve Seven Mile Road. Compensation levels should accord with both job description and job performance.

5. MASCULINITY

God has called men to the glad assumption of sacrificial responsibility in the home and in the church, which includes loving, leading, and providing for their families. Although our culture has built compensation levels assuming dual-income realities, our compensation levels should enable our staff elders and their families to embrace fruitful complementarity as providence dictates.

6. GENEROSITY

One of our clearest opportunities to witness about Jesus is through generosity. Compensation levels should be generous to allow our leaders to be generous and sacrificial.[52]

3. Help your people assess their propensity to give.

Here are the "tests" we put before our people when we send members their annual giving statements, to help them prayerfully assess how they have given in the past year. These are important, because what's true about money inevitability becomes true about everything else in our hands.

1. THE HESITATION TEST

We always need to begin with our hearts. Is there hesitation in my heart about giving generously to Jesus's church? Do I as a member look at this statement and say, "Oh man, I could have used that money somewhere else!" If so, why is that? Is it because I don't trust our good Father to meet my financial needs? Is it because I love this world and the things of this world? If there is any hesitation, we need to check our hearts. We should love to part with our money when it is going to Jesus's church.

2. THE DUTY TEST

Giving is as much an act of obedience as it is an act of worship. Like obedience, worship is supposed to be free, passionate, and glad—not the result of mindless duty. Giving to Jesus's ongoing work should be a joy and privilege.

3. THE LEFTOVERS TEST

When I look at this statement, does it reveal God is getting my leftovers? Do I determine how much I am going to give after determining all that I need to maintain my preferred standard of living? In other words, does God come last? Many of us give this way. We give way less than we could or should, because we work backward.

4. THE DUNKIN' DONUTS TEST

Look at your statement and ask, "What have I spent more money on than I have given to Jesus's church?" Sadly, for some of us, the answer includes pettiness like coffee. Of course, there will be things that fit in this category, like housing, or tuition, or (painfully) taxes. But too many of us spend more money on trivial material pursuits—car washes, cable, Sox tickets, vacations, etc.—than on Jesus's church. These things are not necessarily evil in themselves, of course. But when they trump our giving, something's askew.

5. THE "WHAT THE ... ?" TEST

If someone who has not responded in repentance, faith, and obedience to the gospel looked at your giving statement, would he just shrug his shoulders, or would he do a double take and in wonder, say, "What the ... ? You are serious about this church thing!" No double take means you are not giving enough. Our giving ought to shout wicked-loud about the worth of knowing and serving Christ.

6. THE ISLAND TEST

Does anyone else on this green earth know how much you give? Are you entrusting yourself to the helpful accountability of gospel community, living transparently before some trustworthy brothers and sisters so that you are open to correction and encouragement? In His grace, Jesus has saved us into His family, and we should live with some measure of openness as members. I am not saying to foolishly make your financial life public. I am recommending you confide in a trustworthy community, saying, "Help me be faithful in how I give."

7. THE FACE-TO-FACE TEST

We are going to see Christ face to face. On that day, it will be awesome to say, "Look! Look! I stewarded what You entrusted me with. I gave generously and sacrificially to the work of Your gospel." I would so prefer that than hanging my head regretfully.

22 | KITES

Church can be dependent.
On actually praying.

He knelt down and prayed. —Acts 20:36

SO, MY KIDS ARE BOSTONIANS, BORN and raised.

If they were to draw a map of the world, Massachusetts would be bigger than Europe, Africa, and Asia combined. Ask them where else they'd love to live, and they'd look at you, confused.

Like all Bostonians, they possess an indomitable swagger.

When my oldest son was three years old, we were crossing Lebanon Street to go bike riding in the Wyoming Cemetery. (Not sure if that's legal or not, but our policy was forgiveness rather than permission.) Lebanon Street is a local speed trap, because it runs long, straight, and slightly downhill in a city where most streets bend crooked every forty yards. I was a few steps behind him, pushing his bike with training wheels, when he stepped into the street as a Honda Pilot came barreling toward him at forty miles an hour. He tilted his head, stared the driver right in his eyes, and raised his left hand like he was either a fully deputized officer of the law or Iron Man. It never crossed his mind that the car wouldn't stop simply because he willed it to. I shrieked, and the driver slammed on his brakes, but my son just looked up at me and smirked, as if to say:

"Dad, relax. I got this."

This is how Bostonians see the world. The SATs don't scare us, stock market crashes don't faze us, and escape rooms don't send us into a panic. We chased off the British, invented the telephone, and dug the first subway. We gave the world John Winthrop, Cotton Mather, John Adams, Ralph Waldo Emerson, Mary Baker Eddy (sorry about that), Julia Child, Malcolm X, Steven Tyler (sorry about that, too), Leonard Nimoy (i.e., Spock), and Adam Sandler. Harvard and MIT are both here. We're educated, capable, and accomplished. And prayerless.

We got this.

This swaggering self-sufficiency can seep into our gospel ministry. Any sense of dependence on the Spirit vanishes. We're sure we can get the world to bend to our wishes, accommodate our plans, and get on board with our preferred futures. We begin to rely on gifting, gimmicks, slogans, smoke, lasers, and lattes. We pinball from one conference to another, looking for that silver-bullet technique. We spend $349 on a *How to Break the 200 Barrier* book and DVD set. We employ Planning Center, Gallup polls, Craig Groeschel's Leadership Podcast, Ed Young's Style Guide, and *Harvard Business Review*. We've even read *Center Church*. Twice.

We got this.

This is not how gospel ministry works, though.

This is *never* how it's worked.

• • •

THERE ARE TWO TYPES OF MASSACHUSETTS summer vacationers: those who go up to New Hampshire, and those who head down to the Cape.

Here's what to expect at each:

NEW HAMPSHIRE	THE CAPE
Cabins	Homes
Lakes	Oceans
Hikes in the woods	Strolls on the beach
Tattoos	Capris
Miller Lite	Chardonnay
Led Zeppelin	James Taylor
Live free or die'rs	Limousine liberals

Having spent the first six years of her life living in Venezuela, my wife, Grace, is a certified beach bum and would happily spend all sixty-two days of July and August on the sand and in the sun. So, every summer we round up our four kids, pack the minivan with chairs and umbrellas and frisbees and coolers and super soakers, and rent a home on one of the "Falmouth Fingers" of Cape Cod.

One year, when our kids were little, we bought each of them a kite and walked to the local park to fly them. They were more excited than Bernie Sanders voting on a tax hike. We watched a dozen YouTube videos on how to fly a kite. We read every word on the packaging about how to assemble a kite properly. We were ready.

When we arrived at the park, we followed all the instructions:

Lay the assembled kite, fabric-side up, on the ground.

Stretch the string out ten to twelve yards.

Hold the handle behind you.

Run like the redcoats are coming.

Our perfect technique offered imperfect results. The kites just dragged and bounded through the grass behind us. We spent half an hour trying to achieve lift-off, but our kites wouldn't ascend an inch. With eight sullen eyes staring back at me, I tried to stem everyone's disappointment by promising we'd try again at the beach later that night.

After a full day of swimming in the pool, lounging in the hammock, reading *Calvin and Hobbes*, and racing *Super Mario Kart*, we drove to Falmouth Heights Beach at dusk and replicated our earlier kite-flying efforts.

This time, they took off like rockets. Mine nearly set my hand on fire and tore my arm out of its socket. I am 205 pounds, and I came off the ground for a second. Same preparation. Same mechanics. Same technique. Same kites. But this time, they soared. The only difference: *wind*. We had none in the field that afternoon, but later at the ocean, we had a tempest.

...

THIS SAME PHENOMENON TRANSLATES directly to the gospel life and to our gospel work. Without the presence and power of the Spirit, we bound hopelessly through the dirt. But with the Spirit? Look out.

This is true, of course, for our salvation. Without the Spirit, we know of no wakefulness, no repentance, no faith. Here's how Paul says it in 1 Corinthians: "No one can say, 'Jesus is Lord,' except in the Holy Spirit." When he writes "Jesus is Lord" there, he doesn't mean mouthing the words in a robotic or rote manner. Let's face it: you could put a gun to someone's head and get him to say it. You could teach a one-year-old to say it. Or a parrot. Or Siri. Or Alexa.

When he writes "Jesus is Lord," that's shorthand for a legitimate, all-in, no-holding-back, willing-to-die-for confession of faith in Christ. "Jesus is Lord" means "The gospel is true, and it's true for me. I've been loved by God. I am His and He is mine. I have decided to follow Jesus. No turning back." Nobody says those words on his or her own. Nobody makes that commitment independently. No preacher ever talks anyone into that. No emotional altar call or perfectly crafted apologetic argument makes that happen. Not even listening to Hillsong at dawn on Easter can trigger that. Every time that happens, it's a miracle of divine grace.

That doesn't mean the Spirit doesn't use means. He does. But our prayer and love and evangelism and sermons and apologetics and worship songs do not save. Salvation requires the gale-force wind of the Spirit.

But it's also crucial we understand that what is true in salvation is true in ministry. We need the Spirit to animate—daily, perpetually, relentlessly—all our work. Here is how Jesus said it: "I am the vine; you are the branches. Whoever abides in me and I in him, he it is that bears much fruit, for apart from me, you can do nothing." Let the word *nothing* sink in. "Apart from me, you can do nothing." That doesn't mean literally nothing. Millions of people who don't have the Spirit of Jesus do things every day. Jesus is talking here about gospel work. He is saying these words to His disciples in the context of their commission to follow Him and make disciples. In the life and the work they were called to, nothing could be done without Jesus, by His Spirit.

Think branch on the ground in the forest.

Think kite in a field with no wind.

Without the Spirit, we're dead.

...

THOSE WHO HAVE ACCOMPLISHED GREAT THINGS for God have always known this to be true.

Moses understood this.

Right after the people's awful golden calf rebellion in the wilderness, when the Lord told him to continue to lead them toward the Promised Land, we read this:

Then Moses said to the Lord, "If your Presence does not go with us, do not send us up from here. How will anyone know that you are pleased with me and with your people unless you go with us? What else will distinguish me and your people from all the other people on the face of the earth?" (Exod. 33:15-16 New International Version)

I love Moses's humility, honesty, and desperation in this prayer. "Lord, I am not even leaving my tent to go buy some milk and a couple of scratch tickets if you are not with me. I am certainly not pretending that I could lead your people."

David understood this.

In his gut-wrenching but beautiful prayer of repentance for his myriad sins against the Lord, Uriah, Bathsheba, and the people, David said these words: "Create in me a pure heart, O God, and renew a steadfast spirit within me. Do not cast me from your presence or take your Holy Spirit from me" (Ps. 51:10-11 NIV). In the old covenant, the work of the Spirit was different than it is in the new. The Spirit would rest upon individuals who were tasked with some serious gospel work, such as being the king of Israel. This is why you will often read about David as God's "anointed one." That meant a special, gracious dispensation of the Spirit was on him for the work. So, when David says, "Don't take your Spirit from me," it's not in reference to His salvation per se, but to his work: his ability to rule, to lead, to govern the people well. In other words, David is saying, "I can't be king without your Spirit on me and with me. I am dead if you remove your anointing from me for this work. You can't take your Holy Spirit out of this equation."

Even Jesus understood this.

One of the most surprising and paradoxical facts of the Gospels is that Jesus, God incarnate, prayed. I've always loved how Mark's Gospel opens. It's like a Hollywood blockbuster that has zero opening credits and instead launches in with a high-speed car chase or a helicopter battle. Jesus of Nazareth bursts onto the scene like a lightning bolt, preaching with authority, exorcising demons, healing the sick, and boldly upsetting the status quo of all Israel. He is doing work. But then, right in the middle of all this action, Mark shows us Jesus, up early, far from the crowds, in the silence of the pre-dawn, praying. The correlation is unmistakable: the power and fruitfulness of Jesus's ministry emerged from His time with the Father and the Spirit.

We could multiply examples. Across redemptive history, those who accomplished the most for God's glory and for the good of others were those who depended on God the most. And yet, as American Christians and pastors, we struggle to embrace this.

...

I'M THE WHITEST BIRACIAL GUY YOU'LL ever meet. My dad grew up in Flushing, New York, in the 1950s, racing cars, smoking cigarettes, and doing the twist. He then sported a comb-over for nearly thirty years. Skippy on white bread, sandals over socks: you don't get any whiter.

My mom is full-blooded Puerto Rican. The seventh of nine siblings, she spent her childhood shuttling back and forth between the Islands and the States. She's fluent in Spanish, makes a mean *arroz con pollo*, and was never allowed to wear a skirt above her knees.

They met in 1969, fell in love, and brought two sons into this world.

Among the many complications this has brought to my life (Which ethnicity box do I check? How could I be related to cousins darker than Will Smith?), watching *West Side Story* has routinely caused an existential dilemma. Am I for the Jets or the Sharks? Riff or Bernardo? Then one day I finally realized the right answer: Action. If I were going to be any character in Arthur Laurents's masterpiece, it would be Action, the ready-to-go, let's-get-this-done firebrand. I'm wired to move, go, accomplish. Let's start a church, redecorate this room, hit the gym, read (or write!) a book.

I am a doer, not a prayer.

This is why the end of Paul's speech is precious to me.

. . .

WHAT DO PAUL AND THE EPHESIAN pastors do at the end of his charge? He looks them in the eye and calls them to some serious gospel work. They are to continue in his absence to lead the church deeper and wider. To preach the word. To care for the saints. To love and gospel the city. And what is everyone's response?

I know what *I* would have done: started plotting and planning. A fast fist bump goodbye, and let's get to work. There is vision to cast, strategy to form, people to meet, money to raise, leaders to train, and sermons to prepare. We've got to order the kids' curriculum and build the website and find a worship leader and work on the space.

Yet, the first thing the Ephesian elders do is fall on their knees in prayer: "And when he had said these things, he knelt down and prayed with them all" (Acts 20:36).

I love this.

This occurs in a public place, right on the beach by Miletus port. It was every bit as busy as Boston, with its dozens of docks and landings, tourists, commuters, musicians, and fishermen. And there, right in the middle of the hustle and bustle, the Ephesian pastors huddled together, unashamed, humble, desperate, and prayed: "Jesus, You've got to be with us by Your Spirit. We can't do a thing Paul just said on our own, without You."

This ending doesn't jolt or instruct us like it should. We read this and we just shrug our shoulders and go, "Eh, they're Christians. That's what Christians do. They pray."

I've worked a day job for fifteen years while getting Seven Mile Road up and running. I've never left a meeting about a big project where everyone fell in prayer before God. Never. I've been to multiple weddings in the last few years where a man and woman were stepping into what would be the hardest thing they would ever do, with the opportunity to show off gospel truth in a clearer way than they would ever get to do while single, and there wasn't a single prayer prayed during the ceremony or reception. I've coached basketball teams and attended leadership trainings and observed municipal committees, and prayer has been purposefully absent from all of it. But not with Paul and these pastors. They knew they could never accomplish their work sans the Spirit; they wouldn't step off the sand without seeking the Lord.

. . .

THERE IS A SUPER BRIGHT SIDE to the fact that any and all gospel work requires the animation of the Spirit. Although it's true that without the Spirit, we can do nothing, it's just as true that *with* the Spirit, anything is possible.

At the heart of the Christian gospel is the resurrection of the Son of God. Jesus didn't swoon, pass out, get replaced by Judas, or almost die. He died. Flatlined. This is why the Scriptures and our creeds emphasize so strongly the fact of Jesus's burial. When Eutychus dozed off, backflipped out a third-story window and was "taken up dead," there's some uncertainty there. Was he dead, or knocked out, or what? Not so with Jesus. Three days, in the ground. He was *dead* dead.

This truth is essential, because it means not only the penalty we deserve for our sin has been fully and finally paid, but also that we serve a God who raises the dead. How did the Father raise the Son? No hocus pocus. No incantations. No sleight of hand. It was by the gale-force wind of the Spirit. That same Spirit is with us, and for us. As Paul writes, "The Spirit of him who raised Jesus from the dead is living in you" (Rom. 8:11 NIV). These words should surprise and amaze and energize us, setting us to prayer and to the flying of some gospel kites.

Yes, the doctrine of our full dependence on the Spirit for all things is supposed to foster humility. In God's economy, we're not the star point guard who nailed a game-winning, step-back three with 0.3 seconds left on the clock. We are the scrub on the end of the bench waving our towel at the work of the Spirit.

Yes, it's meant to build patience in us. The Spirit blows when and where He pleases. Some days, we've done everything we ought, and the kite's just sitting there, and that's OK.

But it's also supposed to foster energetic, optimistic, prayerful expectancy in us. We have something the world does not: a Father who loves to answer prayer, a Mediator who carries our prayers to Him, and a Spirit who can turn cemeteries into dance parties. It's inconceivable that we would settle for prayerless pragmatics when we have the Trinity with and for us. This is why Paul and those pastors started in prayer. We must do the same.

. . .

PEOPLE OFTEN ASK ME TO TELL them about where Seven Mile Road got its start.

Sometimes I give the Sunday school answer: "In the mighty heart of God." Although this might sound a bit too cute, it's true.

Sometimes I rap my knuckles on my own chest and say, "Right here." Although somewhat myopic, there's a sense in which this is also true.

Sometimes I chuckle and say, "Right in Pastor Paul McPheeters's tiny little office." That is where the idea of church planting was first expressed verbally, and after that one conversation there was no going back.

Sometimes it's "my parents' living room in Everett," where we held our first series of core team meetings, or "the front porches of the Edgeworth neighborhood in Malden," where I knocked on doors and talked with folks about the gospel, or "the dilapidated but charming Emerson School Hall," where we held our first public services.

But my favorite answer is that Seven Mile Road started in some folding chairs in a cluttered church library at the Forestdale Community Church.

Every Wednesday night for a year, I gathered with Joe Gallagher and Angelo Stathopolous to seek the Lord's grace for this unexpected venture of church planting. Both men were forty years my senior. Joe was an Irish ex-Catholic, Angelo a Greek charismatic. Both had the gifts of faith and encouragement. I'd drive away from those nights of prayer feeling like a cinnamon bun fresh from the oven. Nothing was Instagramable about those times together. We'd alternate reading Scripture, singing hymns, and petitioning the Father. That's it. Our meetings weren't actionable; if the Richter scale had negative numbers, that's how those nights would have registered. But I wouldn't trade an hour of humble, dependent prayer with Joe and Angelo for all the strategy sessions and planning meetings on earth. What the proud gaze of a Bostonian or the naked eye of a pragmatist might label a silly waste of time was the door through which the Spirit blew Seven Mile Road into existence.

God has designed the building of His church to work this way.

He gets the glory.

We call shotgun, start praying, and enjoy the ride.

– BLUEPRINTS –

1. Read the dead guys on prayer.

Our fathers and mothers in the faith knew how to do two things much better than postmodern Americans: fight and pray. Allow their praying to inform yours.

2. Start and surround everything in prayer.

We've sought to deromanticize prayer in the life of Seven Mile Road. Although there is nothing wrong, per se, with all-night prayer vigils, forty days of fasting, or highly publicized and regimented prayer campaigns, we've tried instead to quietly thread prayer through everything we do. We pray multiple times in our liturgy every Sunday. We pray when opening the Scripture in our gospel communities. At the start of each church year, we have a morning of guided prayer, when we cast a vision for our most hopeful ministry and mission initiatives and ask for grace on our work. No team meeting, member forum, or gospel conversation goes unanchored in prayer. We often pause, sometimes multiple times in a meeting or conversation, sometimes even mid-sentence, to pray. The Father is never more than a word away, and we want to foster a prayer-delight in our people.

3. Catalog what you pray for so you can see how the Lord answers.

As true as everything in this chapter is, I'm still a prayer skeptic at heart, so I need to document the things I pray about. For example, here is a list of prayers we prayed when searching for a space solution. The next time I say our Father never answers prayer, or that we are making this whole thing up, punch me in the face.

I prayed …

- that we would not become beholden to a monthly mortgage or building costs.
- that I would not stumble with having space validate my church-planting success.
- that there would be great unity on a solution.
- that space would not become a mission-killer or a magnet but an enabler of sending.
- that God would simply provide us with the money we need.

All were answered:

- We ended up with no mortgage and a manageable annual operations cost.
- We bought an old building in a boring suburb, with a max capacity of 180 people.
- We experienced incredible unity about going for it.
- Built into our "yes" to the building was a commitment to plant in Malden and Wakefield, two adjacent towns.
- We raised $150,000 in forty days and paid cash for the building.

I am not saying prayers are answered only if we tie answers directly to requests. Our Father could have done *none* of these things and still have been answering our overriding prayer that His will be done. But He is our Dad, and sometimes He takes pleasure in giving His children what they ask.

Endnotes

1. I considered adding an appendix of Massachusetts vocabulary to this book. Or maybe just having you watch *The Town* (2010) before reading it.
2. Throughout this book, assume I'm quoting the English Standard Version (ESV) of Scripture unless I tell you otherwise.
3. Scalpers are the guys who yell in your face trying to sell you tickets outside Fenway or the Garden.
4. Now that I've established that dying to self and living in Christ is the foundation of every successful church plant, at the end of each chapter that follows, I'll lay out some of my "blueprints" for building a faithful church in a post-Christian context.
5. St. Dominic Savio Preparatory High School was the Salesian Brothers secondary school on Bennington Street in East Boston that I attended. Spartan pride.
6. *Kid* is a Bostonian term of endearment.
7. Yes, it was the nineties.
8. Unless you are caring for our one- and two-year-olds in the nursery. Then you are breathing in something else entirely.
9. True story: Two minutes into my surgery there was a medical emergency in another room. The doctor left and didn't return for nearly an hour. No one did. I lay there listening to piped-in country music, positive they had forgotten me and that I was about to spend the night strapped to a table.
10. E.L. James, of *Fifty Shades of Grey* notoriety, is the pen name of a real person named Erika Leonard. Her book has been purchased more than 150 million times.

11 Actually, our little New England church doesn't have a single dedicated parking spot. Add parking-lot envy to my sin struggles.

12 A.S.A. Harrison, *The Silent Wife: A Novel* (London: Penguin Books, 2013).

13 "'Confessions' Art Show: Artist Candy Chang Brings Strangers' Secrets To Las Vegas (PHOTOS)," *Huffington Post*, May 3, 2013, https://www.huffpost.com/entry/confessions-art-show-artist-candy-chang-brings-secrets-to-las-vegas-photos_n_3202081.

14 In 2015, the BBC ran an article about the tendency of African presidents to attempt to outdo one another with the length and flamboyance of their titles. My favorite was "Mobutu Sese Seko Kuku Ngbendu Waza Banga," which Joseph Mobutu gave himself and which means "The Warrior who Goes from Conquest to Conquest Leaving Fire in his Wake [*sic*]."

15 1 Corinthians 3:3-9:

> For while there is jealousy and strife among you, are you not of the flesh and behaving only in a human way? For when one says, "I follow Paul," and another, "I follow Apollos," are you not being merely human?
>
> What then is Apollos? What is Paul? Servants through whom you believed, as the Lord assigned to each. I planted, Apollos watered, but God gave the growth. So neither he who plants nor he who waters is anything, but only God who gives the growth. He who plants and he who waters are one, and each will receive his wages according to his labor. For we are God's fellow workers. You are God's field, God's building.

16 That is, if Paul was in fact riding a horse, as Caravaggio and other painters have famously depicted; Scripture is silent on this point.

Endnotes

17 Whenever we read *Jerusalem* in the older covenant we should think "the church" or "Jesus's people."

18 The adverbs *always* and *only* are crucial in this sentence. Belligerence is not the same as faithfulness.

19 His name is Louie Giglio: https://www.louiegiglio.com/.

³ "Blessed shall he be who takes your little ones and dashes them against the rock!"

20 Paul knew his Bible, so he knew Proverbs 26:17: "Whoever meddles in a quarrel not his own is like one who takes a passing dog by the ears." Quarrel-meddlers are dog-ear-grabbing fools. Yet Paul jumped right into Euodia and Syntyche's UFC octagon to say enough's enough. What does this mean? It means there's a right way, and a lot of wrong ways, to break up a fight between believers in your church. (Hint: letting them bloody each other while you blithely pretend the church you're shepherding isn't catching the splatter is one of the wrong ways.)

21 Where I come from, this phrase is usually verbalized as an eye-rolling jab meaning silly, stuck-in-the-Dark-Ages-people who still revere the archaic, error-riddled, misogynistic, passé, pre-enlightenment ridiculousness of the Bible.

22 Two purposeful exceptions: before Herod, and before the Sanhedrin.

23 Apparently, the storms were five times closer than we realized: "Understanding Lightning: Thunder," National Weather Service, accessed October 16, 2019, https://www.weather.gov/safety/lightning-science-thunder.

24 Tim Keller, "Evangelism in the early church," *Redeemer Report,* Redeemer Churches & Ministries, September 2019, https://www.redeemer.com/redeemer-report/article/evangelism_in_the_early_church.

25 The motor vehicle didn't exist when this church was built; neither did parking lots.

26 I am using the word "church" very loosely here. I wish that most of them would find a replacement moniker as they've long-since purged any vestiges of orthodox Christian faith or practice from their communities. It's like Veggie Galaxy calling itself a burger joint.

27 I've always been confused by the "No Place For Hate" signs that dot the landscape on the lawns of homes in our liberal town. Am I to believe that the people living in those homes are hate-free? Try booking Ben Shapiro to speak at the local high school, and we'll see about that. The signs should read: "A Place For Hating Only Those We Deem Hateworthy. In Those Cases, Hate Away."

28 President Trump did something similar with his comments on Mexicans, broad-brushing all those of this ethnic heritage with an epithet I won't repeat.

29 Ray Ortland (@ImmanuelNash), Twitter, February 18, 2017, https://twitter.com/rayortlund/status/833042756431908864?lang=en.

30 People often ask why we plant churches so close to one another. It's a Bostonian geography thing: sometimes you cross a single street and enter an entirely different cultural reality that requires a uniquely contextualized expression of Jesus's church.

31 John Piper, *Risk Is Right: Better to Lose Your Life Than to Waste It* (Wheaton, IL: Crossway, 2013) 17.

32 "Play the guitar" is a vast understatement. John is the single most talented musician I have ever been around. We recorded an original album in his time with us and he performed all the vocals and instrumentation himself, from rhythm to electric to bass to drums and even a little keys.

33 Sergio Mazza (a brother and missionary we sent to the Comoros Island) and I argued until three in the morning whether Jehu was a type of Christ or not.

34 As a general rule, if you are in Jersey you are wanting to get out of Jersey.

35 Proverbs 14:30: "A tranquil heart [a satisfied heart, a heart that is at peace with who it is] gives life to the flesh, but envy makes the bones rot."

36 No offense, but if your southern momma names you Tanner Turley, you're never even supposed to come north of DC, let alone to Medford.

37 John "Way Back" Wasdin was one of the worst pitchers in Red Sox history.

38 Strengths, Weaknesses, Opportunities, Threats.

39 Her.meneutics [*sic*] is a blog hosted by *Christianity Today*.

40 Yes, this website exists.

41 To be clear: When we say *wolves*, we are not talking about well-meaning members who are figuring things out, or awesome brothers and sisters who have a few theological oddities in their arsenal, or young Christians with a million questions, or folks who are new to Jesus and gospel grace and are just wading into the waters of orthodoxy for the first time. We are talking about men and women who will not accept correction but insist on promoting heresy. This chapter is not about establishing a church culture of "Us 24 And No More." Not everyone with theological convictions imperfectly aligned with yours is a heretic. The Christian faith "that was once for all delivered to the saints" is crystal clear on most things; a few things are less clear, like the proper mode of baptism or the timing of Judgment Day. Multiple times in Scripture, we are commanded not to be quarrelsome. Trigger-happy pastors are not the same as bold and faithful shepherds. If you are ordering up replacement shells on Amazon every third week because you've been blasting your shotgun nonstop like you're trying to win a teddy bear at the state fair, you may have lost perspective.

42 I am (hopefully obviously!) not recommending any kind of literal, physical violence here. The intensity of the metaphor is simply meant to convey the intensity of the danger. A zero-tolerance policy for heresy being propagated in the hearts and minds of the people is the aim.

43 It's a lot like the South Medford Business Suit: *The South Medford Business Suit*, 27theMovie.com [website now defunct], image accessed October 13, 2019, https://www.dropbox.com/s/jginr2z9m30s8yp/South%20Medford%20Business%20Suit.jpg?dl=0.

44 I did get a pair of LeBron 11s for Christmas. Although they were three model years old, I couldn't have been happier.

45 Lexico, s.v. "synergy," accessed October 9, 2019, https://www.lexico.com/en/definition/synergy.

46 *Harvard Business Review*'s *10 Must Reads on Teams*, the Craig Groeschel Leadership Podcast, and anything by Patrick Lencioni are good places to start.

47 1 Tim. 5:9-10: "Let a widow be enrolled … having a reputation for good works: if she has brought up children, has shown hospitality, has washed the feet of the saints, has cared for the afflicted, and has devoted herself to every good work."

48 I am using the term *church* very loosely. The church had apostatized from any semblance of gospel orthodoxy in the sixties, and since my encounter with its youth pastor, it has been converted into luxury condominiums.

49 Formerly Clifton StrengthsFinder, featured in Gallup's best-selling book *StrengthsFinder 2.0*, by Tom Rath.

50 "Maximizer," *Gallup Business Journal*, accessed October 11, 2019, https://news.gallup.com/businessjournal/697/maximizer.aspx.

51 Kalos Track is a year-long discipleship community that we run to help our women believe the gospel, understand and

embrace their femininity, and partner with our pastors in making disciples.

52 Don't ever call a pastor who doesn't give generously. If a man doesn't have it in him to give openhandedly from what Jesus enables him to earn, there is no way he will suddenly lead the church to live openhandedly when he is in authority. It is a nonnegotiable for us that our pastors be the most generous givers in the church.